Peterson's

MASTER THE
EMT-BASIC
CERTIFICATION
EXAM

4th Edition

PETERSON'S

Publishing

PETERSON'S
Publishing

About Peterson's Publishing

To succeed on your lifelong educational journey, you will need accurate, dependable, and practical tools and resources. That is why Peterson's is everywhere education happens. Because whenever and however you need education content delivered, you can rely on Peterson's to provide the information, know-how, and guidance to help you reach your goals. Tools to match the right students with the right school. It's here. Personalized resources and expert guidance. It's here. Comprehensive and dependable education content— delivered whenever and however you need it. It's all here.

For more information, contact Peterson's, 2000 Lenox Drive, Lawrenceville, NJ 08648; 800-338-3282 Ext. 54229; or find us online at www.petersonspublishing.com.

Stephen Clemente, Managing Director, Publishing and Institutional Research; Bernadette Webster, Director of Publishing; Mark D. Snider, Editor; Ray Golaszewski, Publishing Operations Manager; Linda M. Williams, Composition Manager

ISBN-13: 978-0-7689-2909-6
ISBN-10: 0-7689-2909-1

Printed in the United States of America

10 9 8 7 6 5 4 3 2 1   12 11 10

Fourth Edition

By printing this book on recycled paper (40% post-consumer waste) 36 trees were saved.

OTHER RECOMMENDED TITLE

Master the Firefighter Exam

Contents

Before You Begin vii
How This Book is Organized vii
Special Study Features vii
You're Well on Your Way to Success viii
Find us on Facebook® & Follow us on Twitter™ viii
Top 10 Ways to Raise Your Score ix

PART I: ALL ABOUT THE EMT

1   Getting Started 3
Levels of Certification 4
Job Description of the EMT–Basic 5
Responding to a Hazardous Material (HAZMAT) Emergency 7
Responding to a Terrorist Attack 11
Clinical Integration 11
Critical Incident Stress Debriefing 14
Preparing for the Written Exam 15
Directed Study 16
Study Guides 16
The Night Before 16
Examination Day 17
What Happens After You Pass Your Exam? 19
Types of EMS–Provider Agencies 21
Summing It Up 23

PART II: DIAGNOSING STRENGTHS AND WEAKNESSES

2   Practice Test 1: Diagnostic 31
Preparing to Take the Diagnostic Test 31
Basics of Emergency Medical Care 33
Airway 39
Assessment 42
Medical 48
Trauma 57
Infants and Children 63
Operations 65
Answer Key and Explanations 68

PART III: EMT–BASIC REVIEW

3 Anatomy and Physiology Review **103**
  Medical Terminology 103
  Topographic Anatomy 116
  Anatomy and Physiology by Body System 117
  Continue to Educate Yourself 132
  Summing It Up 132

4 EMT–Basic Practical Skills Evaluation **133**
  Guidelines for Taking a Practical Skills Examination 133
  The Practical Skills 133
  Practicing Skills 134
  Skills Examination Day 135
  EMT–Basic Skills Performance Sheets 136
  Summing It Up 161

PART IV: PRACTICE TEST

Practice Test 2 .... **167**
  Answer Key and and Explanations 178

APPENDIXES

A Availability of Training **189**

B Professional EMS Organizations and Journals **197**

Before You Begin

HOW THIS BOOK IS ORGANIZED

This book provides a step-by-step tutorial for taking the EMT–Basic Certification Exam, including preparation for both the written exam and the practical skills evaluation.

- **Top 10 Ways to Raise Your Score** gives you a preview of some of the test-taking strategies you'll learn in this book.

- **Part I** provides general information about life as an EMT and how to prepare for the EMT–Basic Certification Exam. You'll learn what it takes to start and maintain a career in emergency medical services, prepare a proper resume, interview properly, and understand the examination process.

- **Part II** is a full-length Diagnostic Test. Taking the test can show you where your skills are strong and where they need some extra work.

- **Part III** is a coaching program. This section provides a comprehensive review of the important topics you will see on the exam.

- **Part IV** contains a full-length practice EMT–Basic Certification Exam, including detailed answer explanations.

- The **Appendixes** contain state-by-state contact information for EMS training facilities and provide a listing of professional EMS organizations and journals.

SPECIAL STUDY FEATURES

Peterson's Master the EMT–Basic Certification Exam is designed to be user-friendly. To this end, the book includes several features to make your preparation easier.

Overview

Each chapter begins with a bulleted overview of the topics covered in the chapter, so you can easily find the topic you need to study.

Summing It Up

Each chapter ends with a point-by-point summary that captures the most important points of the chapter. The summaries are a convenient way to review the content of the chapters.

Also be sure to look in the margins of the book for extra information and advice.

NOTE

Notes highlight critical information about life as an EMT.

TIP

Tips draw your attention to valuable concepts and advice for tackling the EMT–Basic Certification Exam.

ALERT!

Alerts do just what they say—alert you to common pitfalls. This information explores the myths and misconceptions many people have about a career as an EMT and the process for becoming certified.

By taking full advantage of all the Special Study Features, you will become much more comfortable when preparing for and taking the EMT–Basic Certification Exam.

YOU'RE WELL ON YOUR WAY TO SUCCESS

Congratulations on your decision to start a career in Emergency Medical Services (EMS). You have taken the first step in a lifelong career of helping people during their most trying times. As an EMS provider, you will witness and experience things that most of your family and friends will only experience while watching the news. We look forward to helping you raise your scores and improve your chances of becoming a certified EMT. Good luck!

FIND US ON FACEBOOK® & FOLLOW US ON TWITTER™

Join the EMT conversation on Facebook® and Twitter™ at www.facebook.com/emtexam and www.twitter.com/emtexam and receive additional test-prep tips and advice. Peterson's resources are available to help you do your best on this important exam—and others in your future.

Peterson's publishes a full line of books—test prep, education exploration, financial aid, and career preparation. Peterson's publications can be found at high school guidance offices, college libraries and career centers, and your local bookstore and library. Peterson's books are now also available as eBooks.

We welcome any comments or suggestions you may have about this publication. Your feedback will help us make educational dreams possible for you—and others like you.

TOP 10 WAYS TO RAISE YOUR SCORE

1. **Get to the test center early.** Make sure you give yourself plenty of extra time to get there, park your car, if necessary, and even grab some fruit juice or water before the test.

2. **Listen to the test monitors and follow their instructions carefully.**

3. **Read every word of the instructions.** Read every word of every question.

4. **Mark your answers by completely darkening the answer space of your choice.**

5. **Mark only ONE answer for each question, even if you think that more than one answer is correct.** You must choose only one. If you mark more than one answer, the scoring machine will consider you wrong.

6. **If you change your mind, erase completely.** Leave no doubt as to which answer you mean.

7. **Check often to be sure that the question number matches the answer space, that you have not skipped a space by mistake.**

8. **Stay alert.** Be careful not to mark a wrong answer just because you were not concentrating.

9. **Do not panic.** If you cannot finish any part before time is up, do not worry. If you are accurate, you can do well even without finishing. At any rate, do not let your performance on any one part affect your performance on any other part.

10. **Check and recheck, time permitting.** If you finish any part before time is up, use the remaining time to check that each question is answered in the right space and that there is only one answer for each question. Return to the difficult questions and rethink them.

PART I

ALL ABOUT THE EMT

CHAPTER 1   Getting Started

Getting Started

OVERVIEW

- Levels of certification
- Job description of the EMT–Basic
- Responding to a hazardous material (HAZMAT) emergency
- Responding to a terrorist attack
- Clinical integration
- Critical incident stress debriefing
- Preparing for the written exam
- Directed study
- Study guides
- The night before
- Examination day
- What happens after you pass your exam?
- Types of EMS-provider agencies
- Summing it up

In every city and state, Emergency Medical Technicians (EMTs) stand by to answer calls for help. Like you, these people are dedicated to saving lives. Your daily contribution to the preservation of life and, more important, the quality of life is appreciated. The patient whose life you touch will remember you long after you've forgotten about the call. While saving the life of a child can bring you a great sense of accomplishment, nothing is worse than arriving on the scene of an emergency and, despite your own best efforts, losing a patient to an illness or injury. Sometimes training and best efforts are not enough. Fortunately, you do not have to deal with these crises alone.

The life of an Emergency Medical Service (EMS) provider is exciting, exhilarating, and heart-breaking—all at the same time. EMS students must understand that completing an EMS program is just the beginning. A commitment to lifelong learning is a necessity. Passing your exam does not make you an EMT or a paramedic. The real test is not on paper or in a classroom. The real test comes after you pass the course and examinations and are at work in the field. Once you are an EMT, your dedication is tested every day on every call. In the face of disaster, EMS providers must remain calm, retain critical-thinking skills, and rely on their education.

EMS providers meet new challenges daily, so they must constantly seek out opportunities to learn. The world of emergency medicine is constantly changing. EMS providers must stay on the cutting edge of technology. At the same time, EMS providers must be advocates of patient care and stand up for their patients' rights. Remember that patients entrust their lives to EMS providers. EMS providers reciprocate by maintaining the highest standard of skills and knowledge while remaining compassionate and sensitive to patients' needs.

LEVELS OF CERTIFICATION

EMS providers are certified at several different standard levels, though some states have established variations and additional levels of certification. The most common levels are defined in the following section.

Lay Rescuer

A lay rescuer is usually the first person who comes into contact with a patient. The lay rescuer could be a professional, a family member, or a bystander who is trained in CPR or basic first aid. The actions of this person may be crucial to the patient's survival. Several organizations, such as the American Heart Association, the American Red Cross, and some local groups, provide training for lay rescuers. Those who wish to become trained as a lay rescuer should contact a local emergency or first-aid squad for information.

Certified First Responder

Some cities and states offer first-responder programs for certain regions. The New York City Fire Department, for example, trains its engine-company personnel at the first-responder level. First-responder units respond to emergency calls with personnel who are trained in the administration of oxygen, as well as in basic airway and other lifesaving procedures. First responders may also be trained in defibrillation. Using an Automated External Defibrillator (AED), they may defibrillate patients in cardiac arrest within minutes of the emergency. First responders save hundreds of lives each year.

Emergency Medical Technician–Basic

The Emergency Medical Technician–Basic (EMT–Basic) must complete a course based on National Highway Traffic Safety Administration–Department of Transportation (NHTSA–DOT) guidelines. EMT–Basics are trained in the recognition of and intervention in medical and trauma emergencies. This training encompasses airway management, scene assessment, medical emergencies, including the use of the AED and trauma emergencies, as well as pediatric and obstetric/gynecological emergencies. The EMT–Basic is also trained in assisted-medication administration, which requires a basic knowledge of pharmacology. The EMT–Basic training may also encompass advanced airway management. This level of training may be enhanced on a state-by-state basis.

Emergency Medical Technician–Intermediate

The training of the Emergency Medical Technician–Intermediate (EMT–Intermediate) encompasses all the training of the EMT–Basic but includes several additional areas of study. The EMT–Intermediate (based on approval by the certifying state) can be trained in advanced airway management, intravenous (IV) fluid administration, and medication administration (including medications for diabetic as well as cardiovascular emergencies). Several states offer variations in this level of training based on regional needs.

Emergency Medical Technician–Paramedic

The Emergency Medical Technician–Paramedic (EMT–Paramedic) is the highest level of training offered for field EMS providers. The EMT–Paramedic completes an NHTSA–DOT-approved training program that includes a comprehensive knowledge in anatomy and physiology, pharmacology, cardiology, and trauma management and detailed training in pediatrics. EMT–Paramedics are required to complete hundreds of hours of clinical training (usually 1,400 hours or more) as well as a field internship. Some EMT–Paramedics specialize in areas such as critical-care transport, pediatric transport, and air-medical transport.

The EMT–Paramedic usually operates in a well-equipped Mobile Intensive Care Unit (MICU), which can serve as a one-bed emergency room. EMT–Paramedics administer a full spectrum of cardiac medications as well as medications for other emergencies. These professionals are also trained in advanced airway management, emergency surgical procedures, advanced diagnostic interpretation, and advanced emergency pharmacology.

The information provided in this section is a general overview of the training levels of EMS providers. For more comprehensive information, contact your state EMS office.

JOB DESCRIPTION OF THE EMT–BASIC

The following job description is based on the NHTSA–DOT EMT–Basic Curriculum.

Career Requirements

- Responds to emergency calls to provide efficient and immediate care to the critically ill and injured and transports patients to medical facilities
- Drives an ambulance to the address or location given, using the most expeditious route, depending on traffic and weather conditions
- Observes traffic ordinances and regulations concerning emergency vehicle operation
- Upon arrival at the scene of a crash or illness, parks the ambulance in a safe location to avoid additional injury
- Prior to initiating patient care, "sizes up" the scene to determine that the scene is safe, the mechanism of injury or nature of illness, the total number of patients, and to request additional help if necessary
- In the absence of law enforcement, creates a safe traffic environment, such as the placement of road flares, removal of debris, and direction of traffic for the protection of the injured and those assisting in the care of injured patients

- Determines the nature and extent of illness or injury and establishes priority for required emergency care

- Based on assessment findings, renders emergency medical care to adults, infants, and children and to medical and trauma patients. (Duties include, but are not limited to, opening and maintaining an airway, ventilating patients, and cardiopulmonary resuscitation, including use of automated external defibrillators.)

- Provides prehospital emergency medical care of simple and multiple system trauma, such as controlling hemorrhage; treating shock (hypoperfusion); bandaging wounds; immobilizing painful, swollen, and deformed extremities; assisting patients with prescribed medications, including sublingual nitroglycerin, epinephrine auto-injectors, and handheld aerosol inhalers; administering oxygen, oral glucose, and activated charcoal

- Reassures patients and bystanders by working confidently and efficiently

- When a patient must be extricated from entrapment, assesses the extent of injury and gives all possible emergency care and protection to the trapped patient and uses the prescribed techniques and appliances for safely removing the patient, radios the dispatcher for additional help or special rescue and/or utility services, provides simple rescue service if the ambulance has not been accompanied by a specialized unit, and provides additional care in triaging the injured in accordance with standard emergency procedures

- Complies with regulations on the handling of the deceased, notifies authorities, and arranges for protection of property and evidence at scene

- Places stretcher in ambulance and ensures that the patient and stretcher are secured while continuing emergency medical care

- Determines the most appropriate facility to which the patient will be transported, unless otherwise directed by medical direction; reports directly to the emergency department or communications center the nature and extent of injuries, the number being transported, and the destination to assure prompt medical care upon arrival

- Identifies assessment findings that may require special professional services and ensures that assistance be immediately available upon arrival at the medical facility

- Constantly assesses the patient during trip to the emergency facility and administers additional care as needed or directed

- Assists in lifting and carrying the patient out of the ambulance and into the receiving facility

- Reports verbally and in writing about the emergency medical care performed on the patient at the emergency scene and in transit to the receiving facility staff for purposes of records and diagnostics

- Restocks and replaces used linens, blankets, and other supplies; cleans all equipment following appropriate disinfecting procedures; checks all equipment so that the ambulance is ready for the next run; keeps ambulance in efficient operating condition; ensures that the ambulance is cleaned and washed and kept neat and orderly

- In accordance with local, state, or federal regulations, decontaminates the interior of the vehicle after patient transport with contagious infection or hazardous materials exposure

- Determines that the vehicle is in proper mechanical condition by checking items required by service management and maintains familiarity with specialized equipment used by the service

- Attends continuing education and refresher training programs as required by employers, medical direction, licensing, or certifying agencies
- Meets qualifications within the functional job analysis

RESPONDING TO A HAZARDOUS MATERIAL (HAZMAT) EMERGENCY

First responders must be alert for hazardous materials when responding to every call. The dispatcher may provide information such as unusual signs and symptoms (e.g., pungent odor, eye irritation), or the address might suggest that the call involves a chemical release. The presence of hazardous materials may be obvious, as in the case of noxious fumes, gasoline, or corrosive liquid spills. In other situations, the hazardous nature of the chemical(s) may not be immediately apparent, as with odorless but poisonous and/or flammable vapors and liquids or radioactive materials. If a diamond-shaped placard or an orange-numbered panel appears on the side or rear of the vehicle, you should assume that the cargo is hazardous. Unfortunately, not all hazardous materials transport vehicles are clearly marked. Many delivery trucks regularly carry hazardous materials that could be released during a collision, yet the appropriate signage is often missing. Therefore, first responders should use caution when attempting rescues at any incident scene.

Traveling to the Scene

An EMS responding to potential hazardous materials incidents should consider these factors:

- Activities to undertake en route and upon arrival at the scene
- Guidelines for assessment, decontamination, and treatment of affected persons
- Patient transport to the hospital

These steps must be practiced before a hazardous materials emergency occurs. EMS personnel should know their responsibilities and how to perform them. Also, all required equipment should be readily accessible and ready to use.

While in transit to an incident scene, the responder should pay attention to clues that suggest the possibility of hazardous materials. For example, billowing smoke or clouds of vapor could indicate the presence of dangerous substances. The senses, particularly the sense of smell, are among the best tools for detecting chemicals. Should an odor be detected, however, responders are advised to move a safe distance away until they can determine its source. Failure to do so could result in injury, illness, or death. Despite their value, sensory signals, such as smell, color, and nasal or eye irritation, are not always reliable indicators. Their presence depends on the chemical(s) involved and on the surrounding conditions. The nature of an incident is also key to identifying the possibility of hazardous materials. Accidents involving railroad tank cars or tanker trucks or incidents at fixed locations where chemicals are used or stored often indicate the presence of hazardous materials.

Emergency responders should pay attention to factors such as wind direction and topography when approaching a suspected hazardous materials incident and advance upwind and upgrade of suspected chemical emissions. They also need to consider that low-lying areas such as creeks and streambeds

ALERT!

The hazard, or lack thereof, must be determined immediately, before first responders enter a chemically contaminated area.

or urban areas such as courtyards or locations near tall buildings may contain vapor clouds protected from dispersal by the wind.

Responders should attempt to gather as much information as possible while traveling to an incident. A checklist to help determine initial actions should be developed and made available to all EMS personnel. It should include the following information:

- Type and nature of incident
- Caller's telephone number
- Knowledge of whether a chemical(s) may be involved
- Chemical and trade name(s) of substance(s) involved
- Number and ages of victims
- Symptoms experienced by the patient(s)
- Nature of injuries
- State of the material (solid, liquid, gas)
- Method of exposure (inhalation, skin contact, etc.)
- Length of exposure

Using as much information as can be gleaned en route to the event site, emergency responders should relay their observations to a designated resource center (Poison Control Center) for information regarding definitive care procedures. If a hazardous substance has been identified, responders should locate specific information on the chemical(s) by consulting reference guidebooks, Web sites, database networks, telephone hotlines, Material Safety Data Sheets (MSDSs), and the Department of Transportation's *North American Emergency Response Guidebook.*

Chemical-specific information can help identify possible health hazards, including the nature of possible injuries; potential methods of exposure; the risk of secondary contamination; required personal protective equipment (PPE); the need for decontamination; decontamination procedures; and the appropriate safe distance from the hazard to protect EMS personnel, the public, and property from exposure to contaminants or other dangers such as fire or explosion.

Communication with other agencies or services should also be initiated while en route to the event site. If an Incident Command System (ICS)—an on-site incident management concept—has been implemented, the Incident Commander (IC) will identify the best approach route, the possible dangers involved, and the estimated number of injuries. On-site response personnel should maintain contact with receiving facilities to relay as much advance information as possible.

Communication should also be established with local fire and police departments and with the HAZMAT response team, if appropriate.

At the Scene

Upon arrival at a scene, you should conduct an initial assessment of the nature and extent of the incident and request additional support if necessary. A first responder should also confirm that local authorities have been notified and are aware that hazardous materials might be involved.

Unless otherwise directed, responders should park their vehicles pointing away from any incident where hazardous materials are suspected. The vehicle should also be at a safe distance that is upwind and upgrade from the hazardous materials. Responders must also remain alert to the possibility that the incident is the result of an intentional criminal act with the presence of secondary devices intended to injure emergency personnel.

Here are seven general guidelines for responders:

1. Do not drive or walk through any spilled or released materials, including smoke, vapors, and puddles.

2. Avoid unnecessary contamination of equipment.

3. Do not attempt to recover shipping papers or manifests unless adequately protected.

4. Avoid exposure while approaching a scene.

5. Do not approach anyone exposed to contaminated areas.

6. Do not attempt a rescue unless trained and equipped with appropriate PPE for the situation.

7. Report all suspicious packages, containers, or people to the command post.

The first units to arrive at a large industrial or storage facility, transportation accident, or mass gathering location should anticipate a rush of evacuating victims. Proper steps must be taken to keep responders from becoming contaminated or otherwise harmed (e.g., use of a PA system to give instructions).

First responders' top priority is scene isolation. Keep others away! Keep unnecessary equipment from becoming contaminated by giving exact information on safe routes of arrival and vehicle staging locations and by reporting anything suspicious.

First responders should immediately establish an Exclusion (Hot) Zone, making sure not to become exposed during the process. The Exclusion Zone should encompass all contaminated areas, and no unauthorized personnel should be allowed to enter that Zone. Anyone leaving the Exclusion Zone should be considered contaminated, requiring assessment and possible decontamination.

Additional zones, including a Contamination Reduction (Warm) Zone and a Support (Cold) Zone, should be delineated at the first available opportunity. Depending upon available personnel, setting up of such zones may be the primary responsibility of the IC or responders other than EMS.

EMS responders who are not properly trained and equipped should stay out of the Exclusion and Contamination Reduction Zones. While it is recommended that all EMS personnel be trained and equipped to work (at a minimum) in Level C PPE, this does not provide maximum skin or respiratory protection. Entry into a Hot or Warm Zone requires a determination that the level of PPE being worn affords adequate protection.

NOTE

If available, plans should be reviewed to assist with locating proper vehicle staging locations, evacuation routes, and patient treatment centers.

ALERT!

Do not remove non-ambulatory patients from the Exclusion Zone unless properly trained personnel with the appropriate PPE are available and a decontamination corridor has been established.

In addition to providing patient care in the Support Zone, qualified EMS personnel may be asked to assume any of the following roles: Safety Officer, EMS Section Officer (e.g., triage, treatment, transportation, communications), Rehabilitation Officer, or Public Information Officer. EMS personnel also frequently provide medical surveillance for the HAZMAT team.

Considerations for Patient Treatment

For the most part, a contaminated patient is like any other patient except that responders must protect themselves and others from dangers due to secondary contamination. Response personnel must first address life-threatening issues and gross decontamination before taking supportive measures. If spinal immobilization appears necessary, initiate it as soon as possible. Primary surveys should be accomplished simultaneously with decontamination, and secondary surveys should be completed as conditions allow. When treating patients, personnel should consider the chemical-specific information received from the Poison Control Center and other information resources.

Patient Transport to the Hospital

When transporting a contaminated patient by ambulance, special care should be exercised to prevent contamination of the vehicle and subsequent patients. Exposed surfaces that the patient is likely to contact should be protected with disposable sheeting. The use of both chemically resistant backboards and disposable sheeting are highly recommended. If a wooden backboard is used, it should be wrapped in a disposable cover, or it may have to be discarded.

Unnecessary equipment should be stored in a safe location or removed; equipment that does come into contact with the patient should be segregated for decontamination or disposal. The patient should be as clean as possible before transport, and further contact with contaminants should be avoided. No patient should be transported who has not, at a minimum, undergone gross decontamination. Protective clothing should be worn by response personnel, as appropriate. If secondary decontamination cannot be performed prior to transport, responders should attempt to prevent the spread of contamination by wrapping the patient loosely but completely in a large blanket or sheet. Body bags are not recommended for encapsulating patients for physiological and mental health reasons. Consideration should also be given to chemicals that present the added danger of accelerated skin absorption due to heat. The name(s) of the involved chemicals, if identified, and any other data available should be recorded before leaving the scene. Oxygen should be administered for any victim with respiratory problems unless contraindicated. Eyes that have been exposed should be irrigated with available saline or water, and irrigation should be continued en route to the hospital. Personnel should also be alert for any signs of respiratory distress, cardiovascular collapse, or gastrointestinal complaints. Seizures may occur and should be treated according to local protocol.

Patients experiencing pain as a result of their injuries should be treated per medical control or agency protocol. Various types and degrees of burns should be treated per local burn protocol or burn center instructions. If a patient suffers acid and alkaline burns to the eyes, you should continuously irrigate the patient's eyes en route to the hospital. Control and proper disposal of the runoff are necessary to avoid injury to the patient and prehospital caregiver(s). Verbal reassurances and other forms of psychological support are also important to minimize further fear and anxiety.

NOTE

In multiple-patient situations, proper triage procedures should be implemented using local emergency response plans.

During transport, ambulance personnel should use appropriate respiratory protection and provide the maximum fresh-air ventilation (e.g., open windows) that weather conditions permit to the patient's and driver's compartments regardless of the presence or absence of odors.

En route, responders should contact the receiving hospital and provide an update on treatment provided or required and any other pertinent clinical information. Instructions for the procedure to enter the hospital with a contaminated patient should also be requested. Facilities receiving a potential hazardous materials patient will need as much information as possible—as soon as possible.

RESPONDING TO A TERRORIST ATTACK

Guidelines are in place to help EMTs handle large-scale disasters, particularly those associated with terrorist attacks. These guidelines are provided here:

- **Respond to the disaster scene with emergency medical personnel and equipment.**
- **Upon arrival at the scene, assume appropriate role in the ICS.** If ICS has not been established, initiate one in accordance with the jurisdiction's emergency management system.
- **Triage, stabilize, treat, and transport the injured.** Coordinate with local and regional hospitals to ensure casualties are transported to the appropriate facilities.
- **Establish and maintain field communications and coordination with other responding emergency teams (medical, fire, police, public works, etc.) and radio or telephone communications with hospitals as appropriate.**
- **Direct the activities of private, volunteer, and other emergency medical units, as well as bystander volunteers as needed.**
- **Evacuate patients from affected hospitals and nursing homes, if necessary.**

CLINICAL INTEGRATION

In addition to classroom training, EMT–Basic students should have the opportunity to enhance their knowledge by integrating clinical internships. These internships should be provided to all EMT–Basic students regardless of their training program. EMT–Basic students should be aware that clinical requirements vary from region to region. The recommended clinical interface is for EMT–Basic students to complete at least five patient history and physical assessments.

EMT–Basic students should take full advantage of their clinical time. EMS instructors should mandate that students attend a minimum of 20 hours of ambulance clinical time as well as 20 hours of emergency department clinical time. If the EMT–Basic program requires less clinical interaction, students should ask if they may attend additional hours.

Students should make every effort to interact with as many patients as possible during their clinical time. Student interaction should include the following:

Patient History and Physical Examination

This interaction includes a discussion with patients based on their current medical problem as well as a past medical history. The physical examination should be complete.

Medical Interventions

Students should observe any and all interventions as well as seek out the explanations behind these interventions. Students should participate in interventions within their scope of practice. EMT–Basic students should not participate in interventions that are not clearly defined in their scope of practice.

Ambulance Preparation

Students on a field clinical should assist the personnel with their duties regarding ambulance maintenance. Students should check the vehicle's equipment and, if required, ask what each piece of equipment is used for and how it is used. EMT–Basic students should always know where each piece of equipment is located in the event of an emergency.

All interaction among EMT–Basic students should be documented on field clinical assessment forms. These forms are provided by instructors and should be filled out by students or their preceptors at the clinical site. Students should receive a copy of this form to evaluate their performance.

Types of Responses

- **Nonemergency operations** refer to operations in which an EMS response vehicle is out on a nonemergency, also called a *routine operation*. All routine operations are considered nonemergency and are made using headlights only. No light bars, beacons, corner or grill flashers, or sirens are used. During a nonemergency operation, the ambulance shall be driven in a safe manner and is not authorized to use any emergency-vehicle privileges as provided for in the Vehicle and Traffic Law.

- **Emergency operations** refer to any response to the scene or the hospital where the driver of the emergency vehicle actually perceives, based on instructions received or information available to him or her, the call to be a true emergency. Emergency Medical Dispatch (EMD) classifications, indicating a true or potentially true emergency, should be used to determine the initial response type. Patient assessments made by a certified care provider should determine the response type (usually C or U as an emergency) to the hospital. In order for a response to be a true or potentially true emergency, the operator or certified care provider must have a credible reason to believe that emergency operations may make a difference in patient outcome. During an emergency operation, headlights and all emergency lights are illuminated, and the siren is used as necessary.

Emergency Vehicle Operations

- Emergency operations are authorized only to responses deemed emergencies by dispatch protocol and where the risks associated with emergency operations demonstrably make a difference in patient outcome.

- Upon dispatch, emergency operations are only authorized when the dispatch call type justifies an emergency response.

- All operations considered nonemergency shall be made using headlights only—no light bars, beacons, corner or grill flashers, or sirens shall be used. During a nonemergency operation, the EMS response vehicle should be driven in a safe manner and is not authorized to use any emergency-vehicle privileges as provided for in the Vehicle and Traffic Law.

- Emergency operations are authorized at a scene when it is necessary to protect the safety of EMS personnel, patients, or the public.

- EMS response vehicles do not have an absolute right of way. It is a qualified right that should not be taken lightly.

- During an emergency operation, the vehicle's headlights and all emergency lights shall be illuminated and the siren used as required in the Vehicle and Traffic Law.

- Once on the scene, a certified provider should assess the scene and all patients and then determine the type of response for additional EMS vehicles responding to the scene. It is the responsibility of that certified responder to notify the dispatcher or other responding units of the type of response that is warranted, emergency or nonemergency.

- Following assessment of the patient, the EMT in charge of patient care is responsible for determining the response type en route to the hospital.

- Drivers of EMS response vehicles should know and follow their state's laws regarding exceeding the speed limit.

- EMS response vehicles shall not exceed posted speed limits when proceeding through intersections with a green signal or no control device.

- When an EMS response vehicle approaches an intersection, with or without a control device, the vehicle must be operated in such a manner as to permit the driver to make a safe controlled stop if necessary.

- When an EMS response vehicle approaches a red light, stop sign, stopped school bus, or a non-controlled railroad crossing, the vehicle must come to a complete stop.

- In most states, the driver of an EMS response vehicle must account for all lanes of traffic prior to proceeding through an intersection and should treat each lane of traffic as a separate intersection.

- When using the median (turning lane) or an oncoming traffic lane to approach intersections, the EMS response vehicle must come to a complete stop before proceeding through the intersection with caution.

- When traffic conditions require an EMS response vehicle to travel in oncoming traffic lanes, the driver must follow state laws regarding speed in such situations.

- The use of escorts and convoys is discouraged. Emergency vehicles should maintain a minimum distance of 300 to 400 feet when traveling in emergency mode in ideal conditions. This distance should be increased when conditions are less than ideal.

NOTE

Every EMS response vehicle must be driven safely at all times. This means not exceeding the speed limit in most cases. Drivers exercising any of the Vehicle and Traffic Law privileges must do so cautiously and with regard for the safety of all others.

CRITICAL INCIDENT STRESS DEBRIEFING

Critical Incident Stress Debriefing (CISD) is a group technique used after a critical incident. It is designed to minimize the impact of that event and to aid in the recovery of people who have been exposed to disturbing events. Critical Incident Stress Debriefings were designed by Jeffrey T. Mitchell, Ph.D., founder of The International Critical Incident Stress Foundation Inc. Initially developed for firefighters, paramedics, and police officers, the Mitchell Model has been modified and expanded for use in natural disasters, school-based incidents, and in a variety of other settings.

What Is Critical Incident Stress?

Critical incidents are events outside the normal range of a person's experiences. They are usually unexpected and so powerful that an individual is unable to cope with them.

No two people react the same way to an event. Some people may have no reaction. Others may suffer from nightmares, sleep disturbance, nervousness, confusion, anxiety, irritability, inability to concentrate, sadness, depression, and anger. Physical symptoms may include rapid heartbeat, night sweats, headaches, and dizziness.

Job performance may also suffer as will other aspects of the individual's life. Sexual function may be affected, as well as one's ability to interact with family and friends.

Most reactions last only a few days. However, they can sometimes last for weeks or even months. In some instances, symptoms appear immediately. In others, symptoms may be delayed or not appear at all.

Tips to Minimize Critical Incident Stress

The best way to deal with Critical Incident Stress is to prevent it. Since that is sometimes impossible, you can take steps to minimize Critical Incident Stress:

- When possible, know what to expect in advance.
- Make sure you are properly trained for the incident you are sent out to handle.
- Adequate rest breaks should be provided and/or personnel alternated on extended operations.
- Make sure you have access to food and water following the incident.
- Avoid caffeine and alcohol after the incident.
- Understand that it is normal to feel bad for a short time following the incident. Feelings do not disappear immediately; they need time to fade.
- An informal debriefing should be held within a few hours of the incident to allow personnel to vent and share their feelings about what happened. This also helps assess the need for a formal debriefing.

PREPARING FOR THE WRITTEN EXAM

The certification examination is the final test of the ability of a candidate to meet the performance objectives to become an EMT–Basic. You can prepare for this examination in several ways.

Study Habits

An examination is an evaluation tool. The written examination evaluates your aptitude for knowledge retention. You should follow a hard and fast rule of progressive study. As the course begins to run full steam, the amount of study time should increase. Some modules in the EMT–Basic curriculum will require many hours of self-study. As these courses are usually condensed into a short time, you should reserve several hours per week to study for your examination.

Developing good study habits is essential to retaining information and passing the examination.

"Cramming" is not a productive study habit. Studies have shown that cramming reduces retention.

Refer to the study tips below and keep them in mind as you prepare for the exam. You may find that following these five rules decreases your study time and increases your retention.

1. **Never study when you are tired.** Studying when you are tired will almost always be fruitless. Each day your body needs to rest. Attempts at studying when you are tired—especially difficult technical information—are usually weak at best. Allow time for ample rest.

2. **Choose the time when you are usually most awake, and make it your study time.** All people are different: some are more alert in the morning; some are more alert in the evening. You are the best judge of your inner clock. You know when you are most alert. If you are at your best in the morning, study when you wake up. Try to designate at least 45 minutes a day for studying. You may find that 45 minutes of study during your peak time is more efficient than 2 hours when you're tired.

3. **Find a quiet and comfortable place.** Comfort is essential while studying. You should find a place in your home or study area that provides quiet and comfort. Even the temperature of the room can affect your ability to study. Don't study in a hot area as heat tends to make people sleepy. Silence is also important. Attempting to study with the television on or the stereo playing is not a good idea. While background music may relax you, the brain will be distracted since it must retain your studies and process the background music. Studying in a room with other people is also discouraged. Constant disruptions can disturb your concentration and cause confusion.

4. **Never study when you're hungry.** Hunger is a great distracter. If you're hungry, you will think about food and not about your studies. Eat prior to beginning your studies. Try to avoid snacks high in sugar and caffeine, which will provide a temporary rush and then cause you to crash. Fruits, salads, and vegetables are good foods to eat before studying.

5. **Study in short time blocks.** Professional studies show that retention is better in students who study for short blocks of time. The average maximum study time should be about 45 minutes. The brain gets tired after 45 minutes of studying and needs a break. Study for 45 minutes, take a break, rest your eyes, and go for a walk. While in your resting phase, try to mentally review

TIP

Learning to study properly is just as important as learning the material you are trying to study.

the material you just studied. This practice will help you to retain the information. Go back to studying only when your head feels clear again.

DIRECTED STUDY

People tend to study subjects they are comfortable with and avoid subjects they find difficult.

For example, the student who is well-versed in cardiac emergencies will spend more time studying cardiac emergencies because he or she understands the topic and retains the information more readily. The problem is that weaker areas are never approached. This strategy, therefore, may lead to poor scores on the examination.

You can direct your study in several ways. For instance, you can keep a record of your quiz and examination scores for each topic. Focus your study on the topics in which you earned lower scores. This strategy will strengthen your knowledge and make you a well-rounded EMS provider. You can also ask your instructor. Many EMS instructors can provide an item analysis for class final examinations (which you are sure to have before the certification examination). Ask your instructor to share your item analysis with you. With this information, you can identify your weaker areas and know which areas to practice. Most EMS instructors are happy to assist you in this area. To prepare students for the upcoming certification examination, some instructors assign homework based on a student's item analysis.

STUDY GUIDES

Many EMS instructors have written study guides for all levels of EMS provision. Candidates should find one or two study guides that they are comfortable with and stick with them. Purchasing the bookstore's entire stock of EMT–Basic study guides is not necessary to pass your examination. A good review guide, a course textbook and a workbook, and some guidance from your course instructor are all you need to prepare for the examination.

By following these suggestions, you will retain more information. As you develop good study habits, you will notice other things that help you study better. Incorporate what you've learned about your own study habits into these suggestions to develop an effective study plan that is right for you.

THE NIGHT BEFORE

The night before your examination can set the tone for the entire examination. The following list includes several Dos and Don'ts for the night before the examination.

- **DON'T stay up all night cramming.** All-night cramming will make you tired and easily confused during the test. Candidates who stay up all night tend to confuse facts on the examination.
- **DON'T use drugs or alcohol to help you sleep.** Most people who drink alcohol or take drugs to assist sleep are misguided. Alcohol and drugs do not provide a restful sleep. As a matter of fact, alcohol will put you to sleep, only to wake you up in an hour or two. Alcohol prevents restful sleep.

- **DO plan on getting your required amount of sleep—no more, no less.** Most people know exactly how much sleep they need to function properly. If you need 8 hours of sleep to get a good jump on your day, then plan on getting that much sleep. Sleeping too much or too little could negatively affect your performance. Too much sleep can be just as bad as too little.

- **DO avoid stressful situations.** Avoid all stress the night before the examination. Personal issues, especially sensitive ones, should be avoided the night before your examination. They will only serve to distract you, prevent a good night's sleep, and limit study effectiveness.

EXAMINATION DAY

Examination day can be as stressful as any other important day in your life. Some candidates experience so much stress that they arrive at the examination site in a cold sweat. Stress can wear on your ability to answer questions. Adhere to the following tips to do your best on exam day:

- **Eat a good breakfast.** Eating something before the test is advisable; however, a sixteen-ounce steak will probably work against you. When you eat large amounts of food, the body redirects blood from vital organs to the stomach to digest the food. This process makes you tired and inefficient. Eat a light snack, fruit, vegetables, or a salad. Eat just enough to hold you over for the examination. After the examination, you can feast.

- **Avoid high sugars and caffeine.** Foods and drinks containing large amounts of caffeine and sugar will make you alert for a short period of time, but will leave you extremely tired as they wear off. Coffee and tea are diuretics, which can cause frequent trips to the restroom. Fruit juice or water will keep you well-hydrated during the examination.

- **Arrive at the exam site early.** If your examination starts at 9:00 a.m., plan to arrive at 8:00 a.m. Nothing is worse than showing up at an examination late. Leave enough time to account for unforeseen circumstances, such as a lack of parking spaces or a delay caused by an accident on the road.

- **Sit in a well-lit and comfortable area.** This tip is good if you are familiar with the classroom layout. Most examinations are administered in the same room where you took your course. If you are familiar with the layout, find a comfortable seat. Sitting near an open window or under the air conditioning or heating vents can be distracting. Arrive early and size up the examination room, so you can pick a good seat.

Answering Exam Questions

Most exams consist of multiple-choice questions. Here are six proven strategies to help you answer multiple-choice questions effectively:

1. **Read the whole question and all of the answer choices before choosing an answer.** Always read the entire question and all of the answer choices before choosing a response. The question may contain a confusing phrase, and the answer you choose in a hurry may be incorrect.

2. **Look for key words in the questions.** Noticing words printed in bold, italic, or capital letters is often essential to choosing the correct answer. Words like *except, if, and,* and *which* are clues. Make sure to locate the key words in each question.

TIP

If you have studied throughout your course, spend the final night reviewing key terms and concepts.

3. **Read scenario questions carefully.** Most examinations include scenarios with several questions related to them. Read the scenario carefully and completely. Don't jump to the questions until you're confident that you understand the scenario. Answer one question at a time and reread the scenario if you must.

4. **Take your time—but not too much time.** Most examinations are timed, so don't spend too much time on any one question. Figure out approximately how much time you have per question before you begin your test. Examination proctors will usually make "time remaining" announcements. Judge your speed accordingly. In addition, remember not to rush through an examination. No extra points are awarded to the student who finishes first.

5. **If you are unable to answer a question, move on and come back later.** Some questions are answered later in the test. You can use this to your advantage when dealing with difficult questions. Move on and come back. Just make sure you also skip the space on your answer sheet.

6. **When you're finished, go back and check your answers.** If you complete the examination with time remaining, go back and review the questions. No law states that once you're finished, you can no longer look at the examination booklet. Read the questions, answer them again, and check your new answers against the ones on the answer sheet. If they do not match, reread the question, reevaluate it, and choose the answer that seems correct.

Anatomy of a Question

TIP

If you do not know the correct answer, eliminate the answers you know are incorrect.

A question is an evaluation tool—nothing more. Questions are designed to see if you can comprehend information and apply it.

> Which of the following is a late sign of shock?
> (A) Alteration of mental status
> (B) Decreased blood pressure
> (C) Hypoperfusion
> (D) Increased pulse rate
>
> **The correct answer is (B).** Most multiple-choice questions include four answer choices. Only one of the answers is correct. The other three are distracters. A distracter is an answer choice that for one reason or another is incorrect. In the question above, "decreased blood pressure" is the correct answer. Distracters can seem correct, so they distract you from choosing the actual correct answer. Hypoperfusion is the definition of shock; however, under the stress of an examination, you may start thinking, "Is hypoperfusion the definition of late shock or early shock?"

If you were unsure which answer to choose, you could use the process of elimination to help identify the answer. You may know that *alteration of mental status* and *increased pulse rate* are early signs of shock, so you can eliminate them. Now, you have to choose between only two possible answers. Even if you have to guess, having only two options increases your chances of correctly answering the question.

WHAT HAPPENS AFTER YOU PASS YOUR EXAM?

Preparing a Proper Resume

Once you pass your exam and are certified or licensed to work as an EMT–Basic, you should prepare a proper resume and send it to the agencies for which you would like to work.

A proper resume should include your career goal as well as information about your past employment and training. It should also provide a list of any certifications and their expiration dates, so prospective employers are aware of your expertise in the field of EMS.

You may apply to public EMS agencies that deliver emergency care to a specific service area (911 employers) as well as proprietary providers of EMS (private ambulance). Proprietary providers do routine and high-risk transports in addition to some emergencies and 911 calls. They may also offer additional specialty training to help you gain experience.

Another way to gain experience is to volunteer with a local ambulance company. Volunteer agencies usually provide 911 services to their community and are a great way to gain experience and connect with people who have the same interests as you. Many EMT–Basics who move on to paid EMS positions retain their position with their volunteer agency because it offers good experience in emergency medical care and gives them a chance to serve their community.

The following page includes a sample resume you may use as a model when creating your own resume.

NOTE

Your resume should be concise but comprehensive. Proper resumes should be only one page in length and list several years of work experience, even if it is not in the field for which you are now applying.

SAMPLE RESUME

Joseph B. EMT
304 Pleasant Lane
Anywhere, USA 99999
555-555-5555

OBJECTIVE: A career in Emergency Medical Services where the application of my professional knowledge and skills will assist sick and injured patients in accessing emergency medical care in a timely and professional fashion.

EXPERIENCE:
2003–Present   Franks Oxygen Service, Anywhere, USA

Deliver oxygen to health-care facilities, fire departments, and EMS stations

Ensure safety measures are in place

Facilitate safe and efficient delivery of bottled gases, according to state and local laws

EDUCATION: Anywhere High School, Anywhere, USA, 2006

EMT–Basic Certification

Anywhere USA EMS Academy, Anywhere, USA

CERTIFICATIONS: Anywhere State EMT–Basic Provider, # 380076, Expires 8/30/2012

Pre-hospital Trauma Care course

Pre-hospital Pediatric Care course

INTERESTS: Computers, ice hockey, and science fiction

Interviewing

Interviewing for any position can be stressful. Even the most experienced people in the workforce can get nervous before an interview. The secret to a successful interview is to remain calm and talk positively about yourself. Negative comments will not help you gain employment. Stories of negative experiences with a previous employer should be left out of your interview.

On the day of your interview, arrive early, dress appropriately, and bring a copy of your resume. Be patient and polite. Sit down with your potential employer and answer questions slowly and calmly. Try to stay on topic and refrain from talking about personal feelings on any issues. Discuss your good qualities and your work ability. Ask questions that are pertinent to the position and clarify any questions you may have.

When the interview is over, shake hands and thank the interviewer for his or her time. Ask if you may call back in a few days to touch base. Do not say, "Well, do I have the job?" Some employers will hire on the spot, but most will call in a few days after they have conducted several interviews. If you are called back for a second interview, approach it as if it were your first. Repeat your good qualities and answer any questions honestly and concisely.

Don't get discouraged if the first employer does not hire you. Just keep trying. Eventually, you will break into a rewarding and exciting career as an EMT–Basic.

TYPES OF EMS–PROVIDER AGENCIES

You may seek employment at many different types of EMS–provider agencies. Listed below are several types of agencies that provide emergency medical services.

Volunteer Agency

A volunteer EMS agency is made up of area residents who are EMS providers. They are community-minded people who provide a needed and appreciated service to the sick and injured of their community. A volunteer agency is a great place to start even before you become a certified EMT. These agencies sometimes sponsor people in EMS courses. In most cases, you won't get paid for being there, but you will gain much-needed experience in the field of EMS.

Municipal Agency

A municipal agency is usually a city-, state-, or town-run EMS–provider agency. You will come in contact with municipal systems in larger cities and towns. Employment with these agencies usually requires a written examination. Once hired, you will probably attend the EMS academy for additional training. Municipal agencies often offer civil service positions and benefits as well as career mobility.

Hospital-Based Agency

Many hospitals have their own ambulance services, which cover a specific area around the hospital. In many areas, EMS systems were developed by hospital-based agencies and grew into municipalities.

Hospital-based agencies are similar to municipal agencies and often work in the same areas with municipal agencies to deliver emergency medical care.

Proprietary Agency

Proprietary agencies are also called private ambulance companies. Private ambulance companies transport high- and low-risk specialty patients. They are specialized crews assigned to a specific hospital or area and work by contract with that hospital to provide transport. Many proprietary agencies also provide 911 services to contracted service areas. Many large proprietary agencies nationwide hire people for several EMS positions, including air-medical transport.

Other Agencies

Other EMS agencies to consider are first-response agencies, which provide first-responder units to emergency calls; air-medical transports, which provide helicopter and fixed-wing aircraft for patient transport; and specialty assignments like movie sets and shipboard EMS. Overseas employers routinely advertise for EMS providers in the national EMS journals.

As an EMT–Basic, you will find many opportunities to provide patient care in a number of different settings. Keep your options open and find the one that best suits your needs or interests.

SUMMING IT UP

- The five levels of EMT certification are Lay Rescuer, Certified First Responder, EMT–Basic, EMT–Intermediate, and EMT–Paramedic.

- There are steps you can take to help you minimize Critical Incident Stress.

- Developing good study habits is essential to scoring high on the EMT–Basic Certification Exam.

- To effectively answer multiple-choice questions on the EMT–Basic Certification Exam, you must understand the anatomy of a multiple-choice question.

- Preparing a proper resume and interviewing well are important steps in becoming employed as an EMT–Basic.

PART II
DIAGNOSING STRENGTHS AND WEAKNESSES

CHAPTER 2   Practice Test 1: Diagnostic

ANSWER SHEET PRACTICE TEST 1: DIAGNOSTIC

Basics of Emergency Medical Care

1. Ⓐ Ⓑ Ⓒ Ⓓ	11. Ⓐ Ⓑ Ⓒ Ⓓ	21. Ⓐ Ⓑ Ⓒ Ⓓ	31. Ⓐ Ⓑ Ⓒ Ⓓ	41. Ⓐ Ⓑ Ⓒ Ⓓ
2. Ⓐ Ⓑ Ⓒ Ⓓ	12. Ⓐ Ⓑ Ⓒ Ⓓ	22. Ⓐ Ⓑ Ⓒ Ⓓ	32. Ⓐ Ⓑ Ⓒ Ⓓ	42. Ⓐ Ⓑ Ⓒ Ⓓ
3. Ⓐ Ⓑ Ⓒ Ⓓ	13. Ⓐ Ⓑ Ⓒ Ⓓ	23. Ⓐ Ⓑ Ⓒ Ⓓ	33. Ⓐ Ⓑ Ⓒ Ⓓ	43. Ⓐ Ⓑ Ⓒ Ⓓ
4. Ⓐ Ⓑ Ⓒ Ⓓ	14. Ⓐ Ⓑ Ⓒ Ⓓ	24. Ⓐ Ⓑ Ⓒ Ⓓ	34. Ⓐ Ⓑ Ⓒ Ⓓ	44. Ⓐ Ⓑ Ⓒ Ⓓ
5. Ⓐ Ⓑ Ⓒ Ⓓ	15. Ⓐ Ⓑ Ⓒ Ⓓ	25. Ⓐ Ⓑ Ⓒ Ⓓ	35. Ⓐ Ⓑ Ⓒ Ⓓ	45. Ⓐ Ⓑ Ⓒ Ⓓ
6. Ⓐ Ⓑ Ⓒ Ⓓ	16. Ⓐ Ⓑ Ⓒ Ⓓ	26. Ⓐ Ⓑ Ⓒ Ⓓ	36. Ⓐ Ⓑ Ⓒ Ⓓ	46. Ⓐ Ⓑ Ⓒ Ⓓ
7. Ⓐ Ⓑ Ⓒ Ⓓ	17. Ⓐ Ⓑ Ⓒ Ⓓ	27. Ⓐ Ⓑ Ⓒ Ⓓ	37. Ⓐ Ⓑ Ⓒ Ⓓ	47. Ⓐ Ⓑ Ⓒ Ⓓ
8. Ⓐ Ⓑ Ⓒ Ⓓ	18. Ⓐ Ⓑ Ⓒ Ⓓ	28. Ⓐ Ⓑ Ⓒ Ⓓ	38. Ⓐ Ⓑ Ⓒ Ⓓ	48. Ⓐ Ⓑ Ⓒ Ⓓ
9. Ⓐ Ⓑ Ⓒ Ⓓ	19. Ⓐ Ⓑ Ⓒ Ⓓ	29. Ⓐ Ⓑ Ⓒ Ⓓ	39. Ⓐ Ⓑ Ⓒ Ⓓ	49. Ⓐ Ⓑ Ⓒ Ⓓ
10. Ⓐ Ⓑ Ⓒ Ⓓ	20. Ⓐ Ⓑ Ⓒ Ⓓ	30. Ⓐ Ⓑ Ⓒ Ⓓ	40. Ⓐ Ⓑ Ⓒ Ⓓ	

Airway

1. Ⓐ Ⓑ Ⓒ Ⓓ	7. Ⓐ Ⓑ Ⓒ Ⓓ	13. Ⓐ Ⓑ Ⓒ Ⓓ	18. Ⓐ Ⓑ Ⓒ Ⓓ	23. Ⓐ Ⓑ Ⓒ Ⓓ
2. Ⓐ Ⓑ Ⓒ Ⓓ	8. Ⓐ Ⓑ Ⓒ Ⓓ	14. Ⓐ Ⓑ Ⓒ Ⓓ	19. Ⓐ Ⓑ Ⓒ Ⓓ	24. Ⓐ Ⓑ Ⓒ Ⓓ
3. Ⓐ Ⓑ Ⓒ Ⓓ	9. Ⓐ Ⓑ Ⓒ Ⓓ	15. Ⓐ Ⓑ Ⓒ Ⓓ	20. Ⓐ Ⓑ Ⓒ Ⓓ	25. Ⓐ Ⓑ Ⓒ Ⓓ
4. Ⓐ Ⓑ Ⓒ Ⓓ	10. Ⓐ Ⓑ Ⓒ Ⓓ	16. Ⓐ Ⓑ Ⓒ Ⓓ	21. Ⓐ Ⓑ Ⓒ Ⓓ	26. Ⓐ Ⓑ Ⓒ Ⓓ
5. Ⓐ Ⓑ Ⓒ Ⓓ	11. Ⓐ Ⓑ Ⓒ Ⓓ	17. Ⓐ Ⓑ Ⓒ Ⓓ	22. Ⓐ Ⓑ Ⓒ Ⓓ	27. Ⓐ Ⓑ Ⓒ Ⓓ
6. Ⓐ Ⓑ Ⓒ Ⓓ	12. Ⓐ Ⓑ Ⓒ Ⓓ			

Assessment

1. Ⓐ Ⓑ Ⓒ Ⓓ	9. Ⓐ Ⓑ Ⓒ Ⓓ	17. Ⓐ Ⓑ Ⓒ Ⓓ	25. Ⓐ Ⓑ Ⓒ Ⓓ	33. Ⓐ Ⓑ Ⓒ Ⓓ
2. Ⓐ Ⓑ Ⓒ Ⓓ	10. Ⓐ Ⓑ Ⓒ Ⓓ	18. Ⓐ Ⓑ Ⓒ Ⓓ	26. Ⓐ Ⓑ Ⓒ Ⓓ	34. Ⓐ Ⓑ Ⓒ Ⓓ
3. Ⓐ Ⓑ Ⓒ Ⓓ	11. Ⓐ Ⓑ Ⓒ Ⓓ	19. Ⓐ Ⓑ Ⓒ Ⓓ	27. Ⓐ Ⓑ Ⓒ Ⓓ	35. Ⓐ Ⓑ Ⓒ Ⓓ
4. Ⓐ Ⓑ Ⓒ Ⓓ	12. Ⓐ Ⓑ Ⓒ Ⓓ	20. Ⓐ Ⓑ Ⓒ Ⓓ	28. Ⓐ Ⓑ Ⓒ Ⓓ	36. Ⓐ Ⓑ Ⓒ Ⓓ
5. Ⓐ Ⓑ Ⓒ Ⓓ	13. Ⓐ Ⓑ Ⓒ Ⓓ	21. Ⓐ Ⓑ Ⓒ Ⓓ	29. Ⓐ Ⓑ Ⓒ Ⓓ	37. Ⓐ Ⓑ Ⓒ Ⓓ
6. Ⓐ Ⓑ Ⓒ Ⓓ	14. Ⓐ Ⓑ Ⓒ Ⓓ	22. Ⓐ Ⓑ Ⓒ Ⓓ	30. Ⓐ Ⓑ Ⓒ Ⓓ	38. Ⓐ Ⓑ Ⓒ Ⓓ
7. Ⓐ Ⓑ Ⓒ Ⓓ	15. Ⓐ Ⓑ Ⓒ Ⓓ	23. Ⓐ Ⓑ Ⓒ Ⓓ	31. Ⓐ Ⓑ Ⓒ Ⓓ	39. Ⓐ Ⓑ Ⓒ Ⓓ
8. Ⓐ Ⓑ Ⓒ Ⓓ	16. Ⓐ Ⓑ Ⓒ Ⓓ	24. Ⓐ Ⓑ Ⓒ Ⓓ	32. Ⓐ Ⓑ Ⓒ Ⓓ	40. Ⓐ Ⓑ Ⓒ Ⓓ

answer sheet

Medical

1. Ⓐ Ⓑ Ⓒ Ⓓ   15. Ⓐ Ⓑ Ⓒ Ⓓ   29. Ⓐ Ⓑ Ⓒ Ⓓ   43. Ⓐ Ⓑ Ⓒ Ⓓ   57. Ⓐ Ⓑ Ⓒ Ⓓ
2. Ⓐ Ⓑ Ⓒ Ⓓ   16. Ⓐ Ⓑ Ⓒ Ⓓ   30. Ⓐ Ⓑ Ⓒ Ⓓ   44. Ⓐ Ⓑ Ⓒ Ⓓ   58. Ⓐ Ⓑ Ⓒ Ⓓ
3. Ⓐ Ⓑ Ⓒ Ⓓ   17. Ⓐ Ⓑ Ⓒ Ⓓ   31. Ⓐ Ⓑ Ⓒ Ⓓ   45. Ⓐ Ⓑ Ⓒ Ⓓ   59. Ⓐ Ⓑ Ⓒ Ⓓ
4. Ⓐ Ⓑ Ⓒ Ⓓ   18. Ⓐ Ⓑ Ⓒ Ⓓ   32. Ⓐ Ⓑ Ⓒ Ⓓ   46. Ⓐ Ⓑ Ⓒ Ⓓ   60. Ⓐ Ⓑ Ⓒ Ⓓ
5. Ⓐ Ⓑ Ⓒ Ⓓ   19. Ⓐ Ⓑ Ⓒ Ⓓ   33. Ⓐ Ⓑ Ⓒ Ⓓ   47. Ⓐ Ⓑ Ⓒ Ⓓ   61. Ⓐ Ⓑ Ⓒ Ⓓ
6. Ⓐ Ⓑ Ⓒ Ⓓ   20. Ⓐ Ⓑ Ⓒ Ⓓ   34. Ⓐ Ⓑ Ⓒ Ⓓ   48. Ⓐ Ⓑ   62. Ⓐ Ⓑ Ⓒ Ⓓ
7. Ⓐ Ⓑ Ⓒ Ⓓ   21. Ⓐ Ⓑ Ⓒ Ⓓ   35. Ⓐ Ⓑ Ⓒ Ⓓ   49. Ⓐ Ⓑ Ⓒ Ⓓ   63. Ⓐ Ⓑ Ⓒ Ⓓ
8. Ⓐ Ⓑ Ⓒ Ⓓ   22. Ⓐ Ⓑ Ⓒ Ⓓ   36. Ⓐ Ⓑ Ⓒ Ⓓ   50. Ⓐ Ⓑ Ⓒ Ⓓ   64. Ⓐ Ⓑ Ⓒ Ⓓ
9. Ⓐ Ⓑ Ⓒ Ⓓ   23. Ⓐ Ⓑ Ⓒ Ⓓ   37. Ⓐ Ⓑ Ⓒ Ⓓ   51. Ⓐ Ⓑ Ⓒ Ⓓ   65. Ⓐ Ⓑ Ⓒ Ⓓ
10. Ⓐ Ⓑ Ⓒ Ⓓ   24. Ⓐ Ⓑ Ⓒ Ⓓ   38. Ⓐ Ⓑ Ⓒ Ⓓ   52. Ⓐ Ⓑ Ⓒ Ⓓ   66. Ⓐ Ⓑ Ⓒ Ⓓ
11. Ⓐ Ⓑ Ⓒ Ⓓ   25. Ⓐ Ⓑ Ⓒ Ⓓ   39. Ⓐ Ⓑ Ⓒ Ⓓ   53. Ⓐ Ⓑ Ⓒ Ⓓ   67. Ⓐ Ⓑ Ⓒ Ⓓ
12. Ⓐ Ⓑ Ⓒ Ⓓ   26. Ⓐ Ⓑ Ⓒ Ⓓ   40. Ⓐ Ⓑ Ⓒ Ⓓ   54. Ⓐ Ⓑ Ⓒ Ⓓ   68. Ⓐ Ⓑ Ⓒ Ⓓ
13. Ⓐ Ⓑ Ⓒ Ⓓ   27. Ⓐ Ⓑ Ⓒ Ⓓ   41. Ⓐ Ⓑ Ⓒ Ⓓ   55. Ⓐ Ⓑ Ⓒ Ⓓ   69. Ⓐ Ⓑ Ⓒ Ⓓ
14. Ⓐ Ⓑ Ⓒ Ⓓ   28. Ⓐ Ⓑ Ⓒ Ⓓ   42. Ⓐ Ⓑ Ⓒ Ⓓ   56. Ⓐ Ⓑ Ⓒ Ⓓ

Trauma

1. Ⓐ Ⓑ Ⓒ Ⓓ   11. Ⓐ Ⓑ Ⓒ Ⓓ   21. Ⓐ Ⓑ Ⓒ Ⓓ   31. Ⓐ Ⓑ Ⓒ Ⓓ   40. Ⓐ Ⓑ Ⓒ Ⓓ
2. Ⓐ Ⓑ Ⓒ Ⓓ   12. Ⓐ Ⓑ Ⓒ Ⓓ   22. Ⓐ Ⓑ Ⓒ Ⓓ   32. Ⓐ Ⓑ Ⓒ Ⓓ   41. Ⓐ Ⓑ Ⓒ Ⓓ
3. Ⓐ Ⓑ Ⓒ Ⓓ   13. Ⓐ Ⓑ Ⓒ Ⓓ   23. Ⓐ Ⓑ Ⓒ Ⓓ   33. Ⓐ Ⓑ Ⓒ Ⓓ   42. Ⓐ Ⓑ Ⓒ Ⓓ
4. Ⓐ Ⓑ Ⓒ Ⓓ   14. Ⓐ Ⓑ Ⓒ Ⓓ   24. Ⓐ Ⓑ Ⓒ Ⓓ   34. Ⓐ Ⓑ Ⓒ Ⓓ   43. Ⓐ Ⓑ Ⓒ Ⓓ
5. Ⓐ Ⓑ Ⓒ Ⓓ   15. Ⓐ Ⓑ Ⓒ Ⓓ   25. Ⓐ Ⓑ Ⓒ Ⓓ   35. Ⓐ Ⓑ Ⓒ Ⓓ   44. Ⓐ Ⓑ Ⓒ Ⓓ
6. Ⓐ Ⓑ Ⓒ Ⓓ   16. Ⓐ Ⓑ Ⓒ Ⓓ   26. Ⓐ Ⓑ Ⓒ Ⓓ   36. Ⓐ Ⓑ Ⓒ Ⓓ   45. Ⓐ Ⓑ Ⓒ Ⓓ
7. Ⓐ Ⓑ Ⓒ Ⓓ   17. Ⓐ Ⓑ Ⓒ Ⓓ   27. Ⓐ Ⓑ Ⓒ Ⓓ   37. Ⓐ Ⓑ Ⓒ Ⓓ   46. Ⓐ Ⓑ Ⓒ Ⓓ
8. Ⓐ Ⓑ Ⓒ Ⓓ   18. Ⓐ Ⓑ Ⓒ Ⓓ   28. Ⓐ Ⓑ Ⓒ Ⓓ   38. Ⓐ Ⓑ Ⓒ Ⓓ   47. Ⓐ Ⓑ Ⓒ Ⓓ
9. Ⓐ Ⓑ Ⓒ Ⓓ   19. Ⓐ Ⓑ Ⓒ Ⓓ   29. Ⓐ Ⓑ Ⓒ Ⓓ   39. Ⓐ Ⓑ Ⓒ Ⓓ   48. Ⓐ Ⓑ Ⓒ Ⓓ
10. Ⓐ Ⓑ Ⓒ Ⓓ   20. Ⓐ Ⓑ Ⓒ Ⓓ   30. Ⓐ Ⓑ Ⓒ Ⓓ

Infants and Children

1. Ⓐ Ⓑ Ⓒ Ⓓ   4. Ⓐ Ⓑ Ⓒ Ⓓ   7. Ⓐ Ⓑ Ⓒ Ⓓ   10. Ⓐ Ⓑ Ⓒ Ⓓ   12. Ⓐ Ⓑ
2. Ⓐ Ⓑ Ⓒ Ⓓ   5. Ⓐ Ⓑ Ⓒ Ⓓ   8. Ⓐ Ⓑ Ⓒ Ⓓ   11. Ⓐ Ⓑ Ⓒ Ⓓ   13. Ⓐ Ⓑ Ⓒ Ⓓ
3. Ⓐ Ⓑ Ⓒ Ⓓ   6. Ⓐ Ⓑ Ⓒ Ⓓ   9. Ⓐ Ⓑ Ⓒ Ⓓ

Operations

1. Ⓐ Ⓑ Ⓒ Ⓓ   6. Ⓐ Ⓑ Ⓒ Ⓓ   11. Ⓐ Ⓑ Ⓒ Ⓓ   16. Ⓐ Ⓑ Ⓒ Ⓓ   20. Ⓐ Ⓑ Ⓒ Ⓓ
2. Ⓐ Ⓑ Ⓒ Ⓓ   7. Ⓐ Ⓑ Ⓒ Ⓓ   12. Ⓐ Ⓑ Ⓒ Ⓓ   17. Ⓐ Ⓑ Ⓒ Ⓓ   21. Ⓐ Ⓑ Ⓒ Ⓓ
3. Ⓐ Ⓑ Ⓒ Ⓓ   8. Ⓐ Ⓑ Ⓒ Ⓓ   13. Ⓐ Ⓑ Ⓒ Ⓓ   18. Ⓐ Ⓑ Ⓒ Ⓓ   22. Ⓐ Ⓑ Ⓒ Ⓓ
4. Ⓐ Ⓑ Ⓒ Ⓓ   9. Ⓐ Ⓑ Ⓒ Ⓓ   14. Ⓐ Ⓑ Ⓒ Ⓓ   19. Ⓐ Ⓑ Ⓒ Ⓓ   23. Ⓐ Ⓑ Ⓒ Ⓓ
5. Ⓐ Ⓑ Ⓒ Ⓓ   10. Ⓐ Ⓑ Ⓒ Ⓓ   15. Ⓐ Ⓑ Ⓒ Ⓓ

answer sheet

Practice Test 1: Diagnostic

PREPARING TO TAKE THE DIAGNOSTIC TEST

An examination is an evaluation tool. To become certified or licensed in the EMS field, you must satisfactorily complete your final evaluation. Before you take the test, you should evaluate yourself to identify areas of strength and weakness. Taking the Diagnostic Test in this chapter will help you determine your strengths and weaknesses and apportion your study time.

The Diagnostic Test is made up of multiple-choice questions and contains many more questions than you will see on the actual test. The Diagnostic Test provides you with the most comprehensive evaluation tool possible.

We suggest that you answer the questions as if you were taking the actual test. If possible, take the test in one sitting. After you complete the entire test, compare your answers with the correct answers and their corresponding explanations.

As you take the Diagnostic Test, write down any questions you have so you can research them later or ask your instructor for further explanation.

BASICS OF EMERGENCY MEDICAL CARE

Directions: Each question has a maximum of four possible answers. Choose the letter that best answers the question and mark your choice on the answer sheet.

1. Which of the following is NOT a component of the EMS system?

   (A) 911 dispatcher

   (B) Emergency department staff

   (C) Police and fire officers who arrive on the scene

   (D) Bystanders who witness the injury but do not help the patient

2. The EMT–Basic may provide all of the following patient interactions EXCEPT

   (A) spinal immobilization.

   (B) detailed physical assessments.

   (C) ventilation using a bag-valve-mask ventilator.

   (D) field administration of medications in cardiac arrest.

3. Which of the following is the most important responsibility of the EMT–Basic?

   (A) Patient care

   (B) Patient transport

   (C) Patient safety

   (D) Personal safety

4. The term "quality improvement" is best defined as

   (A) a medical director's review of patient call reports.

   (B) an EMT–Basic's documentation of patient interactions.

   (C) the review of system aspects that need improvement based on identified problems.

   (D) the identification of possible problems and methods of correction before the problems surface.

5. The ultimate responsibility for patient care is at the discretion of

   (A) the EMT–Basic on scene.

   (B) the physician medical director.

   (C) the emergency department staff.

   (D) advanced-level providers on scene (if applicable).

6. Many EMS calls can cause a stress reaction in the EMT–Basic. However, some calls cause a higher incidence of stress reaction. Of the following calls, which would have the highest incidence of stress for the EMT–Basic?

   (A) A three-year-old child who is unconscious and not breathing after being hit by a car

   (B) A seventy-five-year-old cardiac patient who feels better after assisted medication

   (C) A seventeen-year-old female who has overdosed on Tylenol

   (D) A fifty-year-old male with an amputated hand

7. As a new EMT–Basic, you're placed with an experienced partner. After a few quiet tours, you notice your partner seems irritable and uninterested in work, complains of difficulty sleeping, and hardly ever eats. What is the most likely explanation for your partner's behavior?

   (A) Your partner may be having a cumulative stress reaction.

   (B) Your partner may be having an acute stress reaction.

   (C) Your partner is just an unfriendly person.

   (D) Your partner dislikes new EMT–Basics.

8. Which of the following is NOT a good a stress-reduction practice?

   (A) Maintaining a properly balanced diet

   (B) Going out for drinks after each shift

   (C) Following a regimen for relaxation

   (D) Exercising a few times each week

9. You respond to a call for a patient with difficulty breathing. Upon your arrival, you find a thirty-eight-year-old male who has been coughing for two weeks and is complaining of night sweats and a low-grade fever. During your assessment, you notice that other people in the house have the same type of cough and fever. Your scene assessment reveals the possibility that this patient may be suffering from

   (A) chronic bronchitis.

   (B) a communicable disease.

   (C) an asthma attack.

   (D) a cardiovascular disease.

10. Gloves should be worn when treating which of the following patients?

    (A) A forty-five-year-old male with AIDS who has been vomiting blood

    (B) A seventy-five-year-old female complaining of excessive vomiting

    (C) A fifteen-year-old female who has a laceration to her right lower leg

    (D) All of the above

11. You respond to an overturned tanker truck. There is no placard on the truck. On the ground, you notice a milky blue liquid that has the distinct odor of onions. The driver of the truck is lying on the ground in this unidentified substance. You should do all of the following EXCEPT

    (A) rapidly extricate the driver, being careful not to step in the puddle of liquid.

    (B) request a hazmat response team to extricate and decontaminate the driver.

    (C) set up a treatment area and await decontaminated patients for treatment.

    (D) set up a triage area in case the incident produces more than one patient.

12. You arrive at the scene of a shooting inside a tavern. On your arrival, you notice two large crowds still fighting with each other in the parking lot. An intoxicated male approaches you frantically, telling you that his friend is inside and was shot in the chest. Your initial actions are to

    (A) ask the male to have his friends provide you protection while you work on the patient.

    (B) request immediate police assistance and remain outside the tavern until they arrive.

    (C) have the man and his friends bring the patient out to you so you can work on him.

    (D) take your equipment inside and attempt to treat the patient as best as you can.

13. Responding to an emergency call, assessing, and providing treatment and transport are all part of the EMT–Basic's

    (A) response to consent.

    (B) treatment protocol.

    (C) scope of practice.

    (D) liability.

14. The term "expressed consent" is best defined as

    (A) a court order that allows medical personnel to treat a patient who refuses treatment.

    (B) treatment of a patient after he or she has made an informed decision to be treated.

    (C) treatment of a patient who is unconscious during the treatment.

    (D) forcibly treating a patient even though he or she refuses care.

15. The term "implied consent" is best defined as

    (A) a court order that allows medical personnel to treat a patient who refuses treatment.

    (B) treatment of a patient after he or she has made an informed decision to be treated.

    (C) treatment of a patient who is unconscious during the treatment.

    (D) forcibly treating a patient even though he or she refuses care.

16. You are on the scene of a diabetic call. On your arrival, the family had already administered glucose paste, and the patient is now coming around. You identify yourself and explain to the patient why you are there. The patient allows a full assessment but refuses transport to the hospital. You should do all of the following EXCEPT

    (A) explain the risks of refusal of transport.

    (B) stay with the patient until a doctor arrives on the scene.

    (C) obtain a patient signature on the refusal form, as well as a witness signature.

    (D) explain that the patient may contact emergency services if the problem happens again.

17. You respond to a call for a twenty-one-year-old patient with hyperventilation syndrome. On your arrival, the patient adamantly refuses assessment. You tell her that it's necessary and do your assessment against her will, even though she keeps telling you to leave her alone. You may be found guilty of

    (A) assault.

    (B) negligence.

    (C) abandonment.

    (D) domestic violence.

18. You and your partner are on the scene of a minor car accident and treating one patient who will require stitches at the local hospital. You hear on the EMS radio that a patient has been shot two blocks away, and the police are asking for an ambulance forthwith. You tell the patient you are treating to seek alternate transport to the hospital and respond to the shooting. You may be charged with

    (A) assault.

    (B) negligence.

    (C) abandonment.

    (D) domestic violence.

19. You are treating a patient for a possible fractured ankle. You and your partner arrive at the hospital and ask the patient to hop over to the wheelchair. In doing so, the patient falls and injures his arm. You may be guilty of

    (A) assault.

    (B) negligence.

    (C) abandonment.

    (D) domestic violence.

20. You transport several children to the hospital after an incident in the school cafeteria produces a toxic gas. When you arrive at the emergency department, you notice a film crew standing at the entrance. The newsperson asks the names and conditions of the children. You freely give the names and conditions. You have done which of the following?

    (A) Breached patient confidentiality

    (B) Committed negligence

    (C) Committed abandonment

    (D) Treated under false implied consent

21. When responding to a crime scene, after scene safety, the first responsibility is

    (A) providing care to any injured parties.

    (B) maintaining the scene evidence.

    (C) questioning bystanders about the perpetrator.

    (D) securing the scene until police arrive.

22. All of the following are considered vital signs EXCEPT

    (A) blood pressure.

    (B) motor function.

    (C) pulse rate.

    (D) respiratory rate.

23. Respiratory rate is assessed by counting

    (A) full-chest rises for fifteen seconds and multiplying by four.

    (B) breaths for thirty seconds and multiplying by two.

    (C) breaths for a full sixty seconds.

    (D) full chest rises for sixty seconds.

24. You are assessing a patient's respirations. You notice stridor, nasal flaring, and accessory muscle use; the patient is sitting in a tripod position. You can state that the patient has _____ breathing.

    (A) regular

    (B) shallow

    (C) labored

    (D) rapid

25. Pulse rate is assessed by counting

    (A) impulses for thirty seconds and multiplying by two.

    (B) impulses for fifteen seconds and multiplying by four.

    (C) breaths for a full sixty seconds.

    (D) full chest rises for fifteen seconds.

FOR QUESTIONS 26–29, MATCH THE SKIN COLOR TO ITS POSSIBLE CAUSES.

26. Cyanosis

    (A) Liver abnormalities

    (B) Inadequate oxygenation

    (C) Impaired perfusion status

    (D) Heat exhaustion

27. Jaundice

    (A) Liver abnormalities

    (B) Inadequate oxygenation

    (C) Impaired perfusion status

    (D) Heat exhaustion

28. Pallor

    (A) Liver abnormalities

    (B) Inadequate oxygenation

    (C) Impaired perfusion status

    (D) Heat exhaustion

29. Flushing

    (A) Liver abnormalities

    (B) Inadequate oxygenation

    (C) Impaired perfusion status

    (D) Heat exhaustion

30. Cool and clammy skin is a sign of _____ , while hot and dry skin is a sign of _____ .
    (A) shock . . . heat exposure
    (B) fever . . . heat loss
    (C) cold exposure . . . heat exposure
    (D) fever . . . heat loss

31. When assessing for normal capillary refill, you should see blood return to the blanched extremity in _____ ; longer blood return times indicate _____ .
    (A) four seconds . . . hypertension
    (B) four seconds . . . poor circulation
    (C) two seconds . . . hypertension
    (D) two seconds . . . poor circulation

32. You respond to a call for an unconscious patient. On arrival, you find a twenty-eight-year-old male unconscious on the floor. His girlfriend states that he was fine and then just passed out. Your assessment reveals constricted pupils. You suspect this patient has overdosed on
    (A) barbiturates.
    (B) alcohol.
    (C) narcotics.
    (D) benzodiazepines.

33. Your patient is unconscious after being struck on the head with a lead pipe. In a patient with severe head injury, you would expect his pupils to be unreactive or
    (A) unequal.
    (B) constricted.
    (C) dilated.
    (D) unaffected.

34. During assessment, you shine your penlight in a patient's eye. You would expect the pupils to respond by
    (A) dilating unilaterally.
    (B) dilating bilaterally.
    (C) constricting unilaterally.
    (D) constricting bilaterally.

35. Contraction of the left ventricle and its resulting blood-flow reading is known as
    (A) diastolic blood pressure.
    (B) systolic blood pressure.
    (C) arterial pressure.
    (D) positive pressure.

36. The blood pressure that signifies the relaxation stage of the ventricles is known as
    (A) diastolic blood pressure.
    (B) systolic blood pressure.
    (C) arterial pressure.
    (D) positive pressure.

37. What are the two different ways to obtain a patient's blood pressure?
    (A) Inspection and palpation
    (B) Inspection and auscultation
    (C) Auscultation and palpation
    (D) Auscultation and percussion

38. All of the following are symptoms EXCEPT
    (A) headache.
    (B) nausea.
    (C) vomiting.
    (D) chest pain.

39. Which of the following is NOT a sign?
    (A) Obvious deformity of an extremity
    (B) Vomiting
    (C) Dilated pupils
    (D) Abdominal pain

40. All of the following are components of the SAMPLE history EXCEPT
    (A) medication.
    (B) allergies.
    (C) signs and symptoms.
    (D) pulse rate.

41. Properly using your body to lift and move a patient is defined as
    (A) body mechanics.
    (B) physical mechanics.
    (C) body-lift technique.
    (D) efficient lifting.

42. All of the following are elements of an effective lift EXCEPT
    (A) lifting with the legs.
    (B) keeping the back straight.
    (C) shifting weight on the lift.
    (D) keeping the weight near your body.

43. You need to transport a stable patient with chest pain down several flights of stairs. Which of the following devices is best suited for this carry?
    (A) Scoop stretcher
    (B) Long backboard
    (C) Stair chair
    (D) Wheeled stretcher

44. When carrying a patient using a stair chair, a third EMS provider should be used as a spotter. Where should the spotter be positioned?
    (A) The top of the stairs above the carry, looking down and advising the crew of obstacles
    (B) The bottom of the stairs below the carry, looking up and advising the crew of obstacles
    (C) Directly behind the person at the lowest point of the carry, hand on his or her back, directing the carry
    (D) On the side of the patient, between the carriers, steadying the chair

45. You and your partner must do a carry down two flights of stairs. Upon opening your stair chair, you notice that it is broken. You do not have time to wait for another unit. Your partner approaches the patient from the rear, places her arms under the patient's arms, and grabs his wrist. You grab the patient under the knees. This type of lift is known as a(n)
    (A) extremity lift.
    (B) two-person patient drag.
    (C) clothing drag.
    (D) patient chair lift.

46. All of the following are examples of emergency moves EXCEPT
    (A) extremity lift.
    (B) sheet drag.
    (C) blanket drag.
    (D) clothing drag.

47. The draw-sheet method, direct ground lift, and direct carry are all examples of
    (A) emergency moves.
    (B) nonemergency moves.
    (C) long-range carrying techniques.
    (D) trauma patient carries.

48. You are the first unit to arrive on the scene of a house fire with a report of trapped occupants. Your partner runs into the house to try to get the people out. After several minutes, your partner appears in the doorway and falls backward, unconscious. Which of the following methods would be the best way to extricate your partner from this situation?
    (A) The fireman's carry
    (B) Extremity carry to a stair chair
    (C) Scoop stretcher
    (D) Long spine board

49. You are transporting an unconscious patient who is extremely intoxicated. Trauma has been ruled out. Which of the following positions would be the best position for transport of this patient?
    (A) Trendelenburg's
    (B) Semi-Fowler's
    (C) Fowler's
    (D) Recovery

AIRWAY

Directions: Each question has a maximum of four possible answers. Choose the letter that best answers the question and mark your choice on the answer sheet.

1. All of the following are structures of the respiratory system EXCEPT

   (A) trachea.

   (B) alveoli.

   (C) esophagus.

   (D) pharynx.

2. Of the following, which is NOT a sign of adequate breathing?

   (A) Abdominal movement

   (B) Equal chest rise and fall

   (C) Muscular retractions in the ribs

   (D) Audible breath sounds

3. You respond to a patient in respiratory distress. On your arrival, you find a sixty-seven-year-old male who has a respiratory rate of thirty-two, nasal flaring, and shallow, irregular respirations. All of these findings are indicative of

   (A) normal respiratory patterns.

   (B) inadequate breathing.

   (C) choking.

   (D) proper ventilation.

4. Which of the following is NOT a cause of inadequate breathing?

   (A) Pulmonary edema

   (B) Allergic reactions

   (C) Airway obstruction

   (D) Conjunctivitis

5. The head-tilt chin-lift airway maneuver can be used in all of the following patients EXCEPT a patient who

   (A) is choking.

   (B) has chest pain.

   (C) was struck by an automobile.

   (D) is suffering from allergic reaction.

6. The exchange of oxygen and carbon dioxide takes place in the

   (A) trachea.

   (B) alveoli.

   (C) bronchus.

   (D) epiglottis.

7. You are assigned to a motor vehicle accident on the interstate. On your arrival, you find a twenty-two-year-old male who is unconscious after being ejected from the vehicle. The initial airway maneuver of choice for the patient would be the

   (A) head-tilt chin-lift.

   (B) insertion of an oropharyngeal airway.

   (C) jaw-thrust maneuver.

   (D) chin pull.

8. The EMT–Basic should never suction a patient for longer than _____ seconds.

   (A) 5

   (B) 10

   (C) 15

   (D) 20

9. While suctioning a patient, suction should be applied

   (A) during insertion of the catheter.

   (B) while advancing the catheter.

   (C) after the catheter is in place.

   (D) while removing the catheter.

10. All of the following adjuncts are used in artificial ventilation EXCEPT the

    (A) bag-valve-mask.

    (B) nonrebreather mask.

    (C) pocket face mask.

    (D) CPR mask.

11. The pocket face mask with supplemental oxygen may deliver up to _____ percent oxygen to the nonbreathing patient.

    (A) 35
    (B) 50
    (C) 85
    (D) 100

12. The bag-valve-mask ventilation device with a reservoir may deliver up to _____ percent of oxygen to the nonbreathing patient.

    (A) 35 to 45
    (B) 50 to 60
    (C) 75 to 85
    (D) 95 to 100

13. You are treating an unconscious patient using an oropharyngeal airway. Proper insertion of this device includes all of the following EXCEPT

    (A) measuring the device from the corner of the mouth to the tip of the earlobe.
    (B) opening of the mouth using crossed-finger technique.
    (C) inserting the airway along the curvature of the mouth.
    (D) checking that the flange properly rests on the patient's lips after insertion.

14. Your seizure patient requires an airway device. Which of the following airway adjuncts would be appropriate, based on the fact that the patient's mouth is clamped shut due to the seizures?

    (A) Oropharyngeal airway
    (B) Nasopharyngeal airway
    (C) Endotracheal tube
    (D) Bag-valve-mask device

15. To ensure proper size, the nasopharyngeal airway is measured from the

    (A) angle of the jaw to the corner of the mouth.
    (B) corner of the mouth to the edge of the nostril.
    (C) edge of the nostril to the angle of the jaw.
    (D) nostril to the top of the ear.

FOR QUESTIONS 16–18, MATCH THE FOLLOWING OXYGEN CYLINDERS TO THEIR APPROPRIATE CAPACITY.

16. D cylinder
    (A) 625 liters
    (B) 350 liters
    (C) 6,500 liters
    (D) 3,000 liters

17. E cylinder
    (A) 625 liters
    (B) 350 liters
    (C) 6,500 liters
    (D) 3,000 liters

18. M cylinder
    (A) 625 liters
    (B) 350 liters
    (C) 6,500 liters
    (D) 3,000 liters

19. The non-rebreather mask can deliver approximately what percent of oxygen when attached to a delivery system at twelve to fifteen liters per minute?

    (A) 35 to 45
    (B) 45 to 55
    (C) 80 to 90
    (D) 100

20. The nasal cannula can provide varied oxygen concentrations. Which of the following liter-flow/liter-per-minute combinations correctly describe the capabilities of the nasal cannula?

    (A) One to six liters, delivering 24 to 44 percent oxygen

    (B) Two to ten liters, delivering 24 to 44 percent oxygen

    (C) Ten to twelve liters, delivering 80 to 90 percent oxygen

    (D) Fifteen liters, delivering 100 percent oxygen

21. Your eighty-two-year-old cardiac patient is complaining of difficulty breathing and chest pain. As you begin to administer oxygen through a non-rebreather mask, the patient fights the mask, saying it is too confining. You should

    (A) inform the patient that he must keep the mask on.

    (B) begin ventilations with a bag-valve-mask ventilator.

    (C) remove the mask and apply a nasal cannula for comfort.

    (D) remove the mask and disregard oxygen administration.

22. The trachea divides into two branches. The bifurcation point at which the branches form is called the

    (A) larynx.

    (B) carina.

    (C) right mainstem bronchus.

    (D) left mainstem bronchus.

23. The leaf-shaped structure that protects the airway is called the

    (A) trachea.

    (B) carina.

    (C) epiglottis.

    (D) vallecula.

24. The vocal cords are located in the

    (A) pharynx.

    (B) carina.

    (C) larynx.

    (D) epiglottis.

25. The anatomical structure that is located posterior to the trachea is known as the

    (A) carina.

    (B) right mainstem bronchus.

    (C) left mainstem bronchus.

    (D) esophagus.

26. Laryngoscope blades come in several different styles. The straight blade is also known as the _____ blade, while the curved blade is known as the _____ blade.

    (A) macintosh . . miller

    (B) miller . . macintosh

    (C) fiber optic . . miller

    (D) fiber optic . . macintosh

27. Which of the following correctly lists laryngoscope blades from smallest to largest?

    (A) 0, 1, 2, 3, 4

    (B) 4, 3, 2, 1, 0

    (C) 8, 6, 4, 2

    (D) 2, 4, 6, 8

ASSESSMENT

Directions: Each question has a maximum of four possible answers. Choose the letter that best answers the question and mark your choice on the answer sheet.

1. You are dispatched to an accident that involves a gasoline tanker and a car. On your arrival, you see several patients lying in the street. Your initial action is to

   (A) approach the patients and begin triage.

   (B) contact the dispatcher for additional resources.

   (C) ensure that the scene is safe for you to operate.

   (D) block access to the scene from civilian traffic.

2. All of the following are important aspects of prearrival dispatch information EXCEPT

   (A) the status of the patient as described by the caller.

   (B) any possibility of specialized equipment needs.

   (C) possibilities of violent activity on the scene.

   (D) name of the patient's private physician.

3. You are assigned to a multivehicle accident that involves a tour bus. You arrive at the scene to find approximately 20 patients with different types of injuries that range from minor to serious. You have determined the scene is safe. Your next action should be to

   (A) begin immediate treatment of the seriously injured patients.

   (B) contact dispatch for additional resources.

   (C) begin triage of all patients.

   (D) set up a treatment area.

4. All of the following are common injury or illness mechanisms encountered by the EMT–Basic EXCEPT

   (A) anaphylactic shock.

   (B) chest trauma secondary to blunt force.

   (C) elderly head injury due to a fall.

   (D) difficulty breathing due to myocardial infarction.

5. Which term best describes the EMT–Basic's assessment of the patient's living conditions, appearance, and complaints?

   (A) The SAMPLE history

   (B) Chief complaint

   (C) General impression

   (D) Initial assessment

6. You arrive at the scene to find that a fifty-three-year-old patient was struck by a motor vehicle. Your assessment reveals that the patient does not readily answer questions; however, he responds to you shouting, "Are you okay?" What is this patient's classification on the AVPU scale?

   (A) Alert

   (B) Voice responsive

   (C) Pain responsive

   (D) Unresponsive

7. Your assessment of a trauma patient finds that the patient suffered severe trauma to the lower jaw after a fall. Due to your findings, you begin to place the patient in spinal immobilization. Your decision to do this is based on which of the following statements?

    (A) Spinal immobilization should be done on patients who sustain trauma above the clavicles.

    (B) Trauma to the lower jaw can be immobilized with a cervical collar.

    (C) Using a cervical collar assists in moving the patient to a soft stretcher.

    (D) Cervical spine immobilization is the protocol for all patients who have suffered trauma.

8. All of the following are assessment methods for patient breathing EXCEPT

    (A) watching the chest for rise during inspiration.

    (B) auscultating lung sounds.

    (C) assessing the patient for accessory muscle use.

    (D) suctioning the airway.

9. You are assessing a patient with asthma. During your assessment, the airway is clear and the lungs have equal expansion. Breath sounds are clear bilaterally because the patient has self-treated with an aerosol medication prior to your arrival. Your treatment of the patient should include

    (A) taking away any medication that the patient may use for self-treatment.

    (B) requesting ALS assistance since there is nothing more you can do.

    (C) administering maintenance oxygen and transport.

    (D) releasing the patient on scene due to total relief.

10. Wheezing, gasping, accessory muscle use, and stridor are all signs of

    (A) a healthy respiratory system.

    (B) inadequate breathing.

    (C) adequate breathing.

    (D) asthma.

11. Your patient is unresponsive. She presents inadequate respirations at a rate of thirty-two breaths per minute. You should immediately

    (A) perform obstructed-airway maneuvers.

    (B) consider contacting ALS for advanced interventions.

    (C) provide 100 percent oxygen using a nonrebreather mask.

    (D) ventilate the patient with a bag-valve-mask device and supplemental oxygen.

12. In assessing the pulse in a conscious adult or child, the EMT–Basic would use which of the following pulse points?

    (A) Carotid

    (B) Femoral

    (C) Radial

    (D) Brachial

13. In assessing the pulse in an infant, the EMT–Basic would use which of the following pulse points?

    (A) Carotid

    (B) Femoral

    (C) Radial

    (D) Brachial

14. Capillary refill is an adequate predictor of perfusion in

    (A) elderly patients and children.

    (B) adults and infants.

    (C) infants and children.

    (D) elderly patients only.

15. During the initial assessment, the EMT–Basic assesses the patient for external bleeding. This is done primarily to

    (A) evaluate the area of injury.

    (B) detect and correct large volumes of blood loss.

    (C) establish criteria for blood transfusions at the hospital.

    (D) make sure the patient isn't lying.

16. All of the following are abnormal findings in skin assessment EXCEPT

    (A) pinkish skin.

    (B) pale skin.

    (C) cyanotic skin.

    (D) ashen skin.

QUESTIONS 17 AND 18 ARE BASED ON THE FOLLOWING PASSAGE.

You and your partner respond to an accident where a car has run into a tree. On your arrival, patient one is a twenty-four-year-old male, unconscious and breathing at thirty-six times per minute. His airway is clear, and he has a pulse of 120. His skin appears pale and diaphoretic. Patient two is a twenty-six-year-old female. She is complaining of pain in the neck and chest. Her pulse is 104, respirations are twenty, and skin is warm and dry.

17. Based on your general impression, how would you prioritize patient one?

    (A) High

    (B) Medium

    (C) Low

    (D) None of the above

18. Based on your general impression, how would you prioritize patient two?

    (A) High

    (B) Medium

    (C) Low

    (D) None of the above

19. Which of the following is NOT a component of the history of present illness?

    (A) Onset of illness

    (B) Quality

    (C) Severity

    (D) Pertinent past history

20. Place the following steps in the correct order for assessing a conscious medical patient.

    1. SAMPLE history
    2. Vital signs
    3. Focused physical examination
    4. History of present illness

    (A) 1, 2, 3, 4

    (B) 4, 1, 3, 2

    (C) 3, 1, 2, 4

    (D) 2, 4, 1, 3

21. Place the following steps in the correct order for assessing an unconscious patient.

    1. SAMPLE history
    2. Vital signs
    3. Rapid physical examination
    4. History of present illness

    (A) 3, 4, 1, 2

    (B) 4, 1, 3, 2

    (C) 3, 1, 2, 4

    (D) 3, 2, 4, 1

22. A patient with no known prior history is complaining of difficulty breathing. Your assessment reveals wheezing in all lung fields. The difference between this patient and a patient with a known history is that a patient with

    (A) a known history will not need ambulance transport.

    (B) no known history will generally respond better to oxygen.

    (C) a known history does not require any sort of physical examination.

    (D) no known history has no prescribed medication you could assist in administering.

23. Which of the following is NOT an indication for transport to the trauma center?

    (A) Death of a passenger in the same vehicle

    (B) Ejection from the vehicle

    (C) Isolated extremity fracture

    (D) Vehicle rollover

24. In using the DCAPBTLS-assessment mnemonic, which of the following terms is NOT associated with this assessment?

    (A) Death

    (B) Contusions

    (C) Burns

    (D) Lacerations

25. Place the following steps in the correct order for assessing a trauma patient with significant mechanism of injury.

    1. SAMPLE history
    2. Rapid trauma assessment
    3. Reconsider mechanism of injury
    4. Vital signs

    (A) 3, 2, 4, 1

    (B) 2, 4, 3, 1

    (C) 1, 2, 3, 4

    (D) 4, 1, 2, 3

26. As you assess a patient from a motorcycle collision, you would start at the head and look for which of the following signs of injury?

    (A) Tenderness

    (B) Deformities

    (C) Abrasions

    (D) All of the above

27. In a medical patient complaining of severe headache, which of the following areas of emphasis would probably produce the most beneficial information in the focused examination?

    (A) Respiratory system evaluation

    (B) Neurological evaluation

    (C) Cardiopulmonary examination

    (D) Abdominal examination

28. Choose the statement below that best describes the detailed physical examination.

    (A) The detailed physical examination is done on all patients.

    (B) The detailed physical examination is done only on critical patients with obvious life-threatening injuries.

    (C) The detailed physical examination is done on patients who may have hidden signs of illness or injury that were not uncovered during the initial examination.

    (D) The detailed physical examination is done at the discretion of the medical director in charge of the service.

29. All of the following are components of the ongoing assessment EXCEPT

    (A) reevaluation of airway, breathing, and circulation.

    (B) reevaluation of vital signs.

    (C) evaluation of treatments and responses.

    (D) initial information gathering on the patient's history.

30. During the ongoing assessment of your patient, you notice that the patient's blood pressure has dropped from 110/70 to 90/58. Because of this pertinent finding, you should

    (A) continue your current mode of treatment.

    (B) completely reassess your interventions.

    (C) immediately administer oxygen to the patient.

    (D) advise your partner to speed up the transport.

31. Which of the following is NOT a responsibility of the EMS dispatcher?

    (A) Prioritizing incoming emergency calls

    (B) Selecting the appropriate receiving hospital

    (C) Assisting callers with emergency medical instructions

    (D) Selecting and assigning the appropriate EMS units to an emergency

32. In using radio communications, which of the following would best describe the transmission of radio messages?

    (A) Radio transmissions should be concise and directly to the point

    (B) Radio transmissions should be comprehensive reports that outline all information about the call

    (C) Radio transmissions should include the patient's name and other personal information

    (D) Radio transmissions should include ten-codes as well as the verbal definitions

33. Which of the following best details the proper order for delivering a verbal report over the air?

    (A) Unit ID, receiving hospital and ETA, age and sex of patient, chief complaint, history of present emergency, findings, treatment, and response

    (B) Patient's name, complaint, ETA to hospital, patient past history, allergies, and medications

    (C) Unit ID, patient's name, complaint, treatment and response, ETA to hospital

    (D) Unit ID, receiving hospital, complaint, findings, treatment and response

34. While assigned to an emergency call, you must make several radio communications. Which of the following is NOT included in communicating with the dispatcher?

    (A) Acknowledgment of the assignment

    (B) Arrival at the scene

    (C) Information-gathering techniques on scene

    (D) Arrival at the hospital

35. Your patient is an elderly male who has fallen in a park. On your arrival, you notice that the patient is wearing hearing aids in both ears and is speaking very loudly. In your communication with this patient, you should

    (A) speak normally as the hearing aids should allow the patient to hear your questions.

    (B) speak slowly and clearly while facing the patient.

    (C) shout loudly into the patient's ear to ensure that he will hear you.

    (D) contact the dispatcher for a specialty responder who knows sign language.

36. The most important aspects in communicating with pediatric patients include all of the following EXCEPT

    (A) allowing the child to remain with his or her parents.

    (B) allowing the child to have his or her favorite toy close by.

    (C) lying to a child if a procedure will cause pain or discomfort.

    (D) remaining honest with the child throughout the duration of the call.

37. All of the following are components of the minimum data set EXCEPT

    (A) chief complaint.

    (B) vital signs.

    (C) perfusion status.

    (D) therapeutic interventions.

38. You respond to a sixty-seven-year-old male who states that he did not call the ambulance. His daughter is at the scene and states that she called because her father was up all night complaining of chest pain. When you question the patient, he states that he is not going to the hospital. All of the following are appropriate actions in the scenario EXCEPT

    (A) allowing the patient to sign a refusal and leave without any examination.

    (B) requesting to do a physical examination of the patient to check for the source of the chest pain.

    (C) examining the patient and explaining your findings and the need for further evaluation at the hospital.

    (D) documenting all findings, discussions with the patient, and alternatives offered to the patient, and having the patient and a witness sign the document.

39. You are reviewing the call report from the last run. You notice that your partner entered three sets of vital signs, and you are only aware that one set was taken. When you ask your partner about it, he states that although he only took one set of vital signs, he added additional sets to "make it look better." As a patient care provider, you should

    (A) change the report personally.

    (B) forget about the issue as it makes no difference.

    (C) discuss the issue with your partner, advise him that it is illegal to falsify documentation, and request that he revise the report.

    (D) take your vehicle out of service as you cannot work with this person anymore and report him to the police.

40. During your proofreading of a patient care report, you notice that you made an error in documenting in the narrative section. You should

    (A) leave the minor error as it is.

    (B) start a new report, making sure to write correctly this time.

    (C) draw a line through the error, write in the correction, and initial the correction.

    (D) completely cross out the error and write the correct line next to or above it.

MEDICAL

Directions: Each question has a maximum of four possible answers. Choose the letter that best answers the question and mark your choice on the answer sheet.

1. All of the following medications may be found on a basic life-support unit EXCEPT

   (A) epinephrine.

   (B) activated charcoal.

   (C) oral glucose.

   (D) diazepam.

2. All of the following are necessary for the correct administration of a medication to a patient EXCEPT

   (A) correct medication.

   (B) correct dose.

   (C) correct route.

   (D) correct needle size.

3. List, in the proper order, the structures of the respiratory system.

   (A) Nose, pharynx, larynx, trachea, bronchi, alveoli

   (B) Nose, larynx, pharynx, bronchi, trachea, alveoli

   (C) Nose, bronchi, larynx, pharynx, trachea, alveoli

   (D) Nose, bronchi, alveoli, pharynx, larynx, trachea

4. Rapid respiratory rate, diminished breath sounds, unequal chest expansion, and tripod positioning are all signs of

   (A) adequate breathing.

   (B) inadequate breathing.

   (C) heart attack.

   (D) asthma attack.

5. Which medication should an EMT–Basic use to treat a patient with breathing difficulty?

   (A) Epinephrine

   (B) Metered dose inhalers

   (C) Nitroglycerin

   (D) Oxygen

6. You respond to a call for a patient having difficulty breathing. On your arrival, you find a twenty-seven-year-old male who has a bluish coloration of the skin. Your assessment reveals an open airway and a respiratory rate of six breaths per minute. The proper device to deliver oxygen and ensure adequate breathing would be a

   (A) nasal cannula at four liters of oxygen per minute.

   (B) nonrebreather mask at eight liters of oxygen per minute.

   (C) bag-valve-mask ventilator with oxygen reservoir and assisted ventilations.

   (D) metered-dose inhaler followed by 100 percent oxygen via nonrebreather.

7. Your conscious patient with adequate ventilations is complaining of difficulty breathing. In which position should you transport this patient?

   (A) Lying down with legs elevated

   (B) In a position that is comfortable to the patient

   (C) Sitting forward with knees flexed

   (D) Lying sideways, to facilitate airway management

8. All of the following are signs of adequate air exchange EXCEPT

   (A) unequal chest expansion.

   (B) regular rhythm.

   (C) rate between twelve and twenty breaths per minute.

   (D) equal, clear breath sounds.

9. You are treating a pediatric patient who is in need of oxygen; however, the child is trying to pull the mask off her face. You should

   (A) immobilize the patient and continue administration of oxygen.

   (B) deliver oxygen by holding the mask in front of the child's face.

   (C) discontinue oxygen administration.

   (D) have the parent hold the child's arms down to facilitate use of the mask.

10. An episodic disease that causes breathing difficulty ranging from mild to severe is

    (A) emphysema.

    (B) chronic bronchitis.

    (C) asthma.

    (D) epiglottitis.

11. Which of the following is a progressive condition that causes poor blood flow to the heart by blocking coronary arteries with calcium and fat deposits?

    (A) Myocardial infarction

    (B) Angina pectoris

    (C) Atherosclerosis

    (D) Ischemia

12. The major difference between angina pectoris and myocardial infarction is the

    (A) pain in myocardial infarction is always brought on by exertion.

    (B) duration of the pain in myocardial infarction is shorter than that of angina pectoris.

    (C) duration of the pain in angina pectoris is shorter and self-correcting after rest.

    (D) pain of myocardial infarction is usually relieved by administration of nitroglycerin.

13. Which of the following describes tachycardia?

    (A) Heart rate below 100 beats per minute

    (B) Heart rate above 100 beats per minute

    (C) Heart rate below 60 beats per minute

    (D) Heart rate between 60 and 100 beats per minute

14. Which of the following describes bradycardia?

    (A) Heart rate below 100 beats per minute

    (B) Heart rate above 100 beats per minute

    (C) Heart rate below 60 beats per minute

    (D) Heart rate between 60 and 100 beats per minute

15. Your patient is a sixty-seven-year-old female with chest pain that occurred at rest. The duration of the pain has been approximately 45 minutes, and she has had no relief with her medications. This type of chest pain most likely indicates

    (A) angina pectoris.

    (B) myocardial infarction.

    (C) upper-respiratory infection.

    (D) influenza.

16. Which of the following would be most effective in the first few minutes of treating a cardiac-arrest patient?

    (A) CPR

    (B) Attachment of an AED and rhythm analysis

    (C) Ventilation

    (D) Transport

17. Which of the following best describes the difference between a semiautomatic defibrillator and a fully automatic defibrillator?

    (A) The fully automatic defibrillator advises a shock and prompts the user to deliver it.

    (B) The semiautomatic defibrillator will deliver a shock on its own after advising all clear.

    (C) The fully automatic defibrillator will deliver a shock on its own after advising all clear.

    (D) A semiautomatic defibrillator will not analyze ventricular fibrillation automatically.

18. Which of the following cardiac rhythms, when producing a pulse, would generate a shock-advise message from an AED?

    (A) Ventricular fibrillation

    (B) Ventricular tachycardia

    (C) Pulseless electrical activity

    (D) Asystole

19. When should you consider transport in treating a patient in cardiac arrest with an AED and CPR?

    (A) After six shocks have been delivered

    (B) After three shocks have been delivered

    (C) Only after ALS care has arrived

    (D) Only after the patient regains a pulse

20. During the analyze mode of AED use, CPR should be

    (A) interrupted to allow the AED to analyze the rhythm.

    (B) continued as it will not interfere with the analyze phase.

    (C) interrupted, but ventilations continued.

    (D) continued at a slower rate.

21. While transporting a patient complaining of chest pain, he becomes unconscious and has no pulse. Which of the following procedures should be followed?

    (A) CPR and ventilations should begin immediately and transport continued.

    (B) The EMT–Basic should attach the AED and set it to analyze while transport continues.

    (C) The EMT–Basic should attach the AED, set it to analyze, and tell the driver to stop the vehicle.

    (D) CPR should be performed for one minute in a stopped vehicle, then the AED attached.

22. All of the following patients are candidates for AED use, with the EXCEPTION of a(n)

    (A) seventy-five-year-old male with no pulse.

    (B) eighty-seven-year-old female with chest pain and a pulse.

    (C) six-year-old drowning patient with no pulse.

    (D) fifty-two-year-old man with no cardiac history who is pulseless and not breathing.

23. Why is it necessary to inspect the AED prior to each shift?

    (A) To ensure that the AED is fully charged and functional

    (B) To ensure that the AED was not used during the previous shift

    (C) To ensure that the EMT–Basic knows how to operate the AED

    (D) None of the above

24. You respond poolside to a cardiac arrest. After attaching the AED, you notice that the patient is lying in a wet area. Treatment of this patient should include

    (A) analyzing and defibrillating the patient where he is lying, as the electricity will not be affected by the water.

    (B) moving the patient to a dry area, using a towel to dry the patient, and attaching the AED.

    (C) drying off the patient with a towel and treating him where he is lying.

    (D) removing the AED and treating the patient with CPR.

25. Common side effects of nitroglycerin include

    (A) general weakness, altered mental status, and bradycardia.

    (B) nausea, dizziness, drop in blood pressure, and headache.

    (C) chills, hypertension, and stupor.

    (D) seizures, coma, and hypertension.

26. Contraindications to administration of nitroglycerin include all of the following EXCEPT

    (A) hypotension.

    (B) previous allergic reaction.

    (C) nausea.

    (D) field treatment of hypertension.

27. All of the following are metabolic causes of altered mental status EXCEPT

    (A) overdose.

    (B) hypothermia.

    (C) CVA.

    (D) diabetic emergencies.

28. The diabetic condition in which there is a rapid onset of altered mental status, which can lead to unconsciousness, seizures, and sometimes even death, is known as

    (A) hypoglycemia.

    (B) hyperglycemia.

    (C) ketoacidosis.

    (D) diabetic coma.

29. All of the following are signs of hypoglycemia EXCEPT

    (A) hunger.

    (B) agitation.

    (C) weakness.

    (D) excessive thirst.

30. Which of the following would contraindicate the use of oral glucose?

    (A) Diabetic history

    (B) Altered mental status

    (C) Unconsciousness

    (D) Consciousness

31. Treatment of the unconscious patient who is suspected of having a diabetic emergency would include all of the following EXCEPT

    (A) administration of oral glucose.

    (B) maintenance of airway and ventilation.

    (C) placement in recovery position.

    (D) requesting ALS assistance.

32. Which of the following is the appropriate treatment for a patient with seizures?

    (A) Protect the patient from injury by moving furniture and other objects out of the way

    (B) Support ventilations and administer high-concentration oxygen

    (C) Do not apply restraints to the seizure patient

    (D) All of the above

33. The condition in which multiple seizures occur one after another without a lucid interval is known as

    (A) prolonged seizure syndrome.

    (B) status epilepticus.

    (C) multiple-seizure disorder.

    (D) grand mal seizure.

34. You are dispatched to a seventy-five-year-old male who is disoriented. On your arrival, the family states that the patient was complaining of a headache before feeling disoriented. Your assessment reveals that the patient is confused, has unequal pupils, slurred speech, and has lost the use of his right side. Your initial assessment reveals a suspicion of

    (A) hypoglycemia.

    (B) stroke.

    (C) seizure.

    (D) intoxication.

35. The major difference between an allergic reaction and anaphylaxis is that a patient with anaphylaxis will have

    (A) itching and hives.

    (B) signs of confusion and altered mental status.

    (C) signs of respiratory distress and shock.

    (D) fever and a rash.

36. You respond to an asthmatic patient who is complaining of difficulty breathing after a bee sting. On your arrival, you notice no other signs of an allergic reaction. Which question would help you determine whether the patient is experiencing an allergic reaction or an asthma attack?

    (A) Does the patient have a rash or feel itchy?

    (B) Has the patient taken any of his medications?

    (C) Is there a family history of allergies to bee stings?

    (D) How long ago did the difficulty in breathing start?

37. In the patient with an anaphylactic reaction (shock), which of the following is the highest priority treatment?

    (A) Administration of the patient's auto-injector of epinephrine

    (B) Airway maintenance, including adjuncts and assisted ventilations, if needed

    (C) Monitoring of vital signs every 10 minutes

    (D) Contact with medical direction for additional instructions

38. All of the following are signs and symptoms of anaphylaxis EXCEPT

    (A) itching.

    (B) respiratory distress.

    (C) fever.

    (D) throat tightness.

39. One of the most common side effects of epinephrine auto-injectors is

    (A) rapid heart rate.

    (B) slow heart rate.

    (C) decreased blood pressure.

    (D) increased difficulty breathing.

40. All of the following are methods of entry into the body for poisons and toxins EXCEPT
    (A) ingestion.
    (B) inhalation.
    (C) absorption.
    (D) proximity.

41. Which of the following questions is not relevant when obtaining a history of a poisoning?
    (A) Has the patient ever taken the substance before?
    (B) When was the substance taken?
    (C) How much of the substance was taken?
    (D) What type of substance was taken?

42. Which of the following should the EMT–Basic focus on when treating a patient who has ingested a poison?
    (A) Preventing absorption
    (B) Inducing vomiting
    (C) Speeding up absorption
    (D) Administering antitoxins

43. You are off duty when your neighbor comes running over, stating that her five-year-old son has ingested a large amount of drain cleaner. On your arrival, you find an unconscious child with foamy blood in his airway. In order to manage the airway and provide ventilations, you should
    (A) open the airway and begin mouth-to-mouth ventilations.
    (B) open the airway and begin mouth-to-mask ventilations.
    (C) attempt to dilute the poison with water.
    (D) attempt to induce vomiting by inserting your fingers into the patient's airway.

44. You have administered activated charcoal to a patient who has ingested a poison. After the administration, the patient vomits the charcoal. What should you do next?
    (A) Transport the patient to the closest hospital
    (B) Begin mouth-to-mask ventilations
    (C) Administer another dose of activated charcoal
    (D) Administer syrup of ipecac

45. All of the following are ways the body can lose heat EXCEPT
    (A) conduction.
    (B) radiation.
    (C) evaporation.
    (D) absorption.

46. The first priority in treating a hypothermic patient is
    (A) management of airway and passive rewarming.
    (B) administration of warm fluids.
    (C) rapid rewarming by applying external heat.
    (D) contacting medical direction for additional instructions.

47. You are called to the scene of an unconscious patient in a factory where the temperatures have been over 100 degrees all week. The foreman states that the patient, a thirty-seven-year-old male, was complaining of dizziness and then passed out. Your assessment reveals that he has hot and dry skin, a rapid pulse, and dilated pupils. This patient is suffering from
    (A) nonemergent hyperthermia.
    (B) emergent hyperthermia.
    (C) diabetic emergency.
    (D) stroke.

48. Cold-water drowning patients should not be resuscitated if they have been submerged in water longer than thirty minutes.

    (A) True

    (B) False

49. All of the following are complications of near-drowning patients EXCEPT

    (A) massive pulmonary edema.

    (B) destruction of red blood cells.

    (C) severe hypoxia.

    (D) hyperthermia.

50. You are treating a patient with a snakebite from a pit viper. All of the following are proper treatment procedures EXCEPT

    (A) ensuring that the scene is safe and the snake is away from the area.

    (B) providing airway support for the patient.

    (C) keeping the patient comfortable and motionless.

    (D) suctioning the venom from the bite area with your mouth.

51. Which of the following factors may cause alterations in a patient's behavior?

    (A) Drug or alcohol abuse

    (B) Blood sugar disorders

    (C) Hypoxia

    (D) All of the above

52. The number one priority in responding to a behavioral emergency is

    (A) the safety of the rescuers.

    (B) airway management of the patient.

    (C) determination of a suicide attempt.

    (D) obtaining the patient's psychological history.

53. Which of the following situations is known to lead to suicide attempts or ideations?

    (A) Recent divorce or loss of a loved one

    (B) High stress levels at home or work

    (C) Drug or alcohol addiction

    (D) All of the above

54. You are called to the scene of a thirty-five-year-old male who is extremely violent. On your arrival, the police have not yet arrived; however, the patient's family states that the patient is in the house threatening to hurt himself or anyone who comes near him. Your first course of action should be to

    (A) enter the home carefully and attempt to treat the patient.

    (B) have a family member go in and tell the patient to come outside.

    (C) request police to the scene and remain in a safe area.

    (D) speak to the patient through a window.

55. All of the following steps should be taken while restraining a patient EXCEPT

    (A) ensuring enough personnel are present to facilitate a rapid and safe restraint.

    (B) having an adequate plan in place before approaching the patient.

    (C) allowing the patient one free arm to maintain balance as she is restrained and placed inside the ambulance.

    (D) informing the patient she'll be restrained and allowing her a chance to enter the ambulance on her own.

56. While interviewing a patient during a behavioral emergency, the EMT–Basic should maintain which of the following attitudes?

    (A) Stern and in charge

    (B) Caring and understanding

    (C) Professional and unemotional

    (D) None of the above

57. All of the following structures are important to childbirth EXCEPT the

(A) uterus.

(B) umbilical cord.

(C) placenta.

(D) fallopian tube.

58. The first stage of labor includes the

(A) delivery of the placenta.

(B) infant entering the birth canal.

(C) beginning of contractions.

(D) cutting of the umbilical cord.

59. The second stage of labor includes the

(A) delivery of the placenta.

(B) infant entering the birth canal.

(C) beginning of contractions.

(D) cutting of the umbilical cord.

60. The third stage of labor includes the

(A) delivery of the placenta.

(B) infant entering the birth canal.

(C) beginning of contractions.

(D) cutting of the umbilical cord.

61. Which of the following is the best indicator of imminent delivery of an infant in the field?

(A) When visual inspection of the vagina is positive for crowning

(B) When contractions are two or fewer minutes apart

(C) When the mother says she can no longer push

(D) When the bag of waters ruptures

62. The predelivery emergency characterized by severe abdominal pain, dark red bleeding, and a hard, rigid uterus is most likely

(A) threatened abortion.

(B) placenta previa.

(C) abruptio placenta.

(D) eclampsia.

63. The predelivery emergency that develops as the cervix dilates and separates from a low-lying placenta is called

(A) threatened abortion.

(B) placenta previa.

(C) abruptio placenta.

(D) eclampsia.

64. During an assisted delivery, you should suction the infant's airway

(A) after the infant is fully delivered.

(B) after the infant's head is delivered.

(C) as soon as you can access the infant's mouth.

(D) only if you are already at the hospital.

65. During suctioning of a newborn's airway, what is the proper order in which suctioning should occur?

(A) Nose and then mouth

(B) Mouth and then nose

(C) Mouth only

(D) Nose only

66. During your assisted delivery, you notice the umbilical cord is twisted around the newborn's neck, and you cannot remove it. This situation is preventing the newborn from delivering. You should

(A) begin rapid transport immediately as this is a true emergency.

(B) request advanced life support to provide advanced airway skills.

(C) clamp the cord and carefully cut it.

(D) proceed as usual as this is quite common.

67. You are preparing to deliver a newborn in the field. Upon inspection of the vagina for crowning, you notice the umbilical cord has delivered out of the vagina. It is pulsating, and you can see the newborn's head. What intervention is most appropriate?

(A) Clamp and cut the cord immediately.

(B) Push the cord back past the newborn's head to facilitate delivery.

(C) Insert your gloved hand into the vaginal opening, creating an airway for the newborn.

(D) Administer high-concentration oxygen, touch nothing, and transport immediately.

68. When dealing with a limb presentation, which of the following is NOT acceptable treatment?

(A) Push the limb back into the birth canal.

(B) Administer high-concentration oxygen.

(C) Elevate the pelvis of the mother.

(D) Begin rapid transport.

69. The diagnosis of eclampsia (in a previously diagnosed mother with preeclampsia) during pregnancy is predicated on the presentation of which of the following events?

(A) Hypertension

(B) Vomiting

(C) Seizures

(D) Headache

TRAUMA

Directions: Each question has a maximum of four possible answers. Choose the letter that best answers the question and mark your choice on the answer sheet.

1. Which type of bleeding is characterized by a rapid pulsatile flow of bright red blood?

   (A) Arterial

   (B) Venous

   (C) Capillary

   (D) Cellular

2. Which type of bleeding is characterized by a steady flow of dark red blood?

   (A) Arterial

   (B) Venous

   (C) Capillary

   (D) Cellular

3. Which type of bleeding is characterized by a slow oozing of blood from an abrasion?

   (A) Arterial

   (B) Venous

   (C) Capillary

   (D) Cellular

4. All of the following are signs of shock due to bleeding EXCEPT

   (A) increased pulse.

   (B) decreased pulse.

   (C) decreased blood pressure.

   (D) altered mental status.

5. All of the following are steps in controlling bleeding in the field EXCEPT

   (A) direct pressure.

   (B) elevation.

   (C) pressure point.

   (D) wire tourniquet.

6. You respond to a multiple-trauma patient at the scene of a motorcycle collision. On arrival, you find a twenty-six-year-old male with large bruises to his abdomen above the liver, a distended abdomen, bleeding from the mouth, deformity in the left lower extremity, and signs of shock. These types of findings are indicative of

   (A) severe bleeding in the head.

   (B) severe internal bleeding.

   (C) severe external bleeding.

   (D) minor internal and external bleeding.

7. The maximum time an EMT–Basic should remain on the scene with a critical trauma patient is

   (A) ten minutes.

   (B) twenty minutes.

   (C) sixty minutes.

   (D) unlimited.

8. The most important intervention the EMT–Basic should make in the treatment of a patient in shock is

   (A) controlling bleeding.

   (B) maintaining an open and secure airway.

   (C) transporting the patient.

   (D) splinting any suspected fractures.

9. Which of the following is NOT a layer of the skin?

   (A) Muscle

   (B) Epidermis

   (C) Dermis

   (D) Subcutaneous

10. Which of the following is the best definition of a contusion?

    (A) A collection of blood under intact skin due to injury

    (B) A large area of heavy bleeding under the skin

    (C) An open area of scraping with oozing blood

    (D) A large open wound with arterial bleeding

11. Which statement best describes the difference between a contusion and a hematoma?

    (A) A hematoma occurs only in the brain.

    (B) There is no difference between these injuries.

    (C) A hematoma is a less severe injury than a contusion.

    (D) A hematoma involves a larger area of injury than a contusion.

12. Your patient has a long, jagged cut on his right arm. Which of the following best describes this type of injury?

    (A) Abrasion

    (B) Contusion

    (C) Laceration

    (D) Avulsion

13. After falling off his bicycle, a six-year-old patient has multiple scrapes and scratches on his arms and legs. This type of injury is known as

    (A) abrasion.

    (B) contusion.

    (C) laceration.

    (D) avulsion.

14. You are assigned to a motor vehicle collision. On arrival, you find the fifty-six-year-old male driver of the automobile has a flap of skin hanging from his head. This injury occurred when the man's head hit the windshield of the car during the collision. The definition of this type of injury is

    (A) abrasion.

    (B) contusion.

    (C) laceration.

    (D) avulsion.

15. You are treating a patient who has a gunshot wound to the right upper chest. The patient is complaining of difficulty breathing. On your assessment, you find that the wound makes a characteristic sucking sound when the patient breathes. The treatment of this type of injury would include all of the following EXCEPT

    (A) administration of high-concentration oxygen.

    (B) splinting of the chest using the patient's right arm.

    (C) application of an occlusive dressing to the injury site.

    (D) monitoring of breath sounds for diminished sounds on the injured side.

16. Which of the following best describes a hemopneumothorax?

    (A) Air trapped in the lungs

    (B) Blood trapped in the lungs

    (C) Air and blood trapped in the pleural space surrounding the lungs

    (D) Chest pain associated with blood in only one of the lungs

17. Which of the following is NOT part of the treatment for an abdominal evisceration?

    (A) Administration of high-concentration oxygen

    (B) Application of an occlusive dressing

    (C) Application of a dry sterile dressing

    (D) Application of a moist sterile dressing

18. Which best describes a full-thickness burn?

    (A) Skin reddening after exposure to the sun

    (B) Blistering of the skin after touching an open flame

    (C) Charring of the skin after contact with a bare electrical wire

    (D) Reddening and blistering of the skin after contact with a caustic chemical

19. Which best describes a partial-thickness burn?

    (A) Skin reddening after exposure to the sun

    (B) Blistering of the skin after touching an open flame

    (C) Charring of the skin after contact with a bare electrical wire

    (D) Reddening and blistering of the skin after contact with a caustic chemical

20. Which of the following best describes a superficial burn?

    (A) Skin reddening after exposure to the sun

    (B) Blistering of the skin after touching an open flame

    (C) Charring of the skin after contact with a bare electrical wire

    (D) Reddening and blistering of the skin after contact with a caustic chemical

21. You respond to a house on fire. On your arrival, you are led to a twenty-seven-year-old woman who was pulled from the fire by the fire department. Your assessment reveals partial-thickness burns on her chest and arms. You also note burns on her lips and soot around her nose. You suspect

    (A) full-thickness burns to the lips.

    (B) critical burns to the chest.

    (C) airway burns.

    (D) possible fluid loss.

22. You are treating a burn patient who has full-thickness burns on both arms as well as his anterior chest and abdomen. Using the rule of nines, the percent of burn area is

    (A) 27 percent.

    (B) 32 percent.

    (C) 36 percent.

    (D) 42 percent.

23. Your patient is a six-year-old child with burns to his anterior chest and back as well as his head. Using the rule of nines for a child, what percentage of his body is burned?

    (A) 36 percent

    (B) 42 percent

    (C) 54 percent

    (D) 61 percent

24. Which of the following is classified as a critical burn?

    (A) A patient with superficial burns over 40 percent of her body

    (B) A child with partial-thickness burns over 15 percent of his body

    (C) A patient with partial-thickness burns to 18 percent of his legs

    (D) A patient with full-thickness burns to her feet

25. Your first priority in the treatment of a patient with an electrical burn who has already been safely removed from danger is

    (A) assessing the patient for entrance and exit wounds from the electrical source.

    (B) assessment and management of the patient's airway.

    (C) applying sterile dressings.

    (D) applying ice to the affected area.

26. You respond to the scene of a fight in a local tavern. On arrival, you find a twenty-three-year-old female with a knife protruding from her upper right abdominal quadrant. Treatment for this patient includes all of the following EXCEPT

    (A) airway maintenance.

    (B) removal of the impaled object.

    (C) administration of high-concentration oxygen.

    (D) application of a bulky dressing around the impaled object.

27. Which of the following is NOT an acceptable treatment of a patient with a partial amputation?

    (A) Wrapping the affected part in dry sterile dressings and bandages

    (B) Removing the intact skin and placing the amputated part in a bag

    (C) Controlling bleeding with pressure point if necessary

    (D) Transporting the patient to an appropriate facility

28. Which of the following is NOT a part of the appendicular skeleton?

    (A) Cranium

    (B) Humerus

    (C) Femur

    (D) Acetabulum

29. All of the following are bones of the upper extremities EXCEPT the

    (A) humerus.

    (B) ulna.

    (C) metacarpal.

    (D) metatarsal.

30. A closed fracture to bones may result in major internal blood loss. Of the following bones, which one can result in the most severe blood loss?

    (A) Humerus

    (B) Femur

    (C) Pelvis

    (D) Radius

31. Effective immobilization of a bone includes which of the following?

    (A) Immobilizing the area above and below the fracture site

    (B) Maintaining manual stabilization throughout the transport

    (C) Immobilizing the joint above and below the fracture site

    (D) Splinting the patient only after she is placed in the ambulance

32. After you apply a splint, the patient complains of a tingling sensation to the immobilized extremity. This is due to

    (A) nerve damage from the injury.

    (B) taking too long to apply the splint.

    (C) applying the splint too tightly.

    (D) the splint irritating the skin.

33. All of the following are contraindications to the application of a traction splint EXCEPT

    (A) pelvic fracture.

    (B) knee injury.

    (C) acetabular fracture.

    (D) open femur fracture.

34. How many vertebrae are in the cervical spine?
    (A) Seven
    (B) Twelve
    (C) Five
    (D) Four

35. The central nervous system consists of
    (A) all nerves and nerve pathways of the body.
    (B) the parasympathetic nervous system.
    (C) the brain and spinal cord.
    (D) the twelve cranial nerves.

36. A concussion is described as
    (A) severe head injury with moderate bleeding.
    (B) mild head injury with a possible loss of consciousness.
    (C) open head injury with deep unconsciousness.
    (D) arterial bleeding of the brain.

37. The primary concern in the patient with severe facial injury is
    (A) severe blood loss.
    (B) airway compromise.
    (C) brain injury.
    (D) cervical spinal injury.

38. You are on the scene of a patient who fell from a window. The patient fell approximately 25 feet and is conscious and complaining of numbness and tingling from his neck down. You suspect
    (A) thoracic spinal injury.
    (B) cervical spinal injury.
    (C) brain injury.
    (D) concussion.

39. The Glasgow Coma Scale examines which of the following?
    (A) Extremity movement, mental status, sensation
    (B) Verbal response, movement, sensation
    (C) Eye opening, verbal response, motor response
    (D) Motor response, verbal response, sensation

40. Which of the following is the required airway maneuver for a patient with suspected spinal injury?
    (A) Modified jaw thrust
    (B) Head-tilt chin-lift
    (C) Jaw lift
    (D) Tongue pull

41. On arrival at a motor vehicle accident, you find a patient seated in a vehicle that has severe damage to the front end. You notice the patient has a laceration to the forehead and the windshield is cracked from where the patient hit his head. The immobilization device of choice is
    (A) rapid extrication on a long spine board.
    (B) a log roll while the patient is still seated.
    (C) a short spine board while the patient is still seated.
    (D) rapid extrication with a cervical collar and long spine board.

42. You arrive at the scene of a rollover vehicle collision. On your arrival, the patient is standing at the scene speaking with police officers. The patient is complaining of neck pain and right-sided tingling. Which of the following is the immobilization technique of choice for this patient?

(A) Short spine board or KED

(B) Rapid takedown

(C) Cervical collar only and transport seated

(D) No immobilization since the patient is already walking

43. Helmet removal should be attempted in which of the following cases?

(A) A football player who suffered a lower back injury and is talking with the EMT crew

(B) A motorcycle rider who is unconscious and wearing a full-face shield

(C) A motorcycle rider who is conscious and wearing a half helmet

(D) A hockey player who went head first into the boards and is complaining of dizziness

QUESTIONS 44–48 ARE BASED ON THE FOLLOWING SCENARIO.

You are called to a private residence for a psychological emergency. On arrival, you find a twenty-eight-year-old male acting violently. The family states that he woke up this morning and was not himself. They also state that the patient was in an accident two days ago in which he sustained a head injury but refused medical care. As you are speaking to the family, the patient collapses.

44. What should be your initial intervention?

(A) Assess breathing

(B) Open the airway with the jaw-thrust maneuver and assess the airway

(C) Assess circulation

(D) Administer glucose paste to the patient and assess blood glucose level

45. After your initial intervention, you should

(A) Assess breathing.

(B) Open the airway with the jaw-thrust maneuver and assess the airway.

(C) Assess circulation.

(D) Administer glucose paste to the patient and assess blood glucose level.

46. After your second intervention, you should

(A) assess breathing.

(B) open the airway with the jaw-thrust maneuver and assess the airway.

(C) assess circulation.

(D) administer glucose paste to the patient and assess blood glucose level.

47. Your findings show that the patient has a stable airway, is breathing, and has a good pulse rate. Your next intervention should be to

(A) do a neurological assessment.

(B) begin a secondary assessment.

(C) immobilize the patient and begin transport.

(D) examine the head for suspected injury.

48. How should this patient be transported?

(A) On a stretcher with head elevated

(B) Immobilized to a long spine board with a cervical collar

(C) Immobilized with a KED to ensure cervical spinal immobilization

(D) On a short spine board, then transferred to the long spine board in the ambulance

INFANTS AND CHILDREN

Directions: Each question has a maximum of four possible answers. Choose the letter that best answers the question and mark your choice on the answer sheet.

1. The major cause of death in children over one year of age is
   (A) respiratory disease.
   (B) trauma.
   (C) respiratory failure.
   (D) cardiovascular diseases.

2. Which pediatric age group has a fear of permanent injury or death?
   (A) Birth to 1 year
   (B) 1 to 3 years
   (C) 3 to 6 years
   (D) 6 to 12 years

3. Which pediatric age group is most likely to be uncooperative with the EMT–Basic during a physical examination?
   (A) 12 to 18 years
   (B) Birth to 1 year
   (C) 6 to 12 years
   (D) 1 to 3 years

4. The major cause of cardiac arrest in the pediatric patient is
   (A) respiratory insufficiency.
   (B) congenital disorders.
   (C) sleep apnea.
   (D) heart disease.

5. The child in respiratory distress should be treated with
   (A) positive-pressure ventilation.
   (B) high-concentration oxygen by mask.
   (C) blow-by oxygen.
   (D) low-concentration oxygen.

6. The child in respiratory failure should be treated with
   (A) positive-pressure ventilation.
   (B) high-concentration oxygen by mask.
   (C) blow-by oxygen.
   (D) low-concentration oxygen.

7. Signs of compensated shock in the pediatric patient include all of the following EXCEPT
   (A) rapid pulse.
   (B) dry mucous membranes.
   (C) decreased output of urine.
   (D) decreased blood pressure.

8. The pediatric patient with an altered mental status, rapid respiratory rate, and delayed capillary refill is probably suffering from
   (A) compensated shock.
   (B) decompensated shock.
   (C) decreased blood sugar.
   (D) head injury.

9. The most common cause of seizures in an otherwise healthy child is
   (A) epilepsy.
   (B) trauma.
   (C) fever.
   (D) hypoxia.

10. Which of the following is NOT an appropriate treatment for a child in shock?
    (A) Elevating the legs
    (B) Maintaining body temperature
    (C) Administering fluids by mouth
    (D) Administering high-concentration oxygen

11. You respond to a private residence for an unconscious child. On your arrival, you find a child lying on the bedroom floor bleeding from the head. You complete your assessment and notice that the child has bruises in various stages of healing. You suspect that

    (A) the child is abused.

    (B) bruising is normal for children.

    (C) the child fell and has a head injury.

    (D) the child has a medical condition that causes bruising.

12. Children with a history of child abuse will usually be outspoken and friendly.

    (A) True

    (B) False

13. In dealing with the death of a child, the EMT–Basic should

    (A) accept that death is part of the job and move on.

    (B) discuss his or her feelings with a partner or coworker.

    (C) spend the night out with friends at the local tavern.

    (D) go home after work, take a sleep aid, and go to bed.

OPERATIONS

Directions: Each question has a maximum of four possible answers. Choose the letter that best answers the question and mark your choice on the answer sheet.

1. Choose the following true statement about the use of excessive speed when responding to an emergency call.
   - (A) Excessive speed is always appropriate for an ambulance.
   - (B) Excessive speed increases the chance of an accident.
   - (C) Excessive speed is indicated in true emergencies.
   - (D) Excessive speed cuts down response time.

2. You are responding to an emergency call down a one-way street with a passing lane when you come upon a school bus that is loading children. Which of the following would be the correct action to take?
   - (A) Make sure your sirens are on and pass the school bus with caution.
   - (B) Announce over the ambulance address system that nobody should move, then pass.
   - (C) Stop your vehicle and wait to accelerate until the bus driver waves you past.
   - (D) There is no requirement on stopping for a school bus.

3. All of the following factors will affect response to an emergency call EXCEPT
   - (A) construction zones.
   - (B) clear, dry roads.
   - (C) rain and wind.
   - (D) icy conditions.

4. Which of the following describes high-level disinfection?
   - (A) The killing of pathogens by application of heat
   - (B) The killing of pathogens by using a potent means of disinfection
   - (C) The killing of pathogens by the application of a pathogenic aerosol or spray
   - (D) Washing and showering after a call where the EMT–Basic was spattered with blood

5. Which of the following describes sterilization?
   - (A) The killing of pathogens by application of heat
   - (B) The killing of pathogens by using a potent means of disinfection
   - (C) The killing of pathogens by the application of a pathogenic aerosol or spray
   - (D) Washing and showering after a call where the EMT–Basic was spattered with blood

6. The written run report is prepared during which phase of response?
   - (A) The transport phase
   - (B) The postrun phase
   - (C) The delivery phase
   - (D) The treatment phase

7. When operating at the scene of a helicopter evacuation, the EMT–Basic should always approach the helicopter from the
   - (A) rear.
   - (B) left side.
   - (C) front.
   - (D) right side.

8. Which of the following is NOT a part of the postrun phase?
   (A) Cleaning the vehicle
   (B) Notification of availability for the next run
   (C) Restocking of supplies in the vehicle
   (D) Patient documentation

9. During extrication of a patient from a motor vehicle, what is the first priority for the EMT–Basic?
   (A) Blocking traffic
   (B) Stabilizing the vehicle
   (C) Establishing a command sector at the incident
   (D) Establishing if vehicle entry is safe for the rescue crew

10. Which of the following is NOT a component of vehicle rescue?
    (A) Hazard management
    (B) Vehicle stabilization
    (C) Patient removal
    (D) Traffic control

11. The initial phase of vehicle extrication begins with
    (A) stabilizing the vehicle.
    (B) patient packaging.
    (C) gaining access.
    (D) size-up.

12. Which of the following best describes a complex access scene?
    (A) A man whose car has fallen on his arm
    (B) A woman with her hand trapped in a machine
    (C) A motor vehicle collision in which the patient's foot is pinned
    (D) A building collapse in which a large piece of cement pins a man by the legs

13. You respond to a call for a man pinned by a tractor. On your arrival, you find that the tractor has flipped over and the man's leg has been pinned under the front of the tractor. His vital signs are stable, and he is complaining of only moderate pain. This scene is known as a/an
    (A) simple access scene.
    (B) complex access scene.
    (C) medium access scene.
    (D) unrated scene.

14. Which of the following statements best describes a disaster?
    (A) A disaster is an incident that produces more than 100 patients in more than one location.
    (B) A disaster affects multiple geographic regions or damages the infrastructure of one region.
    (C) A disaster is any incident that produces multiple patients.
    (D) A disaster occurs naturally, without any human intervention.

15. A mass-casualty incident is best defined as
    (A) any incident that taxes the resources of a given area.
    (B) any incident that produces more than 10 patients.
    (C) any incident that involves mass transportation.
    (D) any incident that involves a terrorist group.

16. All of the following are responsibilities of the EMT–Basic at the scene of a hazardous materials incident EXCEPT
    (A) recognizing the incident.
    (B) establishing scene control.
    (C) mitigating the hazardous material.
    (D) establishing a treatment sector.

17. On the NFPA Hazardous Materials Classification chart, the color blue stands for

    (A) health hazard.

    (B) fire hazard.

    (C) specific hazard.

    (D) reactivity.

18. On the NFPA Hazardous Materials Classification chart, the color red stands for

    (A) health hazard.

    (B) fire hazard.

    (C) specific hazard.

    (D) reactivity.

19. At a mass-casualty incident, the incident commander is responsible for

    (A) command and control of the entire incident.

    (B) command of communications only.

    (C) command of transport only.

    (D) command of patient care only.

20. You are assigned to the treatment area at a mass-casualty incident. You report directly to the

    (A) incident commander.

    (B) triage officer.

    (C) treatment officer.

    (D) transportation officer.

21. Under the triage tag system, the color black refers to a

    (A) dead or unsalvageable patient.

    (B) high-priority patient.

    (C) low-priority patient.

    (D) patient requiring no intervention.

22. Under the triage tag system, the color red refers to a

    (A) dead or unsalvageable patient.

    (B) high-priority patient.

    (C) low-priority patient.

    (D) patient requiring no intervention.

23. At a hazardous materials incident, the hot zone refers to the

    (A) treatment area.

    (B) decontamination area.

    (C) area of the spill or event.

    (D) staging area.

ANSWER KEY AND EXPLANATIONS

Basics of Emergency Medical Care

1. D	11. A	21. A	31. D	41. A
2. D	12. B	22. B	32. C	42. C
3. D	13. C	23. B	33. A	43. C
4. C	14. B	24. C	34. D	44. C
5. B	15. C	25. A	35. B	45. A
6. A	16. B	26. B	36. A	46. A
7. A	17. A	27. A	37. C	47. B
8. B	18. C	28. C	38. C	48. A
9. B	19. B	29. D	39. D	49. D
10. D	20. A	30. A	40. D	

1. **The correct answer is (D).** Choices (A), (B), and (C) are components of the EMS system. The EMS system consists of the following seven components:

   1. patients
   2. public citizens who call 911 and/or provide initial care
   3. 911 dispatcher
   4. first responders (fire, police, or other EMS agency)
   5. EMS personnel (EMT–B, EMT–I, EMT–P)
   6. emergency department staff
   7. allied heath personnel

   All of the above components have direct interaction with the patient once the patient enters an EMS system. Bystanders who witness the injury but do not help the patient are not components of the EMS system.

2. **The correct answer is (D).** The EMT–Basic may provide noninvasive procedures in patient care. In some circumstances, the EMT–Basic may assist in medication ad-

ministration. These circumstances include assistance with the patient's own prescribed medication for asthma, angina, and anaphylaxis. The EMT–Basic does not administer cardiac-arrest medications.

3. **The correct answer is (D).** Although all of these answers are responsibilities of EMT–Basics, their primary responsibility is to assure their own personal safety as well as the safety of their partners. If the EMT–Basic enters an unsafe situation, injury or death becomes a greater possibility.

4. **The correct answer is (C).** The true definition of quality improvement is a review of system aspects that need improvement based on identified problems. Choice (D) refers to quality assurance. Choices (A) and (B) are components of the quality improvement process.

5. **The correct answer is (B).** The EMT–Basic works as an extension of the physician medical director, who assumes responsibility for all patient treatments in the field within the

system for which he or she has oversight. In the field, the highest level of provider is in charge of patient care; however, the medical director is ultimately responsible for patient care.

6. **The correct answer is (A).** EMT–Basics understand that illness and injury know no age boundaries. This question includes descriptions of calls from the routine to the highly stressful. The serious injury of a child always carries a high-stress factor for the EMT–Basic. As an EMT–Basic, you should be aware of the signs of acute and cumulative stress reactions.

7. **The correct answer is (A).** EMS personnel may suffer from a cumulative stress reaction at any time. Usually, these reactions are precipitated by a current event or serious call; however, they may only emerge, as in this question, with a slow and steady onset. The EMT–Basic's responsibility is to his or her partner's well-being. If you find yourself in this situation, discuss these symptoms with your partner or supervisor to ensure your partner receives the necessary treatment.

8. **The correct answer is (B).** EMT–Basics should reduce stress; however, frequent alcohol consumption is ineffective in stress reduction. In fact, alcohol consumption and abuse may worsen the condition. For stress relief, the EMT–Basic should practice relaxation, exercise, and a proper diet.

9. **The correct answer is (B).** A key indicator that this patient has a communicable disease is the fact that others on the premises are suffering from the same symptoms. Most communicable diseases present with a low-grade fever and cough, and many of them present with some form of rash. Use of respiratory protection on this type of call will reduce the incidence of disease spread to EMS providers.

10. **The correct answer is (D).** The EMT–Basic should wear gloves on any call where there is a chance that he or she may come in contact with blood or body fluids. Get into the habit of wearing gloves on all calls. In situations that involve a large amount of bleeding, the EMT–Basic should wear protective gowns, which limit exposure to blood and body fluids.

11. **The correct answer is (A).** The EMT–Basic should never put him- or herself in harm's way. A hazardous materials incident has the potential to produce numerous patients due to product contact in any of its chemical states. The EMT–Basic should immediately request assistance, identify and isolate contaminated patients without becoming contaminated, and set up a triage and treatment area to receive patients after they are decontaminated.

12. **The correct answer is (B).** On the job, you must always consider your own safety. The EMT–Basic is unaware of the status of the patient—or if anyone in the crowd is armed with a weapon. In the interest of safety, the EMT–Basic should not enter the tavern. In this case, a request for bystander assistance is unavailable. One cannot request civilian protection, and one cannot request that someone else bring the patient out because the extent of his injuries is unknown. The EMT–Basic must immediately request police assistance to control this situation.

13. **The correct answer is (C).** The EMT–Basic's scope of practice encompasses response, treatment, and transport of all emergency patients within his or her response area. Treatment protocols outline specific treatments for a given condition. Liability on the part of the EMT–Basic results from failure to act within the scope of practice.

answers diagnostic test

14. **The correct answer is (B).** Expressed consent is the treatment of patients after they make an informed decision, sometimes called informed consent. These patients have had their assessment and treatment plans outlined to them and have agreed to be treated.

15. **The correct answer is (C).** Implied consent occurs when the patient is unconscious. The EMT–Basic will treat under implied consent based on the theory that if the patient were conscious, he or she would agree to be treated.

16. **The correct answer is (B).** In the case of a refusal of treatment, the EMT–Basic should complete a full assessment and inform the patient of the potential risks of not pursuing additional care. In addition—and if the EMT–Basic decides that additional treatment is necessary—medical control should be contacted for assistance. If the patient still refuses, then the EMT–Basic must secure a signed refusal from both the patient and a witness. Finally, the patient should be given options to call again should he or she need assistance.

17. **The correct answer is (A).** Touching any patient against his or her will may bring up a charge of assault. If a fully conscious and aware patient states that he or she does not want assistance, the EMT–Basic should try to verbally convince him or her to be treated. If the patient still refuses, the EMT–Basic should refrain from any physical examinations and contact medical control for additional assistance.

18. **The correct answer is (C).** Once an EMT–Basic makes contact with any patient and begins treatment, he or she is responsible for that patient until the emergency department staff takes over care. If an EMT–Basic begins treatment and leaves before a provider of equal or higher training takes over, he or she is guilty of abandonment.

19. **The correct answer is (B).** An EMT–Basic may be guilty of negligence if he or she fails to provide proper treatment to any patient already being treated. In this scenario, the EMT–Basic was negligent because these three rules were broken:

- The EMT–Basic had a duty to act because the patient had an injury and requested assistance.
- The standard of care was not provided because the patient was made to hop to a wheelchair rather than be transported on a stretcher.
- The actions of the EMT–Basic caused harm to the patient because the patient fell, sustaining additional injury.

20. **The correct answer is (A).** Patient confidentiality is an important issue. EMT–Basic personnel should never release names and patient conditions to anyone other than emergency personnel or emergency department staff. Delivering information to the press is a breach of patient confidentiality.

21. **The correct answer is (A).** The EMT–Basic has a primary responsibility to care for the patient. Although the EMT–Basic should take careful measures not to disturb possible evidence, the first priority is human life. Do not question bystanders about the crime unless your questions involve the kinematics of the patient's injury. The EMT–Basic may not remain on the scene for police arrival if the patient is critical. The EMT–Basic should be aware that he or she should not enter a crime scene until police have secured the scene. This is not always the case when an EMT–Basic is called to a private residence for an injury or assault patient. He or she may be unaware that a crime has been committed until after patient contact.

22. **The correct answer is (B).** Vital signs are defined in the field as blood pressure; pulse rate and quality; respiratory rate and quality; and skin color, temperature, and moisture. Although motor function is assessed, it is not considered a vital sign.

23. **The correct answer is (B).** To assess respiratory rate, the EMT–Basic should count breaths for at least thirty seconds and multiply that number by two.

24. **The correct answer is (C).** Nasal flaring, accessory muscle use, and positioning are all significant signs of labored breathing.

25. **The correct answer is (A).** To assess pulse rate, the EMT–Basic should count impulses for at least thirty seconds and multiply that number by two.

26. **The correct answer is (B).**

27. **The correct answer is (A).**

28. **The correct answer is (C).**

29. **The correct answer is (D).**

30. **The correct answer is (A).** The patient in shock will present with cool or cold, clammy skin; he or she may also have peripheral cyanosis. Patients with heat exposure (heat stroke) will present with hot and dry skin.

31. **The correct answer is (D).** Capillary refill is an effective, rapid perfusion test in infants and children. The test is easily performed by squeezing a fingernail and counting the seconds before blood returns to the nail bed. Any time over two seconds may indicate poor perfusion status.

32. **The correct answer is (C).** The EMT–Basic should always suspect narcotic overdose in the unconscious patient with constricted pupils. This suspicion should be elevated when it is associated with shallow and slow breathing.

33. **The correct answer is (A).** Due to the kinematics of brain injury, injury to the brain will cause bleeding on the injured side of the brain. This, in turn, will put pressure on the optic nerve on the injured side, causing unequal pupils.

34. **The correct answer is (D).** Normal pupil response to light is constriction. In the normal patient, both pupils will respond, regardless of which eye the light is placed in front of. Any other response may be considered abnormal.

35. **The correct answer is (B).** When the heart contracts, blood is forced out into the aorta and out to the rest of the body. When one assesses blood pressure, the systolic pressure, or top number, is a measurement of the pressure in the vessel during contraction.

36. **The correct answer is (A).** The diastolic blood pressure measurement is taken during ventricular relaxation. This reading relates the pressure that remains in the arteries while the heart is at rest.

37. **The correct answer is (C).** The EMT–Basic may obtain a blood pressure using two different methods. When using a stethoscope, the pulsations are counted from the moment one begins to hear them right up until they begin to disappear; this is known as auscultation. Palpation is done by placing the fingers on the pulse point in the wrist or the brachial artery.

38. **The correct answer is (C).** A symptom is something that a patient feels, or a complaint. Headache, nausea, and chest pain are all common patient complaints.

39. **The correct answer is (D).** A sign is something that the EMT–Basic will physically see. Extremity deformities, obvious injuries, pupil dilation, and vomiting are all visible signs. All signs should be documented on the patient call report.

40. The correct answer is (D). Pulse rate is not a component of the SAMPLE history. Pulse rate is part of the physical examination and not a part of the patient's history.

SAMPLE stands for
S = Signs/Symptoms
A = Allergies
M = Medications
P = Past history
L = Last meal
E = Events leading up to current emergency

41. The correct answer is (A). Proper use of one's body, including proper stance and determination of the weight of the patient, is called body mechanics. The EMT–Basic should survey any and all lifts prior to lifting the patient to determine the possibility of injury.

42. The correct answer is (C). During a patient lift, the weight should never be shifted. Shifting weight during a lift may cause the EMT–Basic to become unbalanced and subsequently drop the patient or cause self-injury. The EMT–Basic should be sure of the lift, including balance, before attempting it.

43. The correct answer is (C). When carrying patients down several flights of stairs, especially in older buildings with narrow staircases, the stair chair is the carrying device of choice. The stair chair allows for tight turns and narrow hallways and staircases to be negotiated with relative ease.

44. The correct answer is (C). The spotter should always be behind the person at the lowest point of the carry. This person almost always has his or her back toward the patient and turned away from the carry itself. The spotter will then become a pair of eyes for the person at the bottom of the carry. The spotter may also advise the entire carry crew of obstacles, turns, and narrow hallways in advance. This will add to communication and smooth movement down the staircase.

45. The correct answer is (A). The extremity lift is an excellent technique for moving a patient short distances and when there is no other transport device. This is a commonly used lift for moving a patient from the floor to the wheeled stretcher, stair chair, or other device in a nontraumatic situation.

46. The correct answer is (A). The extremity lift is a nonemergency lift. Emergency moves are used in situations where the EMT–Basic may be in danger of personal injury, such as fires, unstable structures, and other hazardous situations. These moves are not indicated in nondangerous situations, as they may cause additional injury to the patient.

47. The correct answer is (B). All of the moves are nonemergency moves that are designed to facilitate a nontrauma patient's movement onto a stretcher. These moves should never be used on a patient with suspected spinal trauma, for fear of increasing the injury.

48. The correct answer is (A). In this situation, the fireman's carry is the best method of extrication. The fireman's carry is a one-person operation, which takes only seconds to initiate. The extremity carry, scoop stretcher, and long spine board are all two-person operations, which are time-consuming given the situation.

49. The correct answer is (D). The unconscious patient who has no traumatic injury should be transported in the recovery position. The recovery position allows for management of the airway and prevents aspiration in the event that the patient vomits.

Airway

1. C	7. C	13. C	18. D	23. C
2. C	8. C	14. B	19. C	24. C
3. B	9. D	15. C	20. A	25. D
4. D	10. B	16. B	21. C	26. B
5. C	11. B	17. A	22. B	27. A
6. B	12. D			

1. **The correct answer is (C).** The esophagus is a structure of the gastrointestinal system.

2. **The correct answer is (C).** Muscle retractions, known as intercostals retractions, are signs of increased work in breathing. Patients most commonly seen with these retractions are those in severe respiratory distress.

3. **The correct answer is (B).** Increased respiratory rates, nasal flaring, pursed lip breathing, and shallow, irregular respirations are all signs of inadequate breathing.

4. **The correct answer is (D).** Inadequate breathing may be caused by a number of ailments, including pulmonary edema, chest pain, asthma, bronchitis, and head injuries, but not by conjunctivitis.

5. **The correct answer is (C).** The head-tilt chin-lift should never be used on any patient who may be suspected of having a cervical spinal injury.

6. **The correct answer is (B).** Oxygen and carbon dioxide exchange, commonly referred to as gas exchange, takes place in the alveoli. The alveoli are sac-shaped structures that have a membrane that is one cell thick. These membranes are adjacent to capillaries, and the gas exchange occurs at this level.

7. **The correct answer is (C).** The jaw-thrust maneuver is indicated for all unconscious patients who may have a cervical spinal injury. Although an oropharyngeal airway may eventually be indicated, it is not an initial airway maneuver.

8. **The correct answer is (C).** A patient should never be suctioned for longer than 15 seconds. Long periods of suctioning can cause the patient to become hypoxic. Patients who require suctioning will require high-flow oxygen and possibly assisted ventilations after the procedure is completed. When possible, the patient should be hyperventilated prior to suctioning.

9. **The correct answer is (D).** Suction should be applied while removing the catheter. Long applications of suction may result in hypoxia.

10. **The correct answer is (B).** Artificial ventilation is the process of manually forcing air into the patient's lungs. The bag-valve-mask, pocket face mask, and CPR mask are all designed to deliver pressures great enough to produce artificial ventilation. The nonrebreather mask will not develop high pressures to ensure adequate ventilation and should never be used.

11. **The correct answer is (B).** The pocket face mask, when attached to an oxygen supply, can deliver up to 50 percent oxygen to the patient. The pocket face mask alone relies on the expired oxygen of the rescuer, which is normally 16 percent.

12. **The correct answer is (D).** The bag-valve-mask with supplemental oxygen can deliver almost 100 percent oxygen; this fact is based on the device having an oxygen reservoir. If the device lacks a reservoir, the percent of oxygen delivery falls to nearly 50 percent.

13. **The correct answer is (C).** The oropharyngeal airway is inserted upside down along the palate until resistance is felt. After the EMT–Basic feels resistance, the airway is gently rotated 180 degrees to ensure proper placement. Insertion along the curvature of the mouth may result in obstruction of the airway by the tongue.

14. **The correct answer is (B).** The nasopharyngeal airway is the airway of choice in patients who have no access to the mouth. In cases of seizure and oral trauma, it may be impossible to insert an oral airway, including an endotracheal tube. The bag-valve-mask device is not an airway adjunct, but it is a ventilation device.

15. **The correct answer is (C).** The nasopharyngeal airway should be measured from the edge of the nostril to the angle of the jaw. An improperly sized airway may result in kinking from over insertion as well as improper ventilation.

16. **The correct answer is (B).**

17. **The correct answer is (A).**

18. **The correct answer is (D).**

EXPLANATION FOR QUESTIONS 16, 17, AND 18.

Oxygen tanks are produced in several capacities. The D and E cylinders are usually portable, with the D tank being the most popular. The M cylinder is used for a fixed onboard oxygen system.

19. **The correct answer is (C).** The nonrebreather mask can deliver oxygen concentrations as high as 80 to 90 percent when properly hooked up and at the proper liter flow.

20. **The correct answer is (A).** The nasal cannula will deliver a prescribed amount of oxygen based on the liter flow. At one liter, the cannula delivers 24 percent oxygen; at six liters, it delivers 44 percent oxygen.

21. **The correct answer is (C).** When a patient feels confined using a nonrebreather mask, the EMT–Basic should first attempt to calm the patient's fears about the mask and its confining qualities. If that approach fails, the EMT–Basic should remove the mask and apply a nasal cannula. In this instance, the patient is still receiving oxygen and is feeling less anxious about the mask.

22. **The correct answer is (B).** The bifurcation point of the trachea is the carina. The carina is where the right and left mainstem bronchi branch off into the right and left lungs.

23. **The correct answer is (C).** The epiglottis is a leaf-shaped structure above the laryngeal opening. The epiglottis acts like a flap during swallowing, closing off the trachea to foreign bodies such as foods and liquids. The vallecula is the space between the base of the tongue and the epiglottis; this space is important during endotracheal intubation because when the macintosh blade is used, its proper placement is in the vallecula.

24. **The correct answer is (C).** The vocal cords are located in the larynx.

25. **The correct answer is (D).** The esophagus is an organ of the gastrointestinal system that lies directly posterior to the trachea.

26. **The correct answer is (B).** The straight laryngoscope blade is the miller blade, and the curved laryngoscope blade is the macintosh blade. Fiber-optic blades do exist, but they are supplied in both styles of laryngoscope blades.

27. **The correct answer is (A).** Laryngoscope blades are sized from smallest (0) to largest (4).

Assessment

1. C	9. C	17. A	25. A	33. A
2. D	10. B	18. C	26. D	34. C
3. B	11. D	19. D	27. B	35. B
4. A	12. C	20. B	28. C	36. C
5. C	13. D	21. D	29. D	37. D
6. B	14. C	22. D	30. B	38. A
7. A	15. B	23. C	31. B	39. C
8. D	16. A	24. A	32. A	40. C

1. **The correct answer is (C).** The initial action of the EMT–Basic in any situation is to ensure scene safety. The EMT–Basic should do a scene survey from inside the vehicle prior to taking any actions in a rescue attempt. This applies not only to accidents but to all incidents. After the scene is considered safe, the EMT–Basic should call for additional resources and, if necessary, block civilian traffic from entry.

2. **The correct answer is (D).** The EMT–Basic should utilize prearrival dispatch data as an integral part of scene size-up. Information gathered prior to arrival is extremely helpful in assisting the EMT–Basic in knowing what equipment may be needed, if police or firefighters are needed on scene, or if the scene would actually be safe to enter. The name of the patient's physician is important but will not have any impact on the acute phase of patient care.

3. **The correct answer is (B).** Upon arrival at a mass-casualty incident, the first arriving crew should immediately request additional assistance. A mass-casualty incident is defined as any incident that overwhelms the resources of a given system. If the EMT–Basic were to remain on the scene without assistance, he or she would become overwhelmed in a relatively short period of time. After scene safety, resource requests should follow immediately.

4. **The correct answer is (A).** Anaphylactic shock is a relatively uncommon occurrence. The EMT–Basic should be acutely aware that anaphylaxis is a true emergency—but a rare one. Some of the more common mechanisms are head injury due to trauma, chest and abdominal injuries, chest pain, and difficulty breathing, as well as multiple minor injuries.

5. **The correct answer is (C).** The EMT–Basic should complete a full physical examination on every patient; however, the general impression of a patient, or his or her condition, is usually formed within minutes of arrival. The EMT–Basic should evaluate the scene, including the patient's living conditions, as well as the patient's appearance (affect) and complaints.

6. **The correct answer is (B).** This patient, due to his response to your shouting, is classified as verbally responsive, or V, on the AVPU scale. If a patient is awake and answering questions, he or she would be considered A on the scale. Pain-responsive patients are

www.twitter.com/emtexam

answers diagnostic test

considered P. Finally, unresponsive patients are considered U on the AVPU scale.

7. **The correct answer is (A).** Any patient who has experienced trauma above the clavicles should be immobilized with a cervical collar. The cervical collar does not immobilize injury to the lower jaw; however, lower jaw injury is a good indicator that a large amount of energy was expended to the patient's head. This is indicative of cervical spinal injury. The cervical collar does not assist patient movement, especially of a trauma patient, to a soft stretcher.

8. **The correct answer is (D).** Suctioning of the airway is part of airway assessment, not breathing assessment. To assess a patient's breathing, the EMT–Basic should watch for equal chest rise, inspect the chest for any obvious injuries, and auscultate the lungs for injury indicators such as absent breath sound or wheezes, rales, and rhonchi.

9. **The correct answer is (C).** Many times, asthma patients call for ambulances before beginning self-treatment. The EMT–Basic, after completing a history and physical, should provide supplemental oxygen and transport the patient for further evaluation at a hospital.

10. **The correct answer is (B).** Any abnormal respiratory sounds may be signs of inadequate breathing. The EMT–Basic should be aware of respiratory deficiencies and intervene to correct the breathing difficulty.

11. **The correct answer is (D).** This patient is a prime candidate for bag-valve-mask ventilation. The EMT–Basic should begin immediate ventilations for the unconscious patient with inadequate breathing. ALS may be requested, but it is not your immediate intervention. Airway management is especially important in pediatric patients, who commonly suffer cardiac arrest secondary to respiratory insufficiency.

12. **The correct answer is (C).** In assessment of a pulse in a conscious and stable adult or child, the EMT–Basic would use the radial pulse. Located at the wrist of the patient, the radial pulse is the most easily accessible pulse point. In the adult patient, a radial pulse indicates a systolic blood pressure of more than 80 mmHg.

13. **The correct answer is (D).** In an infant, the brachial pulse is the most appropriate pulse point. The EMT–Basic may feel a radial pulse; however, an infant's arms contain more fat than an adult's and may prevent the pulse from being felt. The brachial pulse is stronger and, therefore, easier to assess.

14. **The correct answer is (C).** Capillary refill is an adequate predictor of perfusion in infants and children. In adults, factors other than hypovolemia may alter capillary refill. In assessing capillary refill, the EMT–Basic will gently press on the top of the patient's nail bed, and blood flow should return to the area within two seconds. Any return after two seconds should be considered abnormal.

15. **The correct answer is (B).** Assessment of the patient for external blood loss is part of the initial assessment. The EMT–Basic should detect and correct any major blood loss before continuing to other parts of the assessment.

16. **The correct answer is (A).** Most patients will present with warm and pink skin. Pink skin is a sign of good perfusion: blood vessels are generating warmth on the skin. A patient with pallor, cyanosis, or ashen skin should alert the EMT–Basic to a problem.

17. **The correct answer is (A).** Patient one is a high-priority patient. This patient must receive immediate airway and ventilatory

control as well as a complete initial assessment and immediate transport.

18. **The correct answer is (C).** Patient two is conscious and stable and has no external signs of trauma. However, based on the condition of patient one, she should be transported rapidly. She has a significant mechanism of injury as evidenced from the frontal impact, chest pain possibly attributed to a blunt impact to the chest, and the condition of the other passenger in the vehicle.

19. **The correct answer is (D).** In gathering information for the history of present illness, the EMT–Basic can use the mnemonic device OPQRST:

> **O**nset
> **P**rovocating factors
> **Q**uality
> **R**adiation
> **S**everity
> **T**ime

Pertinent past history is gathered after the history of present illness under the SAMPLE history.

20. **The correct answer is (B).** The correct order in assessment of a conscious medical patient starts with the history of present illness, the SAMPLE history, physical examination, and vital signs.

21. **The correct answer is (D).** The correct order in assessment of an unconscious patient is different from that of a conscious patient. It is important to do a rapid physical assessment first and then obtain a set of vital signs. After the vital signs are assessed, the family may be questioned as to the history of present illness and SAMPLE history.

22. **The correct answer is (D).** When the EMT–Basic is treating a patient with a known history, that patient will more than likely have a prescription medication. The EMT–Basic may assist that patient in taking his or her medication, therefore beginning the treatment process. In a patient with no known history, there is no medication on hand to assist the patient, and the EMT–Basic should, in this case, administer oxygen and transport the patient to definitive care.

23. **The correct answer is (C).** An isolated extremity fracture is not a significant mechanism of injury. Significant mechanism of injury is any circumstance that may lead to a life-threatening condition. Patients with significant mechanism of injury should receive a thorough, detailed physical examination.

24. **The correct answer is (A).** The DCAPBTLS mnemonic reminds the EMT–Basic what to assess during a rapid physical assessment. The terms are as follows: deformities, contusions, abrasions, punctures/penetrations, burns, tenderness, lacerations, and swelling. The term *death* is not associated with the DCAPBTLS assessment.

25. **The correct answer is (A).** The correct assessment priority in a patient with significant mechanism of injury is to reconsider the mechanism of injury, begin a rapid trauma assessment, and obtain vital signs and a SAMPLE history.

26. **The correct answer is (D).** Assessment of the trauma patient would encompass all of the mentioned injury markers. In addition, the EMT–Basic should assess for deformities, lacerations, burns, punctures, penetrating trauma, and any other injury that may occur from that particular mechanism of injury.

27. **The correct answer is (B).** Patients complaining of severe headache will usually be suffering from a neurological impairment. A focused examination of this patient would include a complete neurological examination, including blood pressure and pulse

rate. Blood pressure and pulse rate findings may demonstrate an increase in intracranial pressure.

28. **The correct answer is (C).** The EMT–Basic should perform a detailed physical examination on all patients who may have hidden injuries or signs of illness. This examination can, and sometimes will, be omitted for several reasons, such as if the patient requires critical airway, breathing, or circulatory intervention that does not allow time for a detailed examination.

29. **The correct answer is (D).** The ongoing assessment is completed on a patient so that the EMT–Basic can evaluate the patient status after interventions. This examination also serves to allow the EMT–Basic to reassess all critical areas of his or her initial assessment and compare findings and vital signs to the initial baselines established during an initial examination. The initial patient history is gathered during the initial examination process and is not a component of the ongoing assessment; however, the EMT–Basic is encouraged to talk to a conscious patient during the entire call. Frequent conversation may uncover and clarify pieces of the patient history that were previously left uncovered.

30. **The correct answer is (B).** If during the EMT–Basic's ongoing assessment the patient's condition worsens, the EMT–Basic should reassess the previous interventions and reevaluate critical areas of the initial assessment. Obtaining baseline vital signs during the initial assessment creates a reference point for patient status evaluation after treatment. If the patient status deteriorates, then additional interventions may be needed, including the request for ALS assistance.

31. **The correct answer is (B).** The EMS dispatcher is responsible for choices (A), (C), and (D), as well as other aspects of emergency medical dispatch; however, the EMT–Basic at the scene of the assignment is responsible for making the determination as to which hospital would best treat the patient's condition. The assessment of the EMT–Basic, as well as the patient's response to treatment, will determine if the patient should be transported to a specialty center or the nearest receiving hospital. This responsibility cannot be handled by the EMS dispatcher.

32. **The correct answer is (A).** When communicating with the dispatcher, the EMT–Basic should use concise and direct radio messages. These messages should include only pertinent information that the dispatcher will need to document the call and assign additional emergency responders. Comprehensive radio reports are unnecessary and only serve to confuse all parties, as well as prevent other units from reporting to the dispatcher. The patient's personal information should never be transmitted over the air. Multiple agencies (news, personal, etc.) have access to the emergency frequencies by the use of scanners. The patient's right to privacy should be protected at all times. The use of ten-codes should be used only if all parties are well versed in their definitions. Defining the ten-code after its transmission only serves to extend the transmission.

33. **The correct answer is (A).** The verbal report over the air should be a concise but detailed report that consists of the following information: Unit ID, receiving hospital and ETA, age and sex of patient, chief complaint, history of present emergency, findings, treatments, and responses. This information will be passed on to the receiving hospital to ensure the staff is prepared to receive and treat the patient in an appropriate fashion.

34. **The correct answer is (C).** While on assignment, the EMT–Basic should be informing the dispatcher of his or her status every time

it changes. These status reports should be delivered when assigned, on arrival at the emergency, en route to the hospital (includes verbal report), on arrival at the hospital, and when the unit is available after the call is complete. The EMT–Basic is also responsible for informing the dispatcher if he or she will be out of service for any other reasons, including restocking, cleaning, refueling, tour change, etc.

35. **The correct answer is (B).** Patients who are hearing-impaired will sometimes create a difficult situation when communicating. The EMT–Basic should speak slowly and clearly while facing the patient. Most patients with hearing problems can read lips and make out the words as long as the EMT–Basic is looking at them. Shouting in the patient's ear is inappropriate and may cause the patient to become apprehensive. Normally, hearing aids will allow the patient to hear well enough to understand the EMT–Basic; however, in some cases, these will be ineffective. The use of sign language is an effective tool, provided all parties are knowledgeable in its use.

36. **The correct answer is (C).** It is of the utmost importance to inform pediatric patients of all procedures being conducted and whether or not they will cause pain or discomfort. In not remaining totally honest with the child, the EMT–Basic will lose the trust of the child and render her- or himself ineffective in the treatment of the patient. Children should be allowed to remain with a parent, and their favorite toy should accompany them if requested. A demeanor of total honesty with pediatric patients will develop a trusting atmosphere in which the EMT–Basic may perform his or her duties with a cooperative patient.

37. **The correct answer is (D).** The minimum data set includes all information collected during initial patient contact. This information should be well documented on the prehospital care report. The components of the minimum data set include patient chief complaint, level of consciousness, blood pressure, perfusion status, skin condition (color, temperature, and moisture), heart rate, and respiratory rate. Therapeutic interventions are not part of the minimum data set; however, they should be documented on the prehospital care report.

38. **The correct answer is (A).** The EMT–Basic should never allow a patient to sign a refusal of treatment and leave without first attempting to examine the patient and convince him or her that he or she needs medical care. The patient should receive a complete history and physical, with all necessary evaluations and assessments done based on the history of present illness. After this evaluation, all findings and outcomes should be discussed with the patient. If the patient still refuses, the EMT–Basic may elect to contact medical control for assistance or accept the refusal. All refusals should be well documented.

answers diagnostic test

39. The correct answer is (C). The primary responsibility of the EMT–Basic is to the patient. Inaccurate patient care reports, or those that have been falsified, will provide improper information in the ongoing treatment of the patient. If it was documented that a medication was given that was actually not given, the patient may not receive that medication at the hospital. The EMT–Basic should advise his or her partner that the form should be changed to reflect the pertinent information correctly and follow through to ensure that the information is changed.

40. The correct answer is (C). The EMT–Basic, upon finding an error in documentation, should draw a single line through the error and write the correction above the crossed-out error. In most cases, it is an error in word use that may be confusing to the hospital staff. The EMT–Basic should never leave an error in place, as it may confuse patient care. In addition, completely crossing out the error may raise suspicions that something was omitted purposely.

Medical

1. D	15. B	29. D	43. B	57. D
2. D	16. B	30. C	44. C	58. C
3. A	17. C	31. A	45. D	59. B
4. B	18. B	32. D	46. A	60. A
5. D	19. B	33. B	47. B	61. A
6. C	20. A	34. B	48. B	62. C
7. B	21. C	35. C	49. D	63. B
8. A	22. B	36. A	50. D	64. B
9. B	23. A	37. B	51. D	65. B
10. C	24. B	38. C	52. A	66. C
11. C	25. B	39. A	53. D	67. C
12. C	26. C	40. D	54. C	68. A
13. B	27. C	41. A	55. C	69. C
14. C	28. A	42. A	56. B	

1. **The correct answer is (D).** Most basic life-support units have epinephrine, activated charcoal, and oral glucose. Local protocols determine the availability of most medications. Diazepam, commonly called valium, is a drug used to treat a variety of conditions, including anxiety and seizure disorders. Most basic life-support units do not carry this medication.

2. **The correct answer is (D).** An EMT–Basic always verifies the medication, dose, and route of administration prior to administering any medication. As an EMT–Basic, you should be familiar with any medications you administer to a patient. However, the EMT–Basic does not usually administer injectable medications. When an injectable medication is necessary, the EMT–Basic uses an auto injector, which has the appropriate needle attached.

3. **The correct answer is (A).** The proper order is nose, pharynx, larynx, trachea, bronchi, and alveoli.

4. **The correct answer is (B).** All of the listed items are signs of inadequate breathing. The patient who is having difficulty breathing for any reason will present with some signs of inadequate breathing. The EMT–Basic must be aware that not all patients may present with the same obvious signs. Some patients may exhibit subtle signs or only one symptom of inadequate breathing. The EMT–Basic must be aware of all the signs of inadequate breathing to treat the patient properly.

5. **The correct answer is (D).** The medication of choice in the treatment of breathing difficulty is oxygen. The EMT–Basic should never withhold oxygen from any patient with breathing difficulty. Epinephrine, metered dose inhalers, and nitroglycerin are special-

ized medications for the treatment of specific medical alterations in respiratory status. All patients with breathing difficulty, regardless of the cause, should receive oxygen.

6. **The correct answer is (C).** In all patients with respiratory insufficiency, the EMT–Basic uses a bag-valve-mask ventilator with an oxygen reservoir to assist the ventilations. This patient, in addition to having breathing difficulty, is also suffering from inadequate ventilation. The EMT–Basic must assist oxygenation and ventilation in order for this patient to receive the proper amount of oxygenation. This artificial ventilation should continue until the patient regains the ability to support his own ventilations or until emergency services transfers the patient to another provider for additional treatments.

7. **The correct answer is (B).** The conscious patient with adequate ventilation should sit in a position that is most comfortable. This position (usually leaning forward in a tripod position) will ensure that the patient can maintain adequate ventilations without assistance. The EMT–Basic should administer supplemental oxygen to all patients complaining of difficulty breathing.

8. **The correct answer is (A).** The signs of adequate air exchange are equal chest expansion, clear breath sounds bilaterally, no use of the accessory muscles of breathing, unlabored efforts at ventilation, and signs of adequate oxygenation. The EMT–Basic should evaluate any patient who exhibits abnormal symptoms for conditions that may cause breathing difficulty and treat these conditions promptly.

9. **The correct answer is (B).** Many children will not tolerate an oxygen mask on their face—it may be too confining, and the child will naturally try to remove it. In the event that this occurs, the EMT–Basic can hold the mask a few inches from the child's face

to deliver oxygen to the patient. Efforts in restraining the child are not effective, as they will agitate the child and cause increased difficulty in breathing. The EMT–Basic should never discontinue the administration of oxygen to a patient who requires it.

10. **The correct answer is (C).** Asthma is an episodic disease. Asthmatics may experience attacks that range from mild breathing difficulty to a complete inability to exchange air. These severe patients will need the EMT–Basic to provide ventilator assistance as well as supplemental oxygen. COPD (chronic bronchitis and emphysema) patients are usually short of breath and, in many cases, will not call for assistance unless their breathing difficulty worsens significantly. Epiglottitis is a life-threatening disease caused by a bacterial infection. Medical professionals must treat epiglottitis rapidly, as it may cause an airway obstruction and prevent breathing.

11. **The correct answer is (C).** Atherosclerosis is a major cause of chest pain. Although not the direct diagnosis, atherosclerosis is the causative factor in most cases of angina pectoris, myocardial infarction, and cardiac ischemia (angina). Blood flow to the heart decreases when calcium and fat particles clog the coronary arteries. Ischemia sets in because the heart cells are not receiving enough oxygen. Without medical intervention, this condition will get progressively worse until the patient suffers from a myocardial infarction.

12. **The correct answer is (C).** Patients with angina pectoris usually experience an onset of pain after some type of exertion. The pain usually subsides after rest or administration of oxygen or nitroglycerin. There is not always an obvious cause of pain in myocardial infarction. Nitroglycerin or oxygen administration does not usually relieve the

pain, and the pain will not subside after a period of rest.

13. **The correct answer is (B).** A heart rate above 100 beats per minute could indicate tachycardia. Specifically, a heart rate between 100 and 150 beats per minute signifies tachycardia, with higher heart rates being more specific in origin. A normal heart rate is between 60 and 100 beats per minute, while a heart rate under 60 beats per minute indicates bradycardia.

14. **The correct answer is (C).** A heart rate of fewer than 60 beats per minute indicates bradycardia. The EMT–Basic should know that many athletes have normal resting heart rates below 60. This rate should only cause alarm if the patient exhibits symptoms of poor blood flow to the body, such as low blood pressure.

15. **The correct answer is (B).** Onset and duration are of great importance in a differential diagnosis between angina pectoris and myocardial infarction. In this case, the patient stated that the pain came on at rest. Even after taking nitroglycerin, the patient continued to experience pain for 45 minutes. This information would lead to a diagnosis of myocardial infarction, based on the onset and duration alone. The fact that the medication did nothing to ease the patient's pain helps confirm the diagnosis of myocardial infarction.

16. **The correct answer is (B).** Although CPR and proper ventilation will prolong the window of opportunity to convert a cardiac arrest patient, defibrillation is the definitive treatment of a cardiac arrest patient within the first few minutes of the event. In the first few minutes of cardiac arrest, the heart is in ventricular fibrillation. The EMT–Basic can use defibrillation to help prompt a normal rhythm. In most cases, the EMT–Basic should attach the AED to any pulseless

patient as early as possible. However, the EMT–Basic should consider performing CPR first on patients who have received ineffective or no CPR prior to arrival and in patients with unknown downtimes.

17. **The correct answer is (C).** The fully automatic defibrillator can analyze a patient and deliver a shock without any outside assistance from the user. The fully automatic AED will analyze a cardiac arrest rhythm. If the AED recognizes that the patient needs a shock, it will give an all clear, charge up, and deliver the shock by itself. The semiautomatic AED will analyze and then advise the user to charge and deliver the shock. Both units will be equipped with hands-free pads that the user applies to the patient's chest.

18. **The correct answer is (B).** Different forms of ventricular tachycardia may look the same on a cardiac monitor, but one produces a pulse and one does not. When the AED does not detect a pulse, it will recommend a shock for this rhythm. Delivering a shock to a patient in ventricular tachycardia with a pulse may cause great harm—to the extent of stopping the heart. To prevent this grave error, it is only advisable to attach an AED to a patient who has no pulse.

19. **The correct answer is (B).** The EMT–Basic should consider transport after three unsuccessful defibrillation attempts. If the ALS unit is en route and its ETA is longer than it would take to arrive at the nearest hospital, the EMT–Basic should begin transporting the patient to the hospital. If, for any reason, the ETA of the ALS unit should change, the dispatcher can arrange for the ALS unit to intercept the BLS unit.

20. **The correct answer is (A).** The EMT–Basic should prevent any unnecessary patient movement during the analyze phase of AED use. Although modern AEDs will be able to decipher what is artifact and what is not,

there is always a chance of a false reading and a shock indication where one is unnecessary. The EMT–Basic should understand the serious medical ramifications of delivering an unnecessary shock to a patient.

21. **The correct answer is (C).** The driver should stop the vehicle whenever an AED is in analyze mode or set to shock. Movement of the vehicle may cause interference that could prevent proper analysis of the patient's rhythm. Delivery of defibrillations in a moving vehicle can have dangerous effects, especially if the vehicle turns during a shock and causes the EMT–Basic accidently to touch the patient or defibrillation pads. The EMT–Basic should only deliver an AED treatment after the driver has stopped the vehicle.

22. **The correct answer is (B).** The eighty-seven-year-old female with chest pain and a pulse is not a candidate for AED use. The EMT–Basic should never use an AED on a patient with a pulse. Most AEDs will not recommend a shock if a pulse is detected. The EMT–Basic may treat pulseless pediatric patients with AEDs specially designed for use on younger patients.

23. **The correct answer is (A).** The AED should be inspected prior to the beginning of each shift to ensure that it is fully charged and operational. Failure to do a shift check may result in a charge of negligence on the part of the EMT–Basic if the AED fails to operate at the scene of a cardiac arrest. The EMT–Basic should not take the word of the previous shift that the unit is operational and should check the unit. In addition, regardless of when it was charged and used, it should be tested prior to every shift. Even if a battery shows a full charge at the beginning of the previous shift, temperature conditions and other environmental factors may take a charge from a battery. A defective battery may show a charge, then drop the charge in a few hours.

24. **The correct answer is (B).** When encountering a patient in a wet area, the EMT–Basic should immediately move the patient into a dry area and use a towel to remove excess water from the patient before attaching the AED. This will ensure safety in operation of the unit. Electrical currents can flow through a puddle or wet surface easily, which could possibly injure the rescuers or bystanders. The EMT–Basic should dry the patient with a towel before proceeding to defibrillate.

25. **The correct answer is (B).** Common side effects of nitroglycerin include nausea, vomiting, dizziness, hypotension, headache, and bitter taste in the mouth (from the pill). The patient may feel dizzy and/or lightheaded because nitroglycerin dilates blood vessels, which also causes a drop in blood pressure.

26. **The correct answer is (C).** Previous episodes of nausea after the administration of nitroglycerin are not a contraindication to its administration. True contraindications to the use of nitroglycerin would include hypotension, previous allergic reactions, and using it to treat hypertension in the field.

27. **The correct answer is (C).** Metabolic causes of altered mental states are conditions caused by factors outside of the central nervous system. Many of these factors are from the outside environment. CVA (cerebrovascular accident or stroke) is a structural cause of altered mental status because it occurs in the central nervous system.

28. **The correct answer is (A).** A rapid onset of altered mental status is an indication of hypoglycemia. Blood sugar may drop for multiple reasons, including the patient taking his or her insulin and then failing to eat. After taking insulin, free glucose coverts to stored glucose, which the body cannot use. The

patient may feel disorientated once glucose levels drop. Hyperglycemia, ketoacidosis, and diabetic coma are all definitions of too much sugar in the blood.

29. **The correct answer is (D).** Signs and symptoms of hypoglycemia include hunger, agitation, weakness, alteration of mental status (rapidly deteriorating), and salivation. The onset of hypoglycemia can take just a few minutes. A patient may experience drastic mental changes from the drop in blood sugar. Excessive thirst, excessive urination, and a delayed onset of altered mental status are indicative of hyperglycemia.

30. **The correct answer is (C).** The EMT–Basic should never administer an oral medication to an unconscious patient. Unconscious patients may lose control of their ability to protect the airway and may aspirate the oral glucose, causing severe airway problems. The EMT–Basic should only administer oral glucose to conscious patients with diabetic histories and altered mental states.

31. **The correct answer is (A).** The EMT–Basic should treat an unconscious patient who is having a diabetic emergency with airway and ventilatory maintenance. The EMT–Basic should place the patient in the recovery position to guard against aspiration, and request ALS assistance for administration of intravenous glucose and advance emergency management. The EMT–Basic should never administer oral glucose to an unconscious patient.

32. **The correct answer is (D).** The EMT–Basic must protect a patient suffering from a seizure from injury. In addition, seizures may cause a prolonged period of apnea and can result in hypoxia. The EMT–Basic must be alert for signs of hypoxia and treat accordingly.

33. **The correct answer is (B).** Status epilepticus is the condition where a patient suffers two or more seizures without a lucid interval. Status epilepticus is a dire emergency that requires ventilatory support as well as rapid transport or ALS intervention. The EMT–Basic should assess the patient for status epilepticus and make a decision to transport the patient or request ALS intervention.

34. **The correct answer is (B).** This patient is showing classic signs of a stroke. Slurred speech, confusion, unequal pupils, and hemiplegia are all characteristics of a stroke. Treatment of this patient would include airway and ventilatory support, high concentration oxygen, and transportation in the recovery position to facilitate airway safety.

35. **The correct answer is (C).** The patient suffering from anaphylaxis will exhibit signs of respiratory distress and shock. Allergic reactions are more common than true anaphylactic emergencies. Many people will develop allergies to outside allergens without ever developing anaphylaxis.

36. **The correct answer is (A).** The presence of a rash or an itchy feeling could indicate that the patient is experiencing an allergic reaction. Anaphylaxis usually presents with itching, hives, and generalized swelling on the body. If these signs are not present, then the patient may be suffering from an asthma attack.

37. **The correct answer is (B).** A patient experiencing anaphylactic reaction (shock) will require immediate airway management. This management may need to be aggressive. Anaphylactic shock causes rapid airway swelling, putting the patient in danger of death from hypoxia. Airway maintenance is always the highest priority in this type of patient.

38. **The correct answer is (C).** Patients with anaphylaxis generally do not develop fevers. However, a patient with a fever who is also having an anaphylactic reaction may be on antibiotic medications. Antibiotic medications, especially penicillin derivatives, are major causes of allergic reactions and anaphylaxis.

39. **The correct answer is (A).** Epinephrine commonly increases heart rate. After the injection of epinephrine, the patient may have an increase in pulse rate. Epinephrine will also open airway passages and constrict blood vessels. This will result in increased blood pressure as well as a decrease in breathing difficulty.

40. **The correct answer is (D).** The four common entry routes of poison and toxins are injection, ingestion, inhalation, and absorption. Proximity to a poisonous agent or toxin may not necessarily cause a reaction; however, the EMT–Basic should be aware that certain poisons and toxins (e.g., radiation) might cause a reaction in patients who were near the contaminant but never actually came in physical contact with it.

41. **The correct answer is (A).** When eliciting a history in a poisoning, it is not important to determine if the patient has ever taken the poison before. The EMT–Basic should focus on finding out what the patient took, when the patient took it, how the patient took it, and how much the patient took. This information is essential when contacting poison control or medical direction. In determining the amount and route of ingestion, the medical team can develop a rapid treatment plan to prevent absorption of the substance.

42. **The correct answer is (A).** The EMT–Basic should focus on preventing the absorption of the poison. Speeding up absorption will only increase the severity of the physical effects of the poison. The EMT–Basic will not always induce vomiting in the poisoning patient. Induced vomiting may be hazardous with certain substances. Administration of antitoxins is beyond the scope of the EMT–Basic. Airway management and prevention of absorption are the highest priority for the EMT–Basic.

43. **The correct answer is (B).** The goal of patient management in a poisoning is to support the airway. As an off-duty EMT, you will not have all the essential equipment to deal with this emergency, but you should always have a pocket mask in case of an emergency. You should never attempt mouth-to-mouth ventilations on a poisoning patient because you may accidentally absorb the poison. You should never attempt to dilute poisons or induce vomiting on an unconscious patient.

44. **The correct answer is (C).** If a patient vomits up the first dose of activated charcoal, the EMT–Basic can administer an additional dose. Activated charcoal works in the gastrointestinal system by absorbing and binding poisons and preventing the body from absorbing them. If the patient vomits up the charcoal, the body could still absorb the poison.

45. **The correct answer is (D).** The body can lose heat by conduction, convection, radiation, evaporation, and respiration. The EMT–Basic must be aware of the factors that may affect a patient's ability to maintain heat and work to correct them immediately. The body cannot lose heat through absorption.

46. **The correct answer is (A).** Airway maintenance and passive rewarming is highest priority when treating a hypothermic patient. The EMT–Basic should not administer warm fluids or rapidly rewarm a hypothermic patient.

47. **The correct answer is (B).** Patients exposed to high heat without proper ventilation and

hydration will develop increased internal temperatures, resulting in hyperthermia. In this case, the patient has hot and dry skin. Hot and dry skin is an ominous sign, and the EMT–Basic should move the patient to a cool area and attempt to cool him as rapidly as possible. Emergent hyperthermia is a true emergency that requires rapid transport to the hospital.

48. **The correct answer is (B).** The EMT–Basic should attempt resuscitation of a cold-water drowning patient immediately, regardless of submersion time (with the exception of obvious death). There are documented cases of patients surviving after long periods of submersion in cold water. The EMT–Basic should begin resuscitation efforts immediately at the scene by administering resuscitation, drying off the patient, and starting passive rewarming.

49. **The correct answer is (D).** It is highly unusual for a drowning or near-drowning patient to suffer from hyperthermia because water pulls heat from the body. Near-drowning patients may suffer from pulmonary edema (salt-water drowning), red blood cell destruction (fresh-water drowning), and severe hypoxia from long submersion times.

50. **The correct answer is (D).** The EMT–Basic should provide a snakebite patient with airway and cardiovascular support. In addition, the EMT–Basic should keep the patient as still as possible to avoid rapid movement of the venom through the body. The EMT–Basic should never suck poison from the patient's wound using the mouth. Snake poisons are extremely harmful and could cause injury to the rescuer. If suction is necessary, the EMT–Basic should use a snakebite kit to remove venom from the wound.

51. **The correct answer is (D).** There are many medical causes of behavioral changes. The EMT–Basic should be aware that a behavioral emergency might have a medical cause. It is not acceptable to assume that a behavioral emergency is psychological in nature until you investigate the physical causes.

52. **The correct answer is (A).** As with any response, the safety of rescuers is the highest priority. In behavioral emergencies, this is even more important. EMT–Basics should ensure that every scene entered is safe for themselves and their partners. Behavioral emergencies can rapidly become violent situations. EMT–Basics should be alert to the environment and proceed with caution.

53. **The correct answer is (D).** All three situations may lead to suicidal attempts or thoughts. Suicide, or thoughts of suicide, may be brought on by many factors: high stress, depression, drug or alcohol addiction, recent breakups, or deaths of close relatives and friends. Most suicide attempts are a cry for help. The EMT–Basic should treat the patient physically as well as emotionally.

54. **The correct answer is (C).** Scene safety is the number one concern in any emergency. The EMT–Basic should never enter a home in which a patient is threatening violence. Approaching a window is just as dangerous—if a patient breaks the window, the EMT–Basic may become injured. This will only add to the confusion on the scene. The EMT–Basic should not ask a family member to retrieve the patient, especially during a violent outbreak.

55. **The correct answer is (C).** When restraining a patient is necessary, EMS providers should work with the police in developing a restraint plan before moving in on the patient. The patient should always be given the option of being transported on his or

her own accord; however, if this approach fails, then the restraint procedure should go into effect. One rescuer should be there to talk to the patient while the restraints are applied. The violent patient should never be allowed a free arm or limb. This could result in injury to the rescuers.

56. **The correct answer is (B).** In any patient interaction, the EMT–Basic should maintain a caring and understanding ear. Many behavioral patients are only looking for somebody to talk to. The EMT–Basic can be a major asset to the treatment of the patient if he or she shows compassion. This does not mean that the EMT–Basic should feed into any delusions. In addition, the EMT–Basic may find many clues to the patient's condition during the conversation.

57. **The correct answer is (D).** The EMT–Basic must be familiar with all of the anatomical structures of the female reproductive system in order to assist in the delivery of an infant. These structures include the uterus, vagina, placenta, umbilical cord, amniotic sac, and fetus. A good understanding of all of the functions of these structures is imperative to assist in the delivery of the infant. The fallopian tubes, although a structure in the female reproductive system, serve no purpose in the actual birth of the child.

58. **The correct answer is (C).** Labor can be defined in three stages. The first stage of labor is from the beginning of contractions until the cervix is fully dilated. The second stage of labor is from the time the infant enters the birth canal until the time of birth. The third stage of labor begins after delivery of the infant and ends with the delivery of the placenta.

59. **The correct answer is (B).** See explanation for question 58.

60. **The correct answer is (A).** See explanation for question 58.

61. **The correct answer is (A).** When dealing with the pregnant patient, the EMT–Basic should assess the mother for signs of imminent birth. Some of the indicators are breaking of the bag of water, contractions that are fewer than 2 minutes apart, and the mother's urge to push. However, the best field indicator is direct vaginal visualization for crowning. Crowning is when the head of the infant is showing at the vaginal opening. This is a sure sign of imminent delivery.

62. **The correct answer is (C).** An abruptio placenta is defined as premature separation of the placenta from the uterus. This separation may be partial or complete. The signs of abruption are severe abdominal or back and flank pain, a rigid uterus, and dark red bleeding.

63. **The correct answer is (B).** Placenta previa is characterized by bright red (arterial) and painless bleeding that usually occurs during the last trimester of pregnancy. The placenta is attached to the uterine wall at a lower point than normal; when the cervix begins to dilate, the placenta begins to detach from the uterine wall, causing arterial bright red bleeding.

64. **The correct answer is (B).** The EMT–Basic who is assisting delivery of a newborn should suction the infant's airway after the head is fully delivered. Usually, the head delivers facing down and rotates as it becomes fully delivered. The EMT–Basic can assist in this rotation; however, care must be taken to avoid injury to the infant. Suctioning should commence after delivery of the head to prevent compression of the cord.

65. **The correct answer is (B).** The proper procedure for suctioning a newborn's airway is to suction the mouth first and then suction the nose.

66. **The correct answer is (C).** If during an assisted delivery you notice the umbilical cord is wrapped around the infant's neck, you should initially try and lift it over the head, freeing up the head and continuing delivery. If it is impossible to slip the cord over the infant's head, the EMT–Basic should clamp the umbilical cord and then cut between the clamps to facilitate delivery.

67. **The correct answer is (C).** A prolapsed cord can be a major emergency if it interferes with blood supply to the infant. If the cord gets pinched and blood flow is restricted, the infant will become hypoxic and go into distress. It is imperative that the EMT–Basic provide an open airway for the newborn. This is accomplished by inserting two gloved fingers into the vagina on either side of the newborn's nose. This way, an open airway is provided in case the infant's breathing stimulus is activated due to cord compression.

68. **The correct answer is (A).** A limb presentation must be transported to a hospital immediately. There is no field treatment for this presentation, and the EMT–Basic should never try to insert his or her hand into the birth canal to reposition the infant. The mother should be transported immediately with her pelvis elevated and on high-concentration oxygen.

69. **The correct answer is (C).** Preeclampsia is a condition characterized by hypertension, headache, and sensitivity to light during pregnancy. If the hypertension continues to worsen, seizures may develop. The diagnosis of eclampsia is based on seizure activity.

answers diagnostic test

Trauma

1. A	11. D	21. C	31. C	40. A
2. B	12. C	22. C	32. C	41. C
3. C	13. A	23. C	33. D	42. B
4. B	14. D	24. D	34. A	43. B
5. D	15. B	25. B	35. C	44. B
6. B	16. C	26. B	36. B	45. A
7. A	17. C	27. B	37. B	46. C
8. B	18. C	28. A	38. B	47. A
9. A	19. D	29. D	39. C	48. B
10. A	20. A	30. C		

1. **The correct answer is (A).** Arterial bleeding is characterized by a rapid, spurting, pulsatile flow of oxygenated blood. Arterial bleeding should be considered serious, as patients can lose a large volume of blood from an arterial bleed in a short period of time. The EMT–Basic should apply direct pressure to stop arterial bleeding initially.

2. **The correct answer is (B).** Venous bleeding is characterized by a steady flow of dark, deoxygenated blood. This type of bleeding is common in most soft-tissue injuries. Although not as serious and life-threatening as arterial bleeding, venous bleeding should be controlled immediately to prevent large amounts of blood loss.

3. **The correct answer is (C).** Capillary bleeding is a slow and oozing type of bleeding. Since blood flow in the capillaries is under low pressure, and the capillaries are very small, capillary bleeding does not pose a life threat. Applying direct pressure to the injury site easily controls capillary bleeding.

4. **The correct answer is (B).** Decreased pulse is not a sign of shock. Initial response to hypoperfusion (shock) is that the body will increase pulse rate. As bleeding continues and shock progresses, the patient will develop an altered mental status and his skin color will take on a pallor (paleness). The skin will also become cold and clammy. Decreased blood pressure is a late sign of shock. The EMT–Basic must be aware of the signs of shock. Bleeding control is the definitive treatment of patients with shock.

5. **The correct answer is (D).** Bleeding control is accomplished by first applying direct pressure. If that is unsuccessful, elevate the injured area. If bleeding control is still unsuccessful, a pressure point would be used to slow bleeding to the area. Although a tourniquet may be considered as a last resort, wire should never be used as a tourniquet, as tightening it would cause additional injury to the patient.

6. **The correct answer is (B).** This patient is showing classic signs of severe internal bleeding. After a major traumatic event, abdominal bruising, especially over the site of a major organ, is a definite sign of internal bleeding. A distended abdomen is another sign of internal injuries. Management of

this type of injury includes rapid transport to a hospital for definitive care.

7. **The correct answer is (A).** Critical trauma patients should be rapidly transported to a trauma center for surgical intervention. It is commonly known that the patient must be delivered to a surgical facility within the first hour of his or her injury. This term, known as the golden hour, is an EMS golden rule. The EMT–Basic should rapidly transport all critical trauma patients at the earliest possible opportunity.

8. **The correct answer is (B).** Maintenance of the airway is the highest priority in any aspect of patient care. The EMT–Basic should always make airway management and patient oxygenation the highest priority in trauma care. Following the basics— airway, breathing, and circulation (ABC)— will always be helpful to the trauma patient.

9. **The correct answer is (A).** The skin consists of three layers: epidermis, dermis, and subcutaneous. The muscle lies below the subcutaneous layer. Muscle is not considered part of the skin as it has a different classification of tissue. The subcutaneous tissue is a fatty layer of skin that assists in the protection of underlying tissue, such as muscle.

10. **The correct answer is (A).** A contusion is usually a small isolated area of bleeding under the skin. Contusions are considered a closed wound. Closed wounds are defined as an injury where the skin remains intact. Contusions are usually self-limiting; however, they may require some prehospital treatment. Application of cold compresses is usually indicated in the treatment of a contusion.

11. **The correct answer is (D).** A hematoma is similar to a contusion. A hematoma always involves a larger area of injury with ad-

ditional tissue damage. As in a contusion, the skin remains intact; however, the area of internal injury is more widespread.

12. **The correct answer is (C).** A laceration is a cut that may have jagged edges or a fine, smooth edge. A laceration is a common injury that the EMT–Basic may encounter. Treatment of the patient with an isolated laceration would include direct pressure and elevation of the lacerated extremity. Lacerations are usually superficial and result in venous bleeding; however, they may also be deep, resulting in arterial bleeding.

13. **The correct answer is (A).** Abrasions are defined as scrapes and scratches that affect the skin superficially. Due to the superficial nature of an abrasion, the bleeding is usually slow and oozing from capillaries. These injuries usually contain small stones and dirt. The EMT–Basic should attempt to keep all injuries from becoming contaminated with foreign substances.

14. **The correct answer is (D).** An avulsion is defined as any soft-tissue injury that involves the removal of skin or a flap of skin. Treatment of an avulsion includes folding the flap of skin back to its original position and covering it with a clean dressing.

15. **The correct answer is (B).** A sucking chest wound should be treated immediately with high-concentration oxygen, an occlusive dressing, and breath sound monitoring. The EMT–Basic should monitor the occlusive dressing and the patient's response to the treatment. In some cases, the occlusive dressing may cause increased difficulty in breathing due to a developing tension pneumothorax. If breathing becomes more difficult, the EMT–Basic should release the dressing occasionally to release trapped air. Splinting of the chest using the patient's right arm is not part of the treatment.

16. **The correct answer is (C).** A hemopneumothorax is defined as air and blood trapped in the lungs. Blood in the lungs is especially dangerous, as the lungs are considered a "potential space." This means that excessive bleeding in that area can result in hypoperfusion and shock. This type of bleeding may be difficult to assess from the outside; however, detailed assessment of breath sounds will tip off the EMT–Basic that a hemopneumothorax has developed. Breath sounds in hemopneumothorax are usually absent, and gurgling may be heard on the affected side.

17. **The correct answer is (C).** The treatment of an abdominal evisceration includes administration of high-concentration oxygen, an occlusive dressing, and moist sterile dressings. In addition, the EMT–Basic should assess frequently for shock and transport immediately. Application of a dry sterile dressing is not part of the treatment.

18. **The correct answer is (C).** Burns are classified as superficial, partial thickness, and full thickness. Superficial burns cause the affected area to redden, while partial-thickness burns cause reddening and blistering. Full-thickness burns are characterized by redness, blistering, and charring of the affected area.

19. **The correct answer is (D).** See explanation for question 18.

20. **The correct answer is (A).** See explanation for question 18.

21. **The correct answer is (C).** Whenever a patient is involved in a fire and has associated burn injury, the EMT–Basic should immediately assess the status of the patient's airway. This assessment should include a visual inspection of the area of the mouth and nose for burns and black soot. Included in this assessment should be a visual inspec-

tion of the mouth and monitoring of breath sounds for developing wheezes.

22. **The correct answer is (C).** In this patient, the rule of nines includes both arms and the anterior chest and abdomen. Each arm is 9 percent of the burn area, the chest is another 9 percent, and the abdomen is 9 percent. The total is 36 percent.

23. **The correct answer is (C).** The rule of nines for a child is different from that of an adult. This child has burns on his anterior chest and back as well as the head. The chest accounts for 18 percent, the back is another 18 percent, and the head is 18 percent. This makes the total burn area of this child 54 percent. In the child, the head accounts for a larger surface area due to the fact that a child's head is bigger.

24. **The correct answer is (D).** Burns to the hands, feet, genitalia, and airway are always considered critical. Although they may only account for a small percentage of total body surface areas burned, they need immediate treatment.

25. **The correct answer is (B).** Airway management is always the first priority in the care of any patient. The EMT–Basic should be aware that in an electrical burn, the patient might develop cardiac arrhythmias from the electrical current. The EMT–Basic should be alert for a patient in cardiac arrest from electrical burns. The use of the AED is indicated in the treatment of these patients.

26. **The correct answer is (B).** The EMT–Basic should never attempt to remove an impaled object from any part of the body except the cheek. Removal of an impaled object could result in massive bleeding that may have been prevented by the object. As we cannot know the angle of the object in most cases, removal of the object can also cause additional injury.

27. **The correct answer is (B).** The EMT–Basic should never remove a partially amputated part. The treatment of a partial amputation is to wrap the limb in dry sterile dressings and transport the patient to an appropriate treatment facility.

28. **The correct answer is (A).** The appendicular skeleton consists of all the skeletal parts of the extremities, while the axial skeleton consists of the bones of the skull, spinal column, and ribs.

29. **The correct answer is (D).** The following bones are included in the upper extremities: humerus, radius, ulna, carpals, metacarpals, and phalanges (fingers). Metatarsals are the bones of the foot.

30. **The correct answer is (C).** While any closed fracture may result in blood loss, a fracture to the pelvis can result in a large amount of blood loss. It is not uncommon to lose one to two liters (20 to 33 percent) of blood volume due to this type of injury. Any time the EMT–Basic suspects a fracture to the pelvic area, a consideration should be made as to how much associated blood loss may be endured. The EMT–Basic should assess the patient for signs of shock and treat accordingly.

31. **The correct answer is (C).** To properly immobilize a bone, the EMT–Basic should immobilize the joints above and below the fracture site. This will ensure that no movement of the bone will be possible. Unless the patient has other critical injuries, do not attempt to move the patient until painful and swollen limbs have been properly immobilized.

32. **The correct answer is (C).** If, after a splint is applied, the patient suffers from any type of numbness or tingling in that extremity, the EMT–Basic should reapply the splint a second time with less pressure. Applying a splint too tightly can cause nerve and blood vessel damage.

33. **The correct answer is (D).** The traction splint is indicated for femur fractures. This includes open fractures. Injuries to the pelvis, acetabulum, and knee are not treated with traction splint application.

34. **The correct answer is (A).** The cervical spine consists of seven vertebrae. Injury to higher vertebrae of the cervical spine can cause an immediate threat to the patient's life. It is of the utmost importance that the EMT–Basic identify potential cervical spinal fractures and immobilize them accordingly.

35. **The correct answer is (C).** The brain and spinal cord make up the central nervous system. The nerves and nerve pathways in the body are collectively known as the nervous system. The twelve cranial nerves are part of the central nervous system; however, they are not independently known as the central nervous system.

36. **The correct answer is (B).** A concussion is a mild head injury that may occur after a patient strikes his or her head on another object. Signs and symptoms of a concussion are headache and lethargy as well as possible loss of consciousness. Concussions may range from mild to severe based on symptoms.

37. **The correct answer is (B).** Any patient who suffers from a severe facial injury should be monitored for airway compromise. Broken bones, blood, and teeth may endanger an open airway. The EMT–Basic must prepare to maintain the airway of a patient with a facial injury using any means possible. This may include airway adjuncts and suctioning of the patient's airway at regular intervals during treatment.

answers diagnostic test

38. **The correct answer is (B).** Whenever a patient complains of any loss of sensation, the EMT–Basic should suspect spinal injury above the level of the sensation loss. In this case, the patient is complaining of sensation loss from the neck down. This is a good indication that the injury to the spinal cord is in the cervical area. Treatment of this patient would include aggressive airway management and full spinal immobilization.

39. **The correct answer is (C).** The Glasgow Coma Scale uses a chart and numbering system to assess a patient's status. The scale measures eye opening, verbal response, and motor response to assess the patient's ability to respond to commands.

40. **The correct answer is (A).** In all cases of suspected cervical spine injury and cases in which a patient is unconscious from an unknown cause, the EMT–Basic should open the patient's airway using the jaw-thrust maneuver (modified jaw thrust). This maneuver allows opening of the airway while maintaining cervical spinal stabilization.

41. **The correct answer is (C).** Any patient with a suspected cervical spinal injury should be immobilized with a short board or a KED prior to removal from a seated position in a vehicle. The EMT–Basic should take precautions not to endanger the cervical spine by omitting the use of these devices. Rapid extrication to a long board is indicated only in cases of severe trauma where the patient is critical.

42. **The correct answer is (B).** All patients involved in motor vehicle accidents where there is a rollover should be immobilized, regardless of complaint. The fact that this patient is already standing does not make a difference. The rapid takedown procedure should be used to immobilize any patient who is standing at the scene of a collision with any hint of major mechanism of injury.

43. **The correct answer is (B).** The EMT–Basic should attempt to remove a helmet only if it interferes with airway management. Most helmets today, except full-face-guard helmets, allow the EMT–Basic to maintain an airway while securing the patient to a long board with the helmet on. Immobilize any patient who has a manageable airway and can be immobilized with a helmet on. Removal of a helmet may worsen a previously unidentified spinal injury.

44. **The correct answer is (B).**

45. **The correct answer is (A).**

46. **The correct answer is (C).**

47. **The correct answer is (A).**

48. **The correct answer is (B).**

EXPLANATION FOR QUESTIONS 44–48

This patient is exhibiting inappropriate behavior several days after a head injury. The patient never received medical attention and went home. After the patient loses consciousness, the EMT–Basic should assist him by doing a complete primary assessment. This consists of the A, B, Cs and then a neurological assessment. After the neurological assessment, the patient should be immobilized to a long spine board with a cervical collar applied. Based on the patient's delayed response to injury, the EMT–Basic should be able to effectively rule out an epidural hematoma, as they are rapid arterial bleeds. A concussion will not present with severe symptoms several days later. A cervical spinal injury will not cause inappropriate behavior if it is isolated to the cervical spine. However, a subdural hematoma, which is bleeding slowly from a venous source, can surely cause this type of behavior. A subdural hematoma may take hours or even days to develop, with neurological symptoms being delayed. Treatment for this patient includes high-concentration oxygen, airway management, and rapid transport to the hospital.

Infants and Children

1. B	4. A	7. D	10. C	12. B
2. D	5. B	8. B	11. A	13. B
3. D	6. A	9. C		

1. **The correct answer is (B).** Traumatic injury is the leading cause of death in children of all age groups. Trauma kills more children every year than all other causes of childhood death combined.

2. **The correct answer is (D).** Children 6 to 12 years old have the greatest fear of disfigurement and death. Children in this age group are impressionable and do not fully understand what is going on when they are sick or injured. The EMT–Basic should approach children with honesty and alleviate fears they may have.

3. **The correct answer is (D).** Pediatric patients between the ages of 1 and 3 are not comfortable with being touched by strangers. The EMT–Basic should approach these patients with a calming demeanor and attempt to do an examination from toe to head. It is a good idea to have the parent hold a child in this age group to facilitate a calming atmosphere. At no time should the EMT–Basic separate the child from the parent; this will only worsen the situation.

4. **The correct answer is (A).** The major cause of cardiac arrest in pediatric patients is due to some form of respiratory insufficiency. This can be due to respiratory infections, asthma attacks, or any other pathophysiological or structural defect causing respiratory distress. The EMT–Basic should ensure that the pediatric patient has an open airway at all times and is well oxygenated.

5. **The correct answer is (B).** Any child in respiratory distress should be treated with high-concentration oxygen. In respiratory distress, the child is still breathing on his or her own. The EMT–Basic can deliver supplemental oxygen by mask. High-concentration oxygen is indicated in all cases of respiratory distress. There is no contraindication to oxygen administration in these patients.

6. **The correct answer is (A).** Children in respiratory failure should be treated with positive pressure ventilation by way of a bag-valve-mask ventilator. In respiratory failure, the child has already lost the ability to support his or her own ventilations. Ominous signs are grunting and head bobbing. Positive-pressure ventilation with high-concentration oxygen will support the ventilations of the child until definitive care can be initiated.

7. **The correct answer is (D).** Decreased blood pressure is a late sign of shock in children and adults. The EMT–Basic should be aware of subtle signs of compensated shock in a child. Signs of dehydration are early signs of shock. Compensated shock should be suspected in a child with a history of diarrhea or vomiting. Sunken fontanels in infants are also a sign of dehydration as well as compensated shock.

8. **The correct answer is (B).** The child in decompensated shock will present with alterations of mental status and increased respiratory rate. The EMT–Basic must be aware that falling blood pressure is an ominous late sign and should be avoided at all costs. Interventions should be attempted to prevent blood-pressure drop and circulatory

collapse. Pediatric patients compensate for volume loss longer than an adult, but decompensation is rapid and usually irreversible.

9. **The correct answer is (C).** Pediatric patients who suffer from a seizure and have no history of seizures are usually having a response to fever. The seizure is not related to the actual temperature, but the rate at which the temperature rises. Rapid temperature increase will cause patients to seize. This seizure will present as a tonic clonic seizure, otherwise known as a grand mal seizure. Care for this patient is airway management, cooling, and transport to the hospital. The EMT–Basic must not lose sight of the fact that the seizure may be associated with meningitis, which can also cause fever.

10. **The correct answer is (C).** The EMT–Basic should never attempt to administer fluids by mouth to any patient in shock. This can cause vomiting and airway compromise. The goal in treating the child in shock is to maintain airway, blood pressure, and body temperature. Prevention of hypothermia, even on a warm day, is essential to survival of the child. Airway and oxygenation are of greatest importance in the treatment of pediatric shock patients.

11. **The correct answer is (A).** When you come across a child who has bruises in various stages of healing, especially when the child is unconscious from a head injury, you should suspect child abuse. The EMT–Basic should treat the child and withhold personal feelings toward the parents. The priority is to assist the child and get him or her definitive care, not to confront the parents.

12. **The correct answer is (B).** The child with a history of abuse will usually be quiet, not cry from painful injuries, and generally be withdrawn from the situation. The EMT–Basic should treat any life-threatening injuries and transport the patient to definitive care. On arrival at the emergency department, the EMT–Basic should report all findings to the emergency department staff for investigation by the proper authorities.

13. **The correct answer is (B).** The death of a child is one of the most difficult aspects of a career in EMS. The EMT–Basic will be facing a variety of feelings after the death of a child. The best way to deal with this type of situation is to discuss it with your partner or loved ones. Alcohol and drug use will only compound the problem and add to the grief that the EMT–Basic will be feeling. At no time should he or she accept this or any other traumatic event as part of the job. The EMT–Basic must realize that he or she is human and will respond emotionally to emotional situations. Discussion or participation in critical incident stress debriefing is essential to healthy living in the world of EMS.

Operations

1. B	6. C	11. D	16. C	20. C
2. C	7. C	12. D	17. A	21. A
3. B	8. D	13. A	18. B	22. B
4. B	9. D	14. B	19. A	23. C
5. A	10. D	15. A		

1. **The correct answer is (B).** The use of excessive speed in response to any emergency increases the chances of an accident with another vehicle. Driving an ambulance requires sharp driving skills, and using excessive speed reduces reaction time. There is no indication for the use of excessive speed while responding to or from any emergency call.

2. **The correct answer is (C).** When responding to an emergency call, the driver of the ambulance must drive with due regard for the safety of others. Law requires that an ambulance pause for a stopped school bus and wait until waved on by the bus driver.

3. **The correct answer is (B).** The EMT–Basic is expected to respond to calls in adverse weather conditions. Adverse weather, as well as construction and road closing, will affect response and safety. It is a good idea to find out about planned road closings and adjust your response accordingly. Bad weather conditions call for a slower and safer response. Remember that wet roads increase stopping distances. Careful driving is the key to safety.

4. **The correct answer is (B).** High-level disinfection is the killing of pathogens by using a potent means of disinfection. Application of heat to kill pathogens is known as sterilization, and using a spray or aerosol to kill pathogens is defined as disinfection. The EMT–Basic should have an awareness of when each level of disinfection is appropriate and should initiate the proper levels at all times.

5. **The correct answer is (A).** Sterilization is defined as application of heat to kill pathogens. Many surfaces and contaminated equipment can be cleaned using high-level disinfection or regular disinfection. EMT–Basics should have full knowledge of which equipment must be sterilized and which equipment may be safely disinfected.

6. **The correct answer is (C).** After patient delivery to the hospital, and before the postrun phase begins, the EMT–Basic is required to complete a run sheet to document patient care. This run sheet should not be completed during the transport phase due to the fact that the EMT–Basic should be tending to the patient and not to paperwork. All documentation should be accurate and comprehensive regarding all aspects of the emergency call.

7. **The correct answer is (C).** While operating during a MEDEVAC (helicopter evacuation), the EMT–Basic should always approach the helicopter from the front and only when waved on by the pilot. Helicopter blades have a great degree of tilt and may cause serious injury or even death to the unknowing EMS provider. It is always a good rule to wait for the pilot to give the all-clear signal before approaching.

8. **The correct answer is (D).** Patient documentation should always be done during the delivery phase. After delivery to the hospital and after all paperwork is complete, the EMT–Basic must clean and restock the vehicle for the next emergency call. As soon as the vehicle is ready, the dispatcher should be notified so that the unit may be assigned to another call.

9. **The correct answer is (D).** In all cases of emergency response, safety of the rescuers is the highest priority. EMT–Basics should ensure that the vehicle is properly stabilized, there are no hazardous materials or scene hazards that may cause injury, and the proper protective equipment is worn. In many regions, specialized units perform vehicle rescues and other extrications. If the EMT–Basic is not trained in extrication, then he or she should remain clear of the extrication and await patient delivery.

10. **The correct answer is (D).** The EMT–Basic should not be involved in traffic control unless no police agencies are on the scene and only if traffic poses a potential risk to the operation.

11. **The correct answer is (D).** Size-up of all calls should begin as soon as the assignment is given. The EMT–Basic should perform a scene size-up immediately after arrival at an incident. Size-up includes determination of the number of patients, patient condition, additional resources needed, and scene hazards. A complete size-up should be done at all scenes, and the scene should be reassessed several times during any operation.

12. **The correct answer is (D).** In cases where heavy chunks of debris or heavy machinery are involved and the rescue will take more than the typical rescue equipment, the scene is labeled a complex access scene. A building collapse poses special hazards and complex access. Building stability and the possibility of falling debris are always factors in the safety of the scene.

13. **The correct answer is (A).** This is a simple access scene due to the fact that the patient is pinned by his leg, and basic extrication equipment should be sufficient to safely extricate him. Treatment involves stabilization and extrication from the site.

14. **The correct answer is (B).** A disaster may be a naturally occurring event or an event caused by manmade means. A disaster may not always produce multiple patients. In fact, it may not produce any patients. A disaster will, however, damage the area's infrastructure. Basic communications and even emergency services systems may be incapacitated by the results of a disaster.

15. **The correct answer is (A).** The definition of a mass-casualty incident varies from region to region. In some regions, it is any incident that produces more than a given number of patients. The national definition of a mass-casualty incident is an incident that produces more patients than can be handled by the initial response agency or any incident that taxes the resources of a given area.

16. **The correct answer is (C).** The job of the EMT–Basic is to provide patient care. Any and all responsibilities in regard to caring for the patient fall within that realm. Mitigation is not the job of the EMT–Basic. Hazardous materials specialists are specially trained teams of individuals who will deal with the hazard and secure it safely. The EMT–Basic in an emergency vehicle does not have the necessary equipment to handle a situation such as a hazardous materials incident.

17. **The correct answer is (A).** The NFPA (National Fire Protection Association) has developed the Hazardous Materials Classification chart to assist emergency responders in determining the hazard of a

given material. Although this chart does not identify a specific substance, it can afford a rescuer the information needed to assess the severity of an incident. The color blue is for health hazards, red for fire hazards, yellow for reactivity of the agent (example: reacts violently with water), and white is a specific hazard (example: acid, alkali, etc.). Finding this placard on any material should tip off the EMT–Basic of a hazardous materials incident.

18. **The correct answer is (B).** See explanation for question 17.

19. **The correct answer is (A).** The incident commander is in command of the entire incident. Under the incident command system, sectors are set up to coordinate different activities. These sectors are triage, treatment, staging, transportation, and support. Each of these sectors reports directly to the incident commander.

20. **The correct answer is (C).** When assigned to a sector at a mass-casualty incident, the EMT–Basic would report directly to the officer of that sector. The only people who report directly to the incident commander are the officers from each sector. This system cuts down on radio traffic by allowing face-to-face communications between sector members and radio communication to the incident commander by sector officers.

21. **The correct answer is (A).** The triage tag system (MET-TAG or other) is designed to identify patients of the highest priority. The color system is universal and is as follows:

Black—Dead or unsalvageable
Red—Immediate (High priority)
Yellow—Delayed (Low priority)
Green—Walking wounded, minor

This system is accepted nationally and should be initiated when a mass casualty incident is identified.

22. **The correct answer is (B).** See explanation for question 21.

23. **The correct answer is (C).** Three zones are identified in a hazardous materials incident:

The Hot Zone—area of the incident, spill, or dissemination of the hazardous material

The Warm Zone—area outside, but surrounding the hot zone

The Cold Zone—area that is deemed safe to operate

Decontamination is usually done in the warm zone on the border of the cold zone. The EMT–Basic should be aware of the designated sectors and remain in his or her assigned sector. Without protective clothing (level A or B), the EMT–Basic should never be in the hot or warm zone.

PART III
EMT–BASIC REVIEW

CHAPTER 3   Anatomy and Physiology
Review

CHAPTER 4   EMT–Basic Practical Skills
Evaluation

Anatomy and Physiology Review

OVERVIEW

- Medical terminology
- Topographic anatomy
- Anatomy and physiology by body system
- Continue to educate yourself
- Summing it up

To understand the pathophysiological processes you will encounter in the field, you must first understand the basics of anatomy and physiology.

Anatomy is the study of the structure of a living organism. Physiology is the study of the function of a living organism. This chapter serves as a review of the basic anatomical structure and physiological function of the human body. Your knowledge of anatomy and physiology is the foundation for understanding your patients' disease processes and will help you develop a rational approach to their treatment. The study of anatomy and physiology can be broken into three parts:

1. Medical terminology
2. Topographic anatomy
3. Anatomy and physiology by body system

MEDICAL TERMINOLOGY

As an EMT–Basic student, you should know the meanings of the terms defined in this section. These terms are the foundation for understanding human structure and function.

Common Prefixes and Suffixes Used in Medical Terminology

The following charts show common prefixes and suffixes you will encounter as an EMT–Basic. You should practice using these prefixes and suffixes to develop a comprehensive knowledge of basic medical terminology. Get familiar with the terms in the Example column. You will frequently use them when communicating with fellow EMS providers and emergency department personnel.

Prefix	Meaning	Example	Explanation
a-	absence of	aseptic	absence of contamination
ab-	away from	abduction	movement away from
ad-	toward	adduction	movement toward
an-	without	anuria	without urine output
ante-	prior to	antepartum	prior to childbirth
bi-	two	bilateral	on both sides
brady-	slowed	bradycardia	slow heartbeat
contra-	opposite	contralateral	on the opposite side
cyan-	blue	cyanosis	bluish appearance of skin
diplo-	double	diplopia	double vision
dys-	difficult	dyspnea	difficulty breathing
endo-	inside	endotracheal	inside the trachea
epi-	above	epidural	above the dura mater
erythro-	red	erythrocyte	red blood cell
exo-	outside	exocrine	the external secretion of a gland
hemi-	one side	hemiplegia	one-sided paralysis
hyper-	over	hyperextension	extreme extension of the neck
hypo-	under	hypoglycemia	low blood sugar
inter-	in between	intercostals	between the costal space
intra-	inside of	intravascular	in the vascular space
peri-	surrounding	pericardium	sac surrounding the heart
poly-	multiple	polyuria	frequent urination
post-	after	postpartum	after childbirth
quad-	four-sided	quadriplegia	paralysis of all four limbs
retro-	behind	retroperitoneal	behind the peritoneal cavity
supra-	above	supraventricular	above the ventricles
tachy-	rapid	tachypnea	rapid breathing
trans-	through	transected	went completely through

Common Medical Terminology

The following glossary includes definitions of vocabulary words that the EMT–Basic is required to know. Learning the meanings of these terms will help you understand some of the disease processes you will treat when you become an EMT–Basic. For some terms, sample sentences are provided after the definition.

A

Abdomen: the area between the anatomical line of the rib margin and the pelvis

Abnormal: not a normal finding, as in abnormal blood pressure

Absorbed: to pass through or set in; *Some poisons are absorbed through the skin.*

Abuse: to treat improperly, as in child abuse

Accessory: assist, an adjunct to; *The patient was breathing with her accessory muscles.*

Accident: not on purpose; a motor vehicle collision or other trauma-causing event

Airborne: circulating in the air; *Influenza is an airborne virus.*

Airway: path of air as it enters the body; *The trachea is part of the airway.*

Alert: aware, awake, familiar with surroundings; *The patient was alert on arrival.*

Aligned: in line, correctly matched up; *The physician aligned the bone.*

Alveoli: sacs in the lung where gas exchange takes place

Amniotic fluid: fluid within the sac protecting a fetus; *The fetus is suspended in amniotic fluid.*

Amphetamine: a stimulant; *The patient was experiencing a rapid pulse after taking an amphetamine.*

Amputation: removal of a limb or other body structure; *The patient's vehicle rolled over, causing an amputation of the right leg.*

Analgesic: a pain reliever; *The patient was given an analgesic to ease the pain of his fracture.*

Anaphylaxis: severe allergic reaction; *The patient was having airway problems due to anaphylaxis.*

Aneurysm: a ballooning of a blood vessel, usually an artery; *The patient was diagnosed with an aortic aneurysm.*

Angina: pain in the chest; *The angina attack lasted 5 minutes.*

Angulated: on an angle; *The fracture was angulated.*

Anti-shock: made to prevent shock; *The anti-shock trousers were applied.*

Anxiety: fear, apprehension; *He suffered from an anxiety attack.*

Aorta: largest blood vessel in the body; *The aorta branches into several smaller arteries.*

Appendicitis: inflammation of the appendix

Arrest: to stop; *The patient was in cardiac arrest.*

Artery: a blood vessel that carries oxygenated blood

Asphyxia: to suffocate; *The patient died from asphyxia due to a hanging.*

Aspirin: an analgesic; *The patient stated he took one aspirin prior to our arrival.*

Assessment: an examination; *I did a complete patient assessment.*

Associated: affiliated, related to; *The associated signs and symptoms included pain and an inability to move the extremity.*

Asthma: a reactive airway disease; *The patient had an asthma attack.*

Atrium: an upper chamber in the heart; *The right atrium receives blood from the superior and inferior venae cavae.*

Audible: able to be heard; *The man had audible wheezing on our arrival.*

Auscultate: to listen to the internal sounds of the body. *During a physical examination, an EMT–Basic should auscultate as well as palpate.*

Authorization: permission; *We had authorization from medical control.*

Avulsion: tearing away; *The accident caused an avulsion of the patient's facial skin.*

Axillary: the imaginary line that runs from the armpit to the hip; *The gunshot was located in the axillary region.*

B

BVM: bag-valve-mask; an adjunct for ventilation; *The patient was ventilated using a BVM.*

Bladder: collection area; *Urine is collected in the urinary bladder prior to excretion.*

Bleeding: to bleed; *The laceration had minimal bleeding.*

Blisters: fluid-filled bubbles in the skin; *The second-degree burn caused the injury site to develop blisters.*

Bloodborne: circulating in the blood; *HIV is a bloodborne virus.*

Bone: the tissue that makes up the skeletal system; *Red blood cells are developed in the bone tissue.*

Bowel: term used for lower intestine; *The patient has a history of bowel obstruction.*

Brain: the control center of the central nervous system; *The brain controls most of the functions of the body.*

Breathing: the act of ventilation; *On arrival, the patient was breathing and had a pulse.*

Bruise: a swollen and discolored area resulting from injury; *The area where the patient was struck developed a large bruise.*

Burn: tissue damage resulting from heat energy transfer; *The patient had a third-degree burn.*

C

Cannula: a device used to deliver oxygen; *We placed a nasal cannula on the patient.*

Cardiac: pertaining to the heart; *We treated the patient under cardiac arrest protocols.*

Cardiogenic: pertaining to the cardiovascular system; *He was in cardiogenic shock.*

Carotid: an artery that branches off the aorta, supplying blood to the brain; *We checked for a carotid pulse.*

Caustic: burning, irritating; *The substance was caustic to the skin.*

Cavity: anatomic space; *The heart is located in the thoracic cavity.*

Cells: basic unit of structure in the body; *The heart is composed of specialized cells called cardiac cells.*

Cerebellum: a structure of the brain; *The cerebellum is responsible for balance.*

Cerebrum: a structure of the brain; *The cerebrum has multiple functions; one of these functions is control of sensory input.*

Cervical: a division of the spinal column; *There are seven cervical vertebrae.*

Chamber: an anatomic space; *The ventricle is a chamber in the heart.*

Chronic: longstanding; *Emphysema is a chronic problem brought on by years of smoking.*

Circulation: movement from one place to another; *The red blood cells deliver oxygen by way of circulation in the vascular system.*

Clavicle: bone structure; *The clavicle is sometimes known as the collar bone.*

Clotting: to cake up, coagulate; *The blood contains clotting factors.*

Colon: the large intestine; *The colon is divided into three sections: the ascending, transverse, and descending colon.*

Column: line or division; *The spinal column contains thirty-three vertebrae.*

Combustion: the ignition of flammable materials; *Smoke inhalation is a direct result of poisoning from the products of combustion.*

Congestive: causing congestion; *The patient suffered from congestive heart failure.*

Consciousness: level of awareness; *I determined the patient's level of consciousness.*

Consent: form of permission; *Actual, implied, and informed are just a few of the forms of consent.*

Constriction: tightening; *The patient was wheezing due to constriction of his airway.*

Contusion: bruise; *The patient had a contusion over his left eye.*

Convulsions: a violent, involuntary contraction or series of muscle contractions; *The patient was in convulsions upon our arrival.*

Coronary: pertaining to the heart; *Coronary arteries supply blood to the heart.*

Cranial: pertaining to the skull; *The cranial nerves are located at the base of the skull.*

Crepitus: broken bone ends rubbing together; *Crepitus makes a scratchy rubbing sound when the EMT–Basic is securing a fracture.*

Croup: a viral infection; *Croup is characterized by a seal-bark type of cough.*

Crushing: compressing; *The injury caused crushing to the left arm.*

Cyanosis: bluish appearance of the skin; *The patient's appearance included central cyanosis.*

D

Depressant: a medication that slows down the body systems; *Barbiturates are depressant drugs.*

Deviation: change from normal; *During a tension pneumothorax, the patient will develop tracheal deviation.*

Diabetes: a pancreatic disorder; a condition where the body does not produce insulin and/or use insulin in the correct way

Diaphoresis: sweating; *The patient was having chest pain and diaphoresis.*

Diffuse: spread out over a large area; *While assessing the patient's lungs, I noticed that he had diffuse wheezing.*

Dilation: to make larger, to expand; *Certain medications cause pupil dilation.*

Dislocated: not in its correct location; *His left shoulder was dislocated.*

Dislodged: shaken loose, removed; *The food bolus became dislodged after we performed the Heimlich maneuver.*

Dispatched: sent to, assigned; *We were dispatched to the call at 1:30 p.m.*

Distal: farthest from, distant; *The wrist is distal to the shoulder.*

Distention: swollen, extended; *The patient suffered gastric distention due to poor BVM ventilations.*

Dizziness: vertigo, spinning sensation; *Patients who suffer from high blood pressure may complain of dizziness.*

Dosage: amount or rate of administration; *The patient took the correct dosage of medication.*

Dressing: cover, barrier; *Burns should always be covered with a sterile dressing.*

Drooling: excessive salivation; *One of the major signs of epiglottitis in pediatrics is excessive drooling.*

Dyspnea: difficulty breathing; *The patient having an MI may complain of dyspnea.*

E

Ectopic: irregular, abnormal; *An ectopic pregnancy occurs outside of the uterus.*

Edema: fluid collection, swelling; *Pedal edema is a collection of fluid at the ankles.*

Elbow: joint at the middle of the arm; *The distal humerus and the proximal radius make up the elbow.*

Elevated: lifted higher; *Patients in shock should be transported with their legs elevated.*

Embolism: particle, a piece of fat or bone; *An embolism may break free from the lower extremities and cause a stroke or pulmonary artery blockage.*

Emergency: acute situation, life threatening; *Anaphylaxis is a true emergency.*

Emphysema: obstructive pulmonary disease; *Decreased lung compliance is a symptom of emphysema.*

Epilepsy: seizure condition; *Many patients with epilepsy are treated with Tegretol and Phenobarbital.*

Exchange: to switch; *Air exchange takes place in the alveoli.*

Exertion: stress, increased demand; *Exertion exacerbates angina.*

Exhalation: releasing air from the lungs; *Exhalation is a passive mechanism.*

Expose: uncover; *The EMT–Basic should expose all severe trauma injuries.*

Extremities: limbs, arms, legs; *Most injuries to the extremities are not life threatening.*

F

Facial: relating to the skin or bone structure of the face; *Patients with facial injuries may also have airway complications.*

Febrile: relating to a fever; *Rapid rise in temperature in small children may cause febrile seizures.*

Femur: long bone located in the upper thigh; *Fractures of the femur may cause excessive blood loss.*

Fetus: developing human after the embryonic stage and before birth; *The fetus develops in the uterus.*

Fibrillation: chaotic, unorganized cardiac rhythm; *Ventricular fibrillation is the most common cardiac rhythm in the first few minutes of cardiac arrest.*

Flail: free floating; *A flail segment is three or more ribs broken in two or more places.*

Fluid: solutions made of liquid or plasma; *Dehydration causes loss of large amounts of body fluids.*

Foreign: unrelated to, not part of; *The patient had a foreign body in his eye.*

Fracture: to break; *A skull fracture may be indicative of brain injury.*

Frostbite: superficial cold injury; *Limbs with frostbite should only be rewarmed after the danger of refreezing is gone.*

Frothy: foamy, bubbly; *Patients in pulmonary edema may present with frothy, blood-tinged sputum.*

G

Gallbladder: digestive organ; *The gallbladder stores digestive enzymes.*

Gamma: radiation type; *Gamma radiation has an extreme rate of penetration.*

Gastric: relating to the stomach; *The patient was ventilated improperly and developed gastric distention.*

Gastrointestinal: relating to the digestive system; *Abdominal pain is a common symptom of a gastrointestinal disorder.*

Geriatric: aged, elderly; *Geriatric patients may have no pain during a cardiac event.*

Glucose: form of sugar; *Diabetic patients are given glucose to increase blood-sugar levels.*

H

Hazardous: dangerous; *The EMT–Basic must assess every scene for hazardous conditions.*

Headache: pain in the head; *The patient with a severe headache and altered mental status should be transported to the hospital rapidly.*

Heart: a muscular organ that pumps blood in order to maintain circulation of blood throughout the body; *The heart pumps blood to the cells through the cardiovascular system.*

Hemoglobin: iron compound that transports oxygen; *Hemoglobin is attached to red blood cells.*

Hemorrhage: bleeding; *Blunt abdominal trauma may cause serious internal hemorrhage, usually from the liver and spleen.*

Hepatitis: inflammation of the liver caused by a virus; *All EMS personnel should be vaccinated against Hepatitis B.*

History: past events; prior events related to a patient's medical event; *The patient's history is one of the most important factors in diagnosis.*

Humerus: long bone of the upper arm; *Some humerus fractures should be splinted to the body.*

Hypertension: increased blood pressure; *Hypertension may be caused by cardiovascular disease or head trauma.*

Hyperventilate: rapid ventilation; fast breathing; *Patients may hyperventilate when they are in great pain.*

Hypoglycemia: low blood sugar; *The unconscious patient with a diabetic history should be suspected of being hypoglycemic until proven otherwise.*

Hypoperfusion: lack of perfusion to the tissues; *Shock causes hypoperfusion.*

Hypothermic: having low body temperature; *The hypothermic patient should be handled gently to avoid cardiac arrest.*

Hypovolemia: low blood volume; *Blood loss, burns, or dehydration may cause hypovolemia.*

Hypoxic: lacking oxygen; *Patients with carbon monoxide poisoning present as severely hypoxic.*

I

Illness: form of disease, acute or chronic; *The EMT–Basic responds to the patient suffering from illness or injury.*

Immobilize: to prevent movement; *EMS personnel must immobilize patients with cervical spine injuries to prevent additional damage.*

Impaired: insufficient or incorrect, not considered normal; *Pulmonary contusions cause impaired gas exchange in the lungs.*

Implied: suggested; *The unconscious patient was treated under implied consent, meaning that if the patient were conscious, she would agree to treatment.*

Inadequate: lacking, not enough; *Hypovolemia causes inadequate tissue perfusion.*

Indication: condition or circumstance leading to diagnosis or for which a drug should be given; *Uneven pupils are an indication of brain injury.*

Induce: make happen; *The EMT–Basic induced vomiting in the poisoned patient.*

Infarction: tissue death; *Myocardial infarction is defined as death of heart muscle.*

Inflammation: swelling; *Peripheral edema causes inflammation around the ankles.*

Ingestion: taken internally; *Ingestion is one of the four ways poison can enter the body.*

Injury: damage caused by an outside force; *Determination of the mechanism of injury will help the EMT–Basic identify potential problems.*

Inspiration: the taking in of air; *Inspiration is part of the ventilation process.*

Insulin: a hormone; *Insulin assists in the process of cellular sugar breakdown.*

Intercostal: located or occurring between the ribs. *He was having intercostal retractions.*

Internal: within the body; *Many internal injuries will show no visible signs of injury.*

Intestines: the gastrointestinal tract; *Nutrients are absorbed in the intestines.*

Intracranial: within the cranium, the bony dome that houses and protects the brain; *An intracranial hemorrhage is bleeding within the cranium due to a stroke or leaking of blood from an aneurysm in the brain.*

Ipecac: medication; *Ipecac is used to induce vomiting.*

Irrigate: to wash and/or rinse; *The EMT–Basic should thoroughly irrigate the eyes of a patient with chemical burns.*

Isolated: alone, apart; *Patients with infectious disease should be isolated from the general population.*

J

Joint: structure that permits movement; *Most bone attachments form a joint, which allows movement.*

K

Kidney: organ in the urinary system; *Urine is produced in the kidney.*

L

Labor: process of childbirth; *The EMT–Basic should be aware of the three stages of labor.*

Ligament: connective tissue; *The ligament connects bone to bone.*

Lining: inside covering; *The pleura is a lining of the lung.*

Liter: a unit of measure; *The patient lost a liter of fluid.*

Liver: organ in the digestive system

Lobe: part of, appendage: *The left lung has three lobes.*

Lucid: aware, awake, and alert; *A patient who's had two or more seizures without a lucid interval is said to be suffering from status epilepticus.*

Lumbar: division of the spine; *There are five lumbar vertebrae.*

Lung: organ responsible for air exchange

M

Medical: pertaining to medicine; *Asthma is a medical emergency.*

Membrane: thin, outer tissue, coating; *The mucous membrane covers the inside of the mouth.*

Meningitis: inflammation of the meninges; *Meningitis may be viral or bacterial.*

Metabolic: pertaining to metabolism; *Metabolic acidosis is caused by improper cellular respiration.*

Moistened: made wet; *Burns should be covered with a moistened dressing.*

Mucous: body fluid; *The oral cavity is covered by a mucous membrane.*

Muscle: body tissue; *Movement in the body is a direct result of the contraction and expansion of muscles.*

Myocardial: referring to the heart muscle; *A myocardial infarction is the death of cardiac muscle.*

N

Narcotic: pain medication; *An opioid medication is considered a narcotic.*

Nasal: relating to the nose and/or the nares; *Air is filtered in the nasal cavity.*

Nausea: the feeling that one may vomit; *Nausea is a common side effect of some medications.*

Negligence: failure to perform the correct level of care; *An EMT–Basic is guilty of negligence when he fails to care for a patient in an appropriate manner.*

Nerve: pathway in the nervous system; *A nerve delivers and sends messages to and from the brain and spinal cord.*

Neurogenic: pertaining to the nervous system; *Neurogenic shock causes blood vessel dilation.*

Nitrogen: a gas; *The atmosphere is 78 percent nitrogen.*

Nonrebreather: oxygen mask; *A nonrebreather, powered by ten to fifteen liters of oxygen, can deliver almost 100 percent oxygen.*

Nostril: structure of the nose; *A nostril is also called a nare.*

Noxious: dangerous, poisonous; *The by-products of fire include noxious fumes.*

Numbness: loss of feeling, parasthesia; *A sign of spinal cord injury is numbness below the level of the injury.*

O

Obstructed: blocked; *A myocardial infarction is caused by an obstructed coronary artery.*

Obvious: plain, clear

Occlusive: tending to occlude, block. *An occlusive dressing closes a wound and keeps it from air.*

Onset: beginning, start; *The patient stated that the onset of chest pain came when he was doing heavy work.*

Operation: surgical procedure; *Aortic aneurysms are repaired in an operation.*

Order: physician directive; *Medical control may order you to transport immediately.*

Organ: part of the body systems; *The heart is an organ.*

Oriented: aware; *The patient should be oriented to place and time.*

Overdose: taking too much medication; *An overdose of opioids may cause respiratory arrest.*

Oxygen: gas; *Oxygen is a first-line medication in the treatment of many illnesses and injuries.*

P

Pacemaker: heart-rate controller; *A pacemaker may be artificial or natural (SA node in the heart).*

Palpate: to feel; *During a physical examination, the EMT–Basic should palpate as well as auscultate.*

Pancreas: organ that produces insulin

Paralyze: stop or prevent movement; *Injury to the spinal cord will paralyze a patient.*

Partial: part of, a percentage; *The patient suffered from partial paralysis.*

Pectoris: chest; *A patient with chest pain is said to have angina pectoris.*

Pedal: pertaining to the foot and/or ankle; *Right heart failure causes pedal edema.*

Pediatric: child, infant; *Pediatric patients should be assessed toe to head in nonemergency situations.*

Pelvis: boney structure of the hip; *The pelvis is actually a collection of bones that form the hip.*

Penetrate: to enter; *A bullet penetrates the body, causing penetrating trauma.*

Penicillin: medication; *Penicillin is used as an internal antibacterial agent.*

Perfusion: process of forcing a fluid through an organ by way of the blood vessels. *Hypoperfusion is a lack of perfusion to the tissues.*

Pericardial: covering the heart; *Blood collecting in the sac outside the heart is known as a pericardial tamponade.*

Peripheral: on the edges, outside; *During trauma, the patient's peripheral pulse is a good indicator of perfusion.*

Peritonitis: inflammation of the peritoneum; *A patient with a penetrating wound in the abdomen may develop peritonitis.*

Physician: doctor; *The EMT–Basic works under the direction of a physician.*

Placenta: organ that develops during pregnancy to supply the fetus with blood and nutrients

Pleura: covering of the lungs

Pleuritis: inflammation of the pleura; *A rubbing sound on auscultation of the lungs indicates pleuritis.*

Pneumothorax: air in the chest cavity; *The chest trauma patient may develop a tension pneumothorax.*

Poisoning: toxicological illness; *Poisoning occurs when a foreign substance enters the body and causes cellular reaction.*

Position: placement; *The patient with dyspnea should be transported in a sitting position.*

Preceding: before, prior; *Part of a patient assessment is to obtain information on the events preceding the illness or injury.*

Pregnancy: a normal condition in which a woman carries a fetus

Premature: before its time, early

Pressure: stress, weight; *To stop bleeding, pressure should be applied to an open wound.*

Previous: past, prior to

Primary: first, most important; *The primary survey is always the most important aspect of trauma care.*

Prolonged: delayed, extended; *The patient's transport may be prolonged due to road conditions, weather, or other reasons.*

Prone: the position of lying face down

Psychogenic: pertaining to psychological factors; *Some forms of shock are psychogenic and therefore are self-correcting.*

Pulmonary: lungs and airway; *Chest injury may result in pulmonary contusion.*

Pulsating: beating, regular rhythmic movement of a body part; *Abdominal aortic aneurysms present with a pulsating mass in the abdomen.*

Pulse: heartbeat, distal; *The pulse is a wave formed by the movement of blood through an artery.*

Pumping: beating; *Cardiogenic shock is caused by ineffective pumping of blood by the heart.*

Pupillary: pertaining to pupils; *The shock patient will have delayed pupillary reaction.*

Q

Quadrant: abdominal section; *The liver is located in the upper right abdominal quadrant.*

R

Radiating: moving; *A patient with coronary disease may have chest pain radiating to the arm or jaw.*

Radius: distal bone of the arm; *The radius is located along the thumb side of the arm.*

Rapid: fast, quick; *Shock may cause a rapid pulse.*

Rate: speed; *Taking a pulse determines the heart rate.*

Reaction: response; *Anaphylaxis refers to a serious reaction to a bee sting.*

Record: document; *All findings become a part of a patient's permanent record.*

Redness: discoloration; *An area of redness and swelling may indicate a fracture.*

Reduce: lessen; *Applying pressure to an injury will reduce bleeding.*

Referred: radiation to another area; *Injuries to the liver and spleen may cause referred pain in the shoulders.*

Refill: restock; *A patient may need to refill a prescription.*

Reflex: response; *When people touch very hot items, their first reflex is to pull away.*

Relieved: eased or eliminated altogether; *Administration of oxygen relieved the patient's chest pain.*

Remove: extract; *The EMT–Basic should not remove an impaled object.*

Resistance: force, pressure; *The EMT–Basic may meet resistance when applying a splint.*

Respiratory: pulmonary, relating to the lungs; *Asthma, emphysema, and bronchitis are all respiratory diseases.*

Respond: react; *A patient may or may not respond to treatment.*

Restlessness: agitation, anxiety; *Restlessness is an early sign of hypoperfusion.*

Results: effects; *The results of treatment should be well documented.*

Resuscitate: revive, intervene; *The patient who wishes no medical intervention will have a "Do Not Resuscitate" order.*

Retina: anatomical structure of the eye; *The rods and cones of the retina aid in vision.*

Retractions: muscle activity; *The patient with difficulty breathing will usually have intercostal retractions.*

Return: regain, come back; *The goal of CPR is to gain a return of pulses and respirations.*

Rewarm: bring to normal body temperature; *A frostbitten limb should be rewarmed as soon as possible.*

Ruptured: broken; *Abdominal trauma may result in a ruptured spleen, causing massive internal bleeding.*

S

Sacral: spinal column division; *The sacral bones consist of five fused vertebrae.*

Safety: protection; *The EMT–Basic has a high priority to ensure personal safety.*

Scalp: skin tissue of the head; *Scalp lacerations tend to bleed profusely.*

Scapula: bone structure; *The scapula is the bony protrusion on the superior, posterior part of the thoracic cavity.*

Scene: location; *Scene safety is the highest priority in response to a call.*

Sealed: closed; *Open chest wounds are sealed with an occlusive dressing.*

Secondary: as a result of; *A patient may develop pulmonary edema secondary to an MI.*

Section: part; *An MRI will show a cross-section of the body in a transverse cut.*

Sedentary: slow, inactive; *A sedentary lifestyle is a precursor to cardiac disease.*

Seizure: acute medical condition; *A seizure is caused by a chaotic firing of neurons in the brain.*

Sensation: feeling, sense; *Part of the patient assessment is to assess movement and sensation in all four extremities.*

Septic: toxic, poisoned; *A major infection in the body can lead to septic shock.*

Severe: critical, major; *Anaphylaxis is a severe, life-threatening emergency.*

Shallow: superficial; *A patient with a major chest injury may develop shallow respirations.*

Shellfish: seafood, including shrimp and lobster; *Allergies to shellfish are a major cause of anaphylaxis.*

Shivering: shaking, tremors; *Shivering is an early sign of hypothermia.*

Shock: decreased blood flow through an organ

Shortness: lack; *Dyspnea is another term for shortness of breath.*

Significant: major, pertinent; *Unequal pupils are a significant finding in a patient with head injuries.*

Sign: a finding that can be observed on examination

Site: area, location; *The EMT–Basic should adequately describe the injury site in his transmission to the receiving hospital.*

Skull: cranium; *The skull is the collective term used for the bones of the head.*

Social: personal, habit; *A patient's social history is a pertinent part of the medical history.*

Solid: consisting of matter, not hollow; *The liver and spleen are considered solid organs.*

Spleen: organ that assists in immune system development

Splint: support; *The EMT–Basic should always check for a distal pulse after the application of a splint.*

Spontaneous: proceeding naturally, without aid; *Automatic defibrillation may precipitate spontaneous circulation.*

Spread: move, grow larger; *The rash from chicken pox will begin on the trunk and spread to the extremities.*

Stabilized: equaled, balanced; *The patient who maintains homeostasis after treatment is considered stabilized.*

Stages: parts, sections; *A grand mal seizure has three stages: aura, tonic clonic, and postictal.*

Sterile: devoid of all living organisms; *Sterile gloves should be used for invasive procedures.*

Sternum: breastbone; *The sternum is the anterior attachment for the ribs.*

Stiff: hard, uneasily moved. *Sprains and strains will result in stiff joints.*

Stimulant: substance that increases metabolism; *Cocaine is a stimulant.*

Stomach: organ responsible for extraction of some nutrients in the digestive process

Stool: solid waste; *Stool production is the final phase of digestion.*

Stress: a factor that causes bodily or mental tension

Stroke: decrease or loss of consciousness and/or feeling caused by a rupture or obstruction of a blood vessel in the brain; *A stroke may have three different causes: hemorrhagic, embolic, and thrombotic.*

Struck: hit; *The EMT–Basic should be aware of the mechanism of injury in a patient struck by a vehicle.*

Subcutaneous: below the cutaneous layer of skin; *A patient with significant chest trauma may develop subcutaneous emphysema.*

Substance: chemical, medication; *Morphine is a controlled substance.*

Substernal: behind the sternum

Suction: the process of applying a vacuum; *The EMT–Basic should suction blood or vomitus from a patient's airway during the primary survey.*

Sudden: at once, acute; *An aortic aneurysm is characterized by a sudden onset of tearing pain between the shoulders.*

Suffering: the state of being in unfavorable circumstances such as pain; *The job of the EMT–Basic is to ease suffering.*

Surface: on top; *A first-degree burn is isolated to the surface layer of the skin, causing redness.*

Survey: inspection; *The primary survey is designed to detect and correct life-threatening conditions as they are exposed.*

Suspect: to imagine to be true based on evidence; *When a patient has severe facial trauma, one may suspect cervical spine trauma as well.*

Sustained: continued, prolonged; *During resuscitation, the patient may remain in sustained ventricular fibrillation.*

Swallowing: taking internally; *Swallowing gasoline may cause respiratory complications.*

Swelling: inflammation; *Swelling is associated with soft tissue injury.*

Symptoms: complaints; *Symptoms are what patients state they are feeling—sensations such as headache, chest pain, or nausea.*

Syndrome: disease process, a collection of signs; *Cushing's syndrome is an indicator of increasing intracranial pressure.*

Syrup: medication type; *Certain medications are supplied in syrup form.*

Systolic: related to the contraction of the heart; *The systolic blood pressure is relative to ventricular output.*

T

Tablets: small mass of medication; *Patients with angina may need to be assisted in taking nitroglycerine tablets.*

Tachycardia: rapid pulse; *The patient in shock will present with decreased blood pressure and tachycardia.*

Tachypnea: rapid breathing; *Anxiety and fear will produce tachypnea.*

Tamponade: to close or block; *To control external bleeding, the EMT–Basic should apply direct pressure to the wound—this will tamponade the bleeding.*

Temperature: measurement of heat; *Hypothermia is caused by a decrease in body temperature.*

Tendons: connective tissue; *Tendons connect muscle to bone.*

Tension: pressure, stress; *Air trapped in the chest cavity will cause pressure on the heart and lungs. This is known as a tension pneumothorax.*

Thickness: degree of penetration; *A third-degree burn is considered a full-thickness burn.*

Thoracic: pertaining to the chest cavity; *The heart and lungs lie within the thoracic cavity.*

Tibia: bone of the lower leg; *The tibia forms the knee joint proximally and runs medial down the leg to form the ankle joint distally.*

Tingling: numbness, loss of sensation; *Patients with hyperventilation syndrome may complain of tingling in the extremities.*

Tissues: foundation of body structure; *All organs in the body are made up of specialized tissues.*

Tracheal: related to the trachea

Traction: opposite force, stretch; *The EMT–Basic must apply traction to a fractured femur.*

Transverse: through at a horizontal angle; *A transverse fracture is a fracture that runs horizontally through a bone.*

Trauma: injury to the body; *The patient who has injuries to more than one organ system is referred to as a multisystem trauma patient.*

U

Umbilical: relating to the central abdominal section; *The developing fetus is fed and oxygenated through the umbilical cord.*

Unconscious: not awake or aware; *The unconscious trauma patient must be assessed for severe head injury.*

Unequal: differently sized; *Patients with severe head trauma may present with unequal pupils.*

Unseal: remove a seal; *If, after an occlusive dressing is applied, the patient develops dyspnea, the EMT–Basic should unseal the occlusive dressing.*

Unstable: critical, not homeostatic; *The decompensated shock patient is considered unstable.*

Uterus: reproductive organ; *The fertilized egg attaches to the uterus to develop.*

V

Vacuum: suction, opposite pressure; *The EMT–Basic should be sure that there is proper vacuum in the suction unit.*

Vagina: female birth structure, canal; *During childbirth, the baby travels through the vagina and is delivered.*

Vapor: mist; *Certain medications are delivered in vapor form.*

Vascular: relating to veins and/or arteries; *The liver is an extremely vascular organ; therefore, it will cause a large amount of blood loss when injured.*

Vehicle: means of transportation; automobile; method of administration

Vein: vessel that carries blood; *Deoxygenated blood is returned to the heart in a vein.*

Ventilate: mechanical movement of air in and out of the lungs

Ventricular: relating to the ventricles; *Ventricular tachycardia may present with a pulse or be pulseless.*

Verbal: spoken, communicated; *EMS personnel may receive verbal orders from their base-station physician.*

Vertebrae: spinal bone; *There are twelve thoracic vertebrae.*

Vessels: transport structures for blood; *Arteries and veins are called blood vessels.*

Vicinity: in the area, nearby; *The patient with penetrating injuries in the vicinity of the heart should be monitored for pericardial tamponade.*

Virus: illness, may be airborne (influenza) or bloodborne (HIV, hepatitis); not responsive to antibiotics

Vital: essential; *Normal blood pressure is vital to the sustenance of life.*

Vomitus: vomit, stomach contents; *In poisoning victims, it may be necessary to examine the vomitus.*

W

Wound: injury; *Any external injury that causes bleeding or swelling is called a wound.*

TOPOGRAPHIC ANATOMY

This section defines widely accepted terminology for body locations. Knowledge of this terminology is imperative for several reasons. First, the EMT–Basic needs to understand these terms in order to communicate with other EMS providers. Second, documentation is an important part of the patient chart and necessitates clearly defined information. Finally, the legal aspect of prehospital care requires the EMT–Basic to explain a patient's injury and illness based on accepted terminology of topographic anatomy.

Remember that most topographic anatomy terms are based on anatomic position, which refers to a patient who is standing upright, facing the EMT–Basic with palms facing forward. There are, however, other positions a patient may be described as either being "found in" or "transported in." The following chart describes these positions:

Position	Description
Supine	Patient lying on back, face up
Prone	Patient lying on chest, face down
Fowler's	Patient seated with knees bent
Semi-Fowler's	Patient seated with knees straight
Trendelenburg's	Patient in a lying position with head lower than feet
Shock Position	Patient in a lying position with legs elevated

The following chart describes anatomical locations or references:

Position	Description
Anterior	Toward the front of the body
Posterior	Toward the rear of the body
Medial	Toward the midline
Lateral	Away from the midline
Proximal	A term used to describe two points of reference in relationship to the heart in terms of that which is closer to the heart. *Example:* The elbow is proximal to the wrist.
Distal	A term used to describe two points of reference in relationship to the heart in terms of that which is farther from the heart. *Example:* The wrist is distal to the elbow.
Flexion	The act of bending an extremity
Extension	The act of straightening an extremity
Abduction	To move away from the body
Adduction	To move toward the body
Midline	An imaginary vertical line that separates the body into right and left halves
Axillary Line	An imaginary vertical line that runs on the lateral side of the body that separates the body into front and back halves

Superior	A reference term used to describe position as it refers to the body in terms of that which is closer to the head *Example:* The heart is superior to the liver.
Inferior	A reference term used to describe position as it refers to the body in terms of that which is closer to the feet *Example:* The liver is inferior to the heart.
Unilateral	On one side of the body
Bilateral	On both sides of the body
Ipsilateral	On the same side of the body
Contralateral	On the opposite side of the body
Nipple Line	An imaginary horizontal line across the chest at the same level as the nipple; this can be an important landmark in chest injuries as well as spinal injuries.
Umbilicus	Also known as the navel or belly button, this can be an important reference point regarding abdominal and spinal injuries.

ANATOMY AND PHYSIOLOGY BY BODY SYSTEM

The EMT–Basic must have a comprehensive understanding of the human body systems. This section describes the anatomy and physiology of body systems. All of the body systems work together, but some body systems rely heavily on others to complete certain functions. This section explains those body system relationships in detail.

The Skeletal System

The skeletal system, which comprises 206 bones, provides the body with several important functions.

- Structure: framework for the body
- Protection: shields for vital organs
- Motion: aids movement (along with the muscular system)

The skeletal system is broken down into two divisions: the *axial skeleton*—the skull, spinal column, sternum, and ribs—and the *appendicular skeleton,* which comprises all other bones in the body.

The Axial Skeleton

The Skull

The skull is made up of several different structures, which, after several months of life, fuse together to form a protective shield for the brain. Also known as the cranium, these structures protect the brain, which is located inside the cranial cavity.

NOTE

Each body system works as part of the total functioning unit of the human body.

The EMT–Basic should be familiar with the four different parts of the skull. The *occipital region* is located at the back of the head, just superior to the first cervical vertebrae. The *frontal region* (forehead) is located above the eyes. The *parietal region* is located at the top of the head between the frontal and occipital regions, and the *temporal region* is located on the sides of the head, just above the ears.

Knowing the anatomical position of these regions will help you correctly identify injury sites in head trauma patients and transmit accurate information to the hospital regarding your patients' conditions. Injury to these areas will alert you to possible injuries to underlying structures, such as the brain.

The skull also includes six major facial bones. The first major facial bone is the *mandible,* or lower jaw. The upper jaw, the *maxilla,* comprises two bones, one on the right and one on the left hemisphere of the body. This is also true of the *zygoma,* or cheekbones. The *nasal bone* gives structure and protection to the nose (nares). The eyes, called eye sockets or *orbits*, are circular structures that support the eyeball. The orbit comprises the shared borders of the frontal bone as well as the upper margin of the maxilla and zygoma bones.

The skull contains several internal structures. The *ethmoid bone* is in the frontal area, positioned in the midline of the skull. This bone separates the right and left halves of the skull. The *sphenoid bone* is a butterfly-shaped structure located on the basilar skull above the maxilla. This bone has several bony protrusions that may cause brain injury in severe head trauma. The *foramen magnum* is a large opening in the base of the skull anterior to the occipital region. The foramen magnum allows the spinal cord to pass through the skull and into the spinal column.

The Spinal Column

The spinal column provides structure and support to the body and protects the spinal cord. The spinal column, rib cage, and sternum form the *thoracic cavity*, which gives the chest shape and protects the organs within the cavity. Running through the spinal column is an opening known as the *spinal foramen*. This structure, like the foramen magnum in the skull, allows the spinal cord to pass freely down the length of the spinal column. The bones of the spinal column are called *vertebrae*. Each vertebra is a separate bone joined together by ligaments and other tissue.

Thirty-three vertebrae make up the spinal column. Each vertebra is further broken down into sections. The chart below shows the section and number of vertebrae in each section:

Section	Number of Vertebrae
Cervical	7
Thoracic	12
Lumbar	5
Sacram	5 (fused)
Coccygeal	4 (fused)

The spinal column comprises specially shaped bones that allow anterior, posterior, and lateral bending as well as rotation. Spinal bones (with the exception of the first two cervical vertebrae) are made up of the following structures:

Section	Description
Body	Thick and disc-shaped, weight-bearing portion of the vertebrae
Articular process	A point of attachment for muscle lateral to the spinous process
Spinous process	Posterior midline, bony prominence felt through the skin of the back
Transverse process	A point of attachment for muscle lateral to the articular processes
Vertebral foramen	In the center of the body, allows passage of the spinal cord

Located between each vertebra is a *fibrous disc*, which provides a strong joint as well as absorption of shocks on the spinal column. Structures called the *vertebral foramina* are located between each vertebra. Nerves pass through each section of vertebrae via these foramina, allowing innervation to different parts of the body. Knowing which nerves pass through each section of vertebrae will help you make a direct connection between the nerve passages, spinal cord damage, and levels of paralysis due to cord injury.

The first two cervical vertebrae are called *atlas (C1)* and *axis (C2)*. Atlas and axis are shaped differently to allow the base of the skull to sit properly on the spinal column. The atlas supports the skull, and the axis connects the atlas and skull structure to the rest of the spinal cord. Injury at this level of the spinal column with accompanied cord damage can ultimately result in death.

The *thoracic spine,* which is larger and stronger than the cervical spine, articulates with the ribs to form the thoracic area.

The *lumbar spine,* the strongest section of the spinal column, is larger and thicker than the other sections of the spinal column because it supports the largest portion of body weight. In a full-grown adult, the lumbar region houses a structure called the *cauda equina,* where the spinal cord ends at a bundle of nerves that innervate the lower part of the body.

The *sacrum* and *coccygeal spine* are fused sections of the spine. The sacrum, part of the pelvic girdle, is the posterior support for the pelvis. The coccygeal section, the lowest portion of the spine, projects below the pelvis with a series of spinous processes.

The Sternum

The sternum is a flat bone located in the midline in the anterior thoracic cavity. Also known as the breastbone, the sternum is made up of three sections of bones: the upper section, called the *manubrium;* the middle section, called the *body;* and the lower section, called the *xyphoid process.*

The Ribs

Twelve pairs of ribs make up the *rib cage.* The first seven pairs of ribs are connected directly to the sternum by cartilage. The remaining five pairs are called *false ribs* because they do not directly connect to the sternum. The last two pairs of false ribs are called *floating ribs* because they are not connected to the anterior portion of the rib cage. False ribs are attached posteriorly to the spine and anteriorly to cartilage, which then connects to the sternum. Floating ribs are connected posteriorly to

NOTE

During CPR, the hand is placed on the body of the sternum, avoiding the xyphoid process.

the spine and float free anteriorly. Spaces between the ribs are called *intercostal spaces*. It is within these spaces that one witnesses *intercostal retractions,* which occur when negative intrathoracic pressure pulls tissue inward.

The Appendicular Skeleton

To give you a better understanding of the appendicular skeleton, the bones in this section are described as they are found in the body. The description begins with the upper appendicular skeleton and moves on to the lower appendicular skeleton.

The Scapula

The scapula is a flat, triangular bone that attaches posteriorly to the rib cage and forms the connecting point for the structures of the upper skeleton to the axial skeleton. Attached to the scapula is the *clavicle*. The point of attachment is called the acromioclavicular joint.

The Clavicle

The clavicle attaches to the scapula at the midaxillary line and attaches to the sternum in the area of the manubrium, creating the sternoclavicular joint, also known as the *collarbone*.

Bones of the Upper Arm and Hand

The *humerus* is the largest bone of the upper skeleton and is attached to the scapula at its head. The humerus attaches distally with the radius and ulna bones of the lower arm, creating the elbow joint. The radius runs along the thumb side of the arm. Therefore, the term *radial pulse* is associated with the radial artery on that side of the lower arm.

The ulna runs along the "pinky" side of the lower arm, and both the radius and ulna attach to the bones of the hand distally, creating the wrist. The bones of the hand from proximal to distal are the *carpal bones, metacarpal bones,* and *phalanges* (fingers).

The Pelvis

Several bones make up the pelvis, forming a support structure and connecting point between the lower extremity and the spinal column. The bones of the pelvis include left and right halves. Each half includes the *ilium,* or upper half (hip bone); the *ischium,* or lower half (forming part of the attachment point for the femur); and the *pubis bones*. These bones attach posteriorly to the coccygeal spine, forming the pelvic girdle. Anteriorly, they connect at the pubic symphysis.

The Femur

The femur, the largest bone in the body, attaches to the pelvis at the femur's proximal end or head. The attachment between the head of the femur and the shaft is called the *femoral neck*. This attachment should be examined when treating elderly patients with hip fractures, as the fractures often occur in

NOTE

Collarbone fractures are very common in falls on the outstretched hand.

this area. The femur attaches distally to the bones of the lower leg—the *tibia* and *fibula.* Anteriorly at this connecting point sits the *patella,* or knee cap. This articulation point (connection point) is collectively called the knee.

The Tibia

The larger of the two bones of the lower leg, the tibia is more commonly known as the shinbone. This bone connects proximally to the knee joint and distally to the bones of the foot. The tibia supports body weight.

The Fibula

Like the tibia, the fibula connects proximally at the knee joint and distally to the bones of the foot. At its distal connection point, the anklebone is created.

Bones of the Foot

The bones of the foot, similar to the bones of the hand, are the *tarsals,* which connect to the talus (the connection point of the distal tibia and fibula), the metatarsals, and phalanges (toes).

The Muscular System

The muscular system is a complex arrangement of tissue and chemical reactions beyond the scope of the EMT–Basic. This section briefly describes the points of the muscular system the EMT–Basic encounters in field interactions.

Muscles, with bone, provide body movement. The muscles contract and relax, causing parts of the body to move up and down, rotate, and move laterally and medially. Muscle tissue accounts for approximately half of a person's total body weight. Three types of muscle tissue exist: *skeletal muscle, cardiac muscle,* and *smooth muscle.*

Skeletal Muscle

Skeletal muscle is muscle that attaches to bones (skeleton). The primary function of skeletal muscle is to provide movement. Skeletal muscle is *voluntary muscle,* meaning it can be made to move as a result of the person's will. In other words, a person moving his or her arm is using voluntary muscle to create movement.

Cardiac Muscle

Cardiac muscle is *involuntary muscle.* As its name suggests, cardiac muscle makes up most of the heart. Cardiac muscle has a unique feature in that it can produce and conduct electrical stimulation. The ability of cardiac muscle to create electrical impulses is called *automaticity.* Simply stated, any part of the cardiac muscle can take over as a cardiac pacemaker should the normal system fail.

Smooth Muscle

Smooth muscle is specially developed muscle usually found in the walls of blood vessels and organs. Generally considered involuntary muscle, smooth muscle is not consciously controlled. The body controls smooth muscle in that it can facilitate peristalsis (the digestive process of physically moving food through the digestive system), blood vessel constriction and dilation, and other expansions and contractions that regulate bodily function.

The Brain, Spinal Cord, and Nerves (Nervous System)

The nervous system controls all functions of the body. The brain constantly processes data from internal and external stimuli and reacts to it for the benefit of survival. Every day, the brain makes millions of unconscious decisions to maintain body temperature, increase or decrease breathing and heart rate, and react to outside threats.

Picture yourself withdrawing cash at an automated teller machine. A masked man holding a gun approaches you from behind and demands your money. As you turn around, your heart begins to race, you sweat, and you feel nauseous. However, your vision is sharp and your mind develops ideas about your next move. All of these responses happen without your thinking. This is the brain and nervous system in action. The approach of the man with the gun and your initial response set off a chain reaction of events within the nervous system.

The brain interprets the man with a gun as a threat and responds by stimulating the sympathetic nervous system. Heart rate quickens, pupils dilate, breathing increases, and blood flowing to the gastrointestinal tract shifts its direction toward areas of greater importance under the circumstances— the muscles and nervous system, the heart, and the pulmonary system. This entire chain of events is known as the fight-or-flight response.

The Brain

The human brain is one of the largest organs in the body. The average adult brain weighs approximately 3 to 3½ pounds. The following section defines the four major parts of the brain. Remember, however, that the brain comprises multiple subparts.

The following chart defines the four major parts of the brain and their basic functions:

Structure	Function	Description
Brain stem	Controls involuntary function	Controls heart rate, respiratory rate, swallowing, and coughing
Diencephalon	Sensory processing and body function control	Processes sensory information and controls body functions from the spinal cord; controls autonomic nervous system; regulates hunger and thirst; regulates body temperature; regulates emotional response
Cerebrum	Largest portion of the brain; sensory control	Controls the five senses: hearing, vision, taste, touch, and smell; controls speech; controls personality
Cerebellum	Coordination of balance	Interprets signals from the body and brain to maintain correct balance; coordinates skilled motor activities like painting or skating

The brain is located in the *cranial cavity,* a sealed structure in normal adults. In newborns, the cranial cavity is not yet sealed but remains loosely bound for several months, usually sealing within eighteen months. Several coverings offer protection to the brain. Collectively, these coverings are called the *meninges,* which comprise three layers. The outermost layer is called the *dura mater,* the middle layer is the *arachnoid mater,* and the inner layer is called the *pia mater.*

Within the cavity, and between the *pia* and *arachnoid mater*, cerebrospinal fluid protects the brain. This fluid circulates throughout the brain and spinal cord. Cerebrospinal fluid serves two functions: It provides nourishment and a protective barrier to the brain. For example, in a fall where a man hits his head, the cerebrospinal fluid cushions the shock, preventing injury. Without the cerebrospinal fluid, the brain would bounce off the hard interior surface of the skull and suffer damage.

The Cranial Nerves

Twelve pairs of cranial nerves are located at the base of the brain and control motor and sensory functions. These nerves do not attach to the spinal cord but pass through different openings in the skull and perform motor and sensory functions. The chart below describes the twelve cranial nerves and their functions.

Number	Name	Motor/Sensory	Function
I	Olfactory	Sensory	Controls sense of smell; loss of this sense could indicate injury to this nerve
II	Optic	Sensory	Controls vision; damage to structure of the eye, pathways in the brain, or orbital fractures may result in vision loss
III	Oculomotor	Motor	Controls movement of the eyeball and eyelid; damage to this nerve may cause double vision as well as other multiple defects
IV	Trochlear	Motor	Controls movement of the eyeball; damage to this nerve may cause double vision as well as other multiple defects
V	Trigeminal	Both	Controls movement of the lower jaw; controls facial muscles involved in the act of eating
VI	Abducens	Motor	Controls lateral eye movement; controls eye movement looking outward or peripherally
VII	Facial	Both	Controls facial expressions; controls salivation and tearing
VIII	Vestibulocochlear	Sensory	Controls hearing; controls equilibrium
IX	Glossopharyngeal	Both	Controls salivation; controls taste
X	Vagus	Both	Controls parasympathetic nervous system
XI	Accessory	Motor	Controls swallowing; controls head movement
XII	Hypoglossal	Motor	Controls tongue movement; controls sensory muscles of the mouth, which send signals through the sensory nerves to the brain—usually when eating, drinking, or engaging in other sensory activity

The Nervous Systems

Three complex systems of nerves exist in the body. The brain and spinal cord make up the *central nervous system*, while the *peripheral nervous system* comprises all other nerves. Two separate divisions, called the *sympathetic* and *parasympathetic branches*, make up the *autonomic nervous system*.

The branches of the autonomic nervous system control increases and decreases in bodily function. Generally, the sympathetic nervous system controls the speeding up of body functions. This includes increased heart rate, increased breathing, and dilation of pupils. We call this set of reactions the fight-or-flight response. The parasympathetic nervous system works in an opposite fashion, slowing down body functions. The parasympathetic nervous system slows heart rate and breathing and increases the rate of peristalsis.

A good example of the parasympathetic nervous system in action is the way your body responds after you eat a big meal. You become sluggish as the parasympathetic nervous system coordinates digestion, moving blood flow from the brain and other vital organs to absorb nutrients in the process of digestion. The decreased blood flow to vital organs, although not dangerous, makes you feel tired.

The Spinal Cord

The spinal cord passes through the foramen magnum in the skull and continues down through the spinal foramen. As the spinal cord passes down, nerves branch off through openings in the spinal column. These nerves control different motor and sensory activity. The nerves and their locations have a direct relation to paralysis after spinal cord injury. A person who is paralyzed from the waist down often suffered a spinal cord injury at the level of the twelfth thoracic vertebrae. Patients paralyzed from the nipple line down most likely experienced an injury at the level of the first thoracic vertebrae.

The *reflex arc* is located in the spinal cord. Some impulses in the body do not generate a response from the brain. Instead, they are controlled in the spinal cord. The reflex arc is a perfect example of the spinal cord creating a primitive motor response to an outside stimulation. An example of this is when a person is near a hot stove and accidentally places his hand on the flame. An impulse is sent through the nervous system to the spinal cord. This impulse is interpreted as pain. The spinal cord, in response to this pain message, sends back a message to the arm, and in an involuntary response, the hand pulls away from the source of the pain—the hot stove. This entire process happens instantaneously. The reflex arc decreases the size of the injury by interpreting the sensory signal and eliciting a motor response to avoid that pain source.

Cardiovascular System

The heart, blood vessels, and blood all work together to support the body in its maintenance of homeostasis. All three of these components of the cardiovascular system must operate properly to maintain homeostasis.

The Heart

The heart is a four-chambered pump composed of a specially designed muscle called *cardiac muscle,* which generates electrical impulses. The upper chambers of the heart are called *atria,* while the lower chambers are called *ventricles.* The heart can pump more than 3,000 gallons of blood per day.

Two different systems allow the heart to pump blood. Coming from the right side of the heart, blood is pumped into the *pulmonary circulation.* Coming from the left side of the heart, blood is pumped into the *systemic circulation.*

The pulmonary circulation system begins when blood is pumped from the right atrium into the pulmonary arteries. The pulmonary arteries carry deoxygenated blood from the heart and into the lungs, where it can be oxygenated. After the blood is oxygenated, it is returned to the heart by way of the pulmonary vein. The pulmonary vein returns blood to the left atria.

The systemic circulation begins when blood is pumped from the left atrium into the pulmonary vein. Once the blood leaves the left atrium, it travels through the systemic circulation, supplying oxygen and nutrients to the body cells. Blood returns to the heart from the systemic circulation by way of the inferior and superior venae cavae.

Within the heart, valves separate the four separate chambers. The valve between the right atria and the right ventricle is called the *tricuspid valve.* The valve between the left atria and left ventricle is called the *bicuspid valve,* or *mitral valve.* The valve between the right ventricle and the pulmonary circulation is called the *pulmonic valve.* The valve between the left ventricle and the systemic circulation is called the *aortic valve.* Blood returning to the heart fills the atria passively, and no valves return from either the systemic or pulmonary circulation to the atria.

The heart is protected by a tough, nonelastic fibrous tissue called the *pericardium.* This layer of tissue serves several purposes. The first purpose is to provide protection to the heart muscle. The second purpose is to prevent the heart from overstretching. The third purpose is to anchor the heart to the mediastinum.

The Blood Vessels

The body contains several types of blood vessels. Each vessel performs a different function in regulating blood supply to the body. As blood leaves the left ventricle and moves into the systemic circulation, it is carried by arteries, which then break down into smaller vessels called *arterioles.* Arterioles branch off into the body tissues and further break down into vessels called *capillaries,* vessels that are only one cell thick. Within the capillaries, gas exchange takes place as oxygen is delivered to the cells and carbon dioxide is removed from the cells. The capillaries also deliver nutrients to the cells.

Just past the capillary level begins the return of blood flow back to the heart. Vessels coming off the capillaries and back to the heart begin as *venoules.* As the vessels expand in size, they turn into *veins.* As the venous return continues back toward the heart, the vessels expand in size until they reach the *inferior* and *superior venae cavae.* These vessels are responsible for all blood returned to the heart. Both of these vessels return blood into the right atrium.

ALERT!

The EMT–Basic should be aware that in some cases of severe chest trauma, the pericardium could fill with blood due to a ventricular rupture.

The EMT–Basic should be aware of the following physiological functions:

- **Arteries** carry blood away from the heart.
- **Arterioles** are smaller arteries that enter the organs and tissues.
- **Capillaries** are vessels that are one cell thick where gas and nutrient exchange take place.
- **Venoules** carry blood from the capillaries on its return trip to the heart.
- **Veins** are larger vessels that ultimately return all blood to the heart.

The EMT–Basic should also know the following terms as they relate to the cardiovascular system:

- **Cardiac output** is the volume of blood pumped by the heart in one minute.
- **Stroke volume** is defined as the amount of blood pumped from the heart in one beat.
- **Blood pressure** is the pressure of circulating blood against the walls of the blood vessels.
- **Systolic pressure** is the highest pressure within the bloodstream, occurring during heartbeats.
- **Diastolic pressure** is the lowest pressure within the bloodstream, occurring between heartbeats.

The Blood

Blood consists of multiple elements essential to maintaining functions that support life. The following chart outlines elements of blood and their functions:

Element	Function
Red blood cell	Red blood cells contain hemoglobin, which transports oxygen and carbon dioxide in the blood.
White blood cell	White blood cells are specialized cells that attack foreign substances as they circulate in the blood. They fight disease and infection.
Platelet	Platelets are responsible for blood clot formation and vaso-spasm after injury has occurred.
Plasma	Plasma is the liquid portion of blood that carries all the elements of blood through the vascular system.

The Endocrine System

The endocrine system coordinates functions of the body by releasing substances called *hormones,* messengers delivered to cells to create reactions in the body that will help support homeostasis. The *pituitary gland, pineal gland, parathyroid glands, thyroid gland,* and *adrenal glands* are all part of the endocrine system.

The body's organ systems also contain *endocrine tissue.* The *pancreas* is an organ that contains endocrine tissue. The pancreas secretes both *insulin* and *glucagon,* two important hormones responsible for regulation of blood sugar in the body.

Insulin helps the body convert sugar into a form that is usable by the cells, while glucagon breaks down stored sugars for use by the body as energy.

The EMT–Basic should be aware that the endocrine system is a complex system that regulates multiple bodily functions. The functions listed above are those most commonly encountered in dysfunction while in the field. Diabetic patients who have an insulin-regulation problem will sometimes become unconscious from either *hypoglycemia* (low blood sugar) or *hyperglycemia* (high blood sugar), based on their levels of insulin.

Another important function of the endocrine system is the release of *epinephrine* and *norepinephrine* by the adrenal glands. Epinephrine and norepinephrine are the hormones responsible for increased heart rate and contraction, vasoconstriction, and pupil dilation.

You may remember these as the responses of the sympathetic nervous system discussed earlier. During the fight-or-flight response, epinephrine and norepinephrine are secreted by the adrenal glands.

Finally, the endocrine system is also responsible for sexual development. The testicles produce testosterone, which help in male development, and the ovaries secrete estrogen and progesterone, which help in female development.

The Respiratory System

The respiratory system is responsible for bringing oxygen into the body and eliminating carbon dioxide. Knowing the definitions of the following terms will help you fully understand the function of gas exchange.

Ventilation

Ventilation is the actual mechanical function of moving air into and out of the lungs. The diaphragm and the muscles of the chest wall affect this process. As a patient inhales, the diaphragm contracts and moves downward, and the chest muscles contract and move outward.

This creates a larger area inside the chest wall, decreasing the pressure inside the lungs. As the pressure decreases, outside air is drawn into the lungs to stabilize it with the atmospheric pressure. Exhalation is produced by the diaphragm moving upward (expanding) and the chest muscles moving inward. This function increases the pressure inside the lungs, and air is forced out.

Respiration

Respiration is an internal function often broken down into two categories: *external respiration* and *internal respiration.*

External respiration occurs when air is exchanged between the alveoli and the capillaries (gas exchange at the alveolar level). Oxygen is taken into the capillaries by the red blood cells that contain hemoglobin, and carbon dioxide is removed from the red blood cells and sent back into the lungs for expiration.

Internal respiration occurs at the tissue cellular level. Oxygen is delivered to the cells by the red blood cells. The red blood cells pick up the waste products of cellular respiration (carbon dioxide) and return them to the lungs during external respiration.

The respiratory system is broken down into two distinct sections: the *upper respiratory system* and the *lower respiratory system.* The upper respiratory system consists of the nose and pharynx and their associated structures. The lower respiratory system consists of the larynx, trachea, bronchi, and lung tissue (including alveoli). The following chart refers to the structures of the respiratory system and their functions:

Structure	Function
Nose	Filters and moisturizes air; olfactory (smell) tissue in the nose allows the sense of smell
Pharynx	Passageway for air, assists in voice function; balances air pressures between the ears and the throat
Larynx	The "voice box," a passageway between the laryngopharynx and the trachea
Vallecula	The depression between the epiglottis and the base of the tongue
Epiglottis	A leaf-shaped structure that provides protection to the airway during swallowing; prevents aspiration of foreign bodies and liquids into the airway
Trachea	Made up of rings of cartilage and forms the air passage into the smaller airways; divides into the right and left branches; point of division is called the carina; anything beyond the point of division is called the mainstem bronchi
Bronchi	Two main bronchi that branch off from the trachea on the right and left side; travel deeper into the lungs, bringing inhaled air into the lower airways
Bronchioles	The smallest part of the airway; attach the hard structure of the airway to the alveoli, where air exchange takes place
Alveoli	Structures shaped like bunches of grapes; capillary membrane surrounds each alveolus, where the exchange of air and waste products takes place; the only place in the entire airway that air exchange can occur; alveoli collapse is called atelectasis

The Lungs

Situated in the thoracic cavity, the lungs are separated in the center by the heart and other anatomical structures.

The lungs are divided into *lobes;* the right lung has three lobes and the left lung has two lobes.

The heart, which sits predominantly on the left side, is located in a space created by the left lung, which has a sharper lower border at the midline to accommodate the heart. This is the reason that in the trachea, the left mainstem bronchus has a much more acute angle than the right mainstem.

Each lung is covered by a two-layered membrane called the *pleura.* These membranes protect the lungs from injury and help create a smooth expansion and contraction during inspiration and expiration. As a two-layered membrane, the pleura has two parts: the *visceral pleura,* attached to the lung, and the *parietal pleura,* attached to the chest wall. Between these layers is a serous fluid that lubricates the layers to aid smooth expansion and contraction. Be aware that a potential space exists between these layers. In lung injury, this space may fill with air or blood, causing a *pneumothorax* or a *hemothorax.* The EMT–Basic should be aware of this possibility while caring for a patient with a chest injury. Lung sounds should be frequently monitored.

NOTE

Each lung works independently of the other, so if one lung gets damaged, the other lung will remain functional.

Within the lungs are the *alveoli*, rounded sacs (see previous chart) that have a capillary membrane attached. Gas and waste product exchange take place at the level of this membrane. This process, known as external respiration, is essential for the maintenance of homeostasis. If gas exchange is impaired for any reason, hypoxia will develop, and the patient may suffer permanent damage to the brain or to other organs. This condition may result in death.

The lungs have the capacity to contain a large volume of air. Normal total lung capacity is 6,000 ml of air, although normal *tidal volume* (the amount of air taken in during one breath) is about 500 ml of air. These numbers are important for the EMT–Basic to keep in mind during assisted ventilation. While normal tidal volume is 500 ml, only about two thirds of that volume ever reach the alveoli. The other one third remains in the structural components of the airway, which is called "anatomic dead space." During assisted ventilation, the adult bag-valve-mask device delivers 800 ml of air when properly used. Therefore, it is imperative that the EMT–Basic performs ventilatory assistance correctly and efficiently. This involves maintaining a proper mask seal, using proper ventilation techniques, and attaching the device to an oxygen source.

The Gastrointestinal System

The gastrointestinal system, also known as the *digestive system,* provides essential nutrients to the body. These nutrients are converted into various sources of energy as well as other components that are usable by the body. Breakdown of food is a two-step process. The first step is *actual digestion,* the breakdown of food into molecules the body can use. The second step is *absorption,* where the molecules are absorbed by the body for use.

The digestive system is divided into two parts: the *gastrointestinal tract* and the *alimentary canal.* The gastrointestinal tract includes all of the organs and structures of the digestive system. The alimentary canal is the path that food takes through the gastrointestinal tract during the digestive process.

Structure	Function
Mouth	Food is ingested into the mouth, beginning the digestive process.
Teeth	The teeth grind up food in a process known as mechanical digestion.
Tongue	The tongue moves food in the mouth to enable chewing, shapes the food, and forces it into the back of the mouth for swallowing.
Parotid Glands	Parotid glands produce saliva, which contains digestive enzymes and assists in mechanical digestion in the mouth by beginning to break down food.
Pharynx	The pharynx serves as a duct between the mouth and the esophagus.
Esophagus	A muscular tube that secretes mucous and expands and contracts to move food down into the stomach. No digestive processes occur in the esophagus.
Stomach	The stomach serves as a holding area for digestion. Protein digestion takes place in the stomach. The stomach secretes digestive enzymes that further break down food. Once digestive enzymes are secreted, the stomach mixes them with the food and produces a substance called chyme, which is passed into the small intestine for further absorption.

Small Intestine	The small intestine is approximately ten to twelve feet long and is responsible for most digestion and absorption in the body. It contains three parts: the duodenum, jejunum, and the ileum. The small intestine connects with the large intestine at the ileocecal valve.
Large Intestine	The final stages of digestion occur in the large intestine. Water absorption is finalized, and food becomes more solid. Normal bacteria in the large intestine convert proteins into substances appropriate for absorption and elimination.
Liver	The liver produces bile, which helps break down fats and metabolizes carbohydrates and proteins. It also removes toxins, stores glucose in the form of glycogen, and stores vitamins.
Gallbladder	The gallbladder stores bile produced by the liver. When needed, bile is excreted into the small intestine through the cystic duct
Pancreas	The pancreas secretes digestive enzymes and hormones that regulate blood sugar.
Anus and Rectum	The rectum is the final holding area for digested food. The anus is the muscular sphincter that separates the rectum from the outside. Highly muscular, the anus relaxes so digested products can be eliminated from the body.

The EMT–Basic should understand that gastrointestinal emergencies are extremely hard to isolate, effectively diagnose, and treat in the field. Due to the complexity of the structures and the multiple organs involved, many emergencies share the same medical presentation. The most common of these presentations is abdominal pain. Treatment of abdominal pain is best handled at the emergency department, where comprehensive imaging and medical testing can pinpoint the diagnosis.

The Urinary System

The urinary system, another system that helps the body to eliminate waste, is made up of two kidneys, two ureters, the bladder, and the urethra. The kidney's main function is to filter toxins out of the blood and send them to the bladder for excretion from the body. Kidneys also maintain blood volume, which in turn regulates blood pressure. Kidneys assist in the regulation of the body's pH and are one of the components of the buffer system of the body.

The kidneys are highly vascular organs that need a constant blood supply to avoid damage.

This is especially pertinent information when you are treating a patient in a state of *hypoperfusion*. Hypoperfusion causes the body to shunt blood away from the kidneys to supply the heart, lungs, and brain. Without blood flow, the kidneys shut down, causing additional pathophysiological process in the trauma or hypovolemic patient. Patients who have kidney failure can contract many different illnesses due to the buildup of toxins in the blood.

Patients who have chronic kidney failure are treated by the use of *hemodialysis*. These patients are usually seen three times a week and are attached to a dialysis machine, which filters the blood through a highly technical process. Interaction with any patient who has a history of kidney failure should involve transport for further evaluation.

TIP

With a large number of gastrointestinal emergencies requiring surgical intervention, the EMT–Basic best serves the patient by providing a safe, comfortable ride to the emergency department while monitoring vital signs and treating the patient symptomatically to relieve pain and anxiety.

CONTINUE TO EDUCATE YOURSELF

The human body is a complex machine consisting of multiple organ systems and chemical reactions necessary to maintaining a homeostatic balance. Failure of the respiratory system to properly deliver blood to the capillaries for distribution to the cells will result in multiorgan hypoxia and create cellular changes as the organs resort to alternate forms of respiration to produce energy necessary for their survival.

You should gain and retain as much knowledge as possible about the anatomy and physiology of the body systems as well as the pathophysiology of these systems. This understanding will help you properly assist and treat patients to offset the chain reactions that occur in the body during a period of illness or injury. This is not by any means an elective topic, and the information in this text is only the tip of the iceberg as far as understanding these complex body systems. Continue your education in this area, since the understanding of the structure and function of the body is tantamount in the understanding of the treatment of its disease processes.

SUMMING IT UP

- An understanding of basic anatomy and physiology is the foundation for success as an EMT–Basic.
- The EMT–Basic must have thorough knowledge of the most commonly used medical terminology.
- The EMT–Basic should understand topographic anatomy in order to communicate with other providers, document patient charts, and adhere to legal and ethical protocols.
- The EMT–Basic must fully understand the working mechanisms of the body, including the skeletal system, muscular system, nervous system, heart, blood vessels, endocrine system, respiratory system, gastrointestinal system, and urinary system.

EMT–Basic Practical Skills Evaluation

OVERVIEW

- Guidelines for taking a practical skills examination
- The practical skills
- Practicing skills
- Skills examination day
- EMT–Basic skills performance sheets
- Summing it up

GUIDELINES FOR TAKING A PRACTICAL SKILLS EXAMINATION

To receive certification, all EMT–Basic candidates must demonstrate competence in the performance of the practical skills needed to treat patients in the field. Candidates should have sufficient opportunity to obtain a working knowledge of these skills during the training program. Most states do not allow candidates to sit for a written examination until they demonstrate competence in skills performance. This chapter explains how to develop these skills and offers advice on how to succeed on the practical skills examination.

THE PRACTICAL SKILLS

Typically, the required practical skills for the EMT–Basic include:

1   Patient Assessment/Management–Trauma
2   Patient Assessment/Management–Medical
3   Cardiac Arrest Management/AED
4A Spinal Immobilization–Seated Patient
4B Spinal Immobilization–Supine Patient
5A Immobilization Skills–Long-Bone Injury
5B Immobilization Skills–Joint Injury
5C Immobilization Skills–Traction Splinting
5D Bleeding Control/Shock Management
5E Airway, Oxygen, and Ventilatin Skills–Upper Airway Adjuncts and Suction
5F Mouth-to-Mask with Supplemental Oxygen
5G Oxygen Administration

Some states add additional requirements to the examination. Check with your instructor for more information on state-specific requirements.

Candidates perform many of these skills at the same testing station. For example, the examiner might ask you to demonstrate your airway skills at a scenario-based testing station that assesses a variety of practical skills. These types of practical examinations base the testing station on a single scenario, allowing the EMT–Basic to assess and manage a patient with a predetermined medical emergency. In the aforementioned example, the EMT–Basic must assess the airway and perform the correct interventions to pass the station.

Many training institutions prepare candidates for final testing by running scenario-based practice stations similar to those used during the practical skills examination.

TIP

You can increase your chances of passing the practical skills examination by learning how examiners administer the test and finding out what they expect from each candidate.

PRACTICING SKILLS

EMT–Basic candidates should use every available opportunity to practice their skills. This will not only increase your chances of passing the practical skills examination, but will also help you become a more confident EMT in the field.

Students often find it difficult to get the practice they need during classroom skills sessions. Instructors often place students in large groups and only allow them a short amount of time to practice a single skill. The following four tips can help you make the most of your practice opportunities in and outside the classroom:

1. **Take full advantage of practice time afforded in class.** Pay attention while others are practicing. You can learn a great deal from observing the successes and mistakes of other students. When it's your turn to practice a skill, take your time and follow all the steps on the skills performance sheet.

2. **Make a note of all critiques offered by the station instructor and work to correct deficiencies.** If you need more practice, talk with your senior instructor. Many institutions will set up remediation sessions or allow you to show up early for additional practice.

3. **If you belong to an EMS agency, ask a senior member to help you practice.** Many senior members will be happy to assist you. Most EMS agencies have training equipment that you can use to practice your skills whenever you have free time.

4. **Practice your assessment skills on family members.** You can run through the steps of assessment while your relative rests comfortably on the couch. As you go through the steps, ask your family member to look at the performance sheet and advise you of any missed items or omissions of intervention.

ALERT!

Always follow the steps on your performance sheet when you practice a skill. You can start practicing without the sheet after you memorize all the steps.

Memorizing the skills performance sheets is an essential part of mastering your practical skills examination. Your instructor will provide you with these sheets early in your training to ensure that you have ample time to memorize them. Memorizing these sheets can be difficult, so ask a friend, family member, or fellow student to assist you. An assistant can stop you when you omit a step and reinforce a good performance. Attempts at skills practice prior to memorization will only confuse you.

Your fellow students are another wonderful resource. Get together with other candidates to compare notes and study for the exam. Choose a study partner who is serious about passing the examination and avoid talking about outside topics while studying.

If you misunderstand the theory behind a skill, consult your textbook. Most EMS textbooks will have a full explanation of skill theories as well as pictures of professionals performing the skills.

SKILLS EXAMINATION DAY

You can prepare for the practical skills examination in the same way that you would prepare for a written examination. Get plenty of rest the night before the examination and don't stay up all night reading the skills sheets. Make time to study well in advance of examination day. If you plan to review the skills the night before your exam, make sure that the session is shorter than your previous reviews. An intense review session will only make you nervous.

When you arrive at the testing site, make sure you have all the equipment that you will need for the examination. Although most examination sites will supply everything needed to complete the skills examination, some sites also advise you to bring your personal equipment, such as a stethoscope, penlight, pocket mask, and a pair of trauma shears.

Entering the Skills Station

The first thing you should do after entering the skills station is compose yourself. Stress and anxiety could negatively affect your performance. If you feel nervous, take a deep breath and clear your mind as you wait for the examiner's instructions. Skills examiners have been in your position, so they understand how you feel.

Once you receive your instructions, the examiner will ask you to inspect the equipment. Make sure you have everything you need to perform the skills without stopping and asking for additional equipment. In general, skills examiners do not intentionally remove essential pieces of equipment during testing, but they may accidentally leave something out. Double check all of the equipment before you begin.

Students must take proper infection control precautions at all skills stations. Make sure that you put on gloves at every station. Forgetting to wear gloves often results in an immediate failure of the skills station. WEAR GLOVES AT ALL STATIONS.

The most important aspect of the skills examination is the successful completion of the skill. When using a mannequin, it may be hard for the examiner to know what you are doing during an assessment. Verbalize everything you are doing during the assessment to help the examiner understand your actions. The examiner may refer to this practice as voice treating. As you begin your skill, try using statements such as, "I am opening the airway. Is it open?" The examiner will respond appropriately. Continue verbalization throughout the examination.

If the examiner asks you a question, remain calm. It may be part of the test, or the examiner may be giving you a hint that you missed something. Examiners do not usually give hints, but this may happen. Think about what you did in the last twenty seconds and try to remember if you missed a

TIP
Look over your performance skills sheets as you wait for the examiner to call on you. Try not to focus on any particular skill, as the examiner may ask you to demonstrate any number of skills during the exam. Just give the sheets a quick glance as you wait.

step. If you don't think you missed anything, don't dwell on it—answer the question and move on. Dwelling on previous questions will only break your concentration.

When you complete the station, state that you have completed it. You may leave once the examiner releases you. Once you leave a station, focus all of your attention on the next station. Clear the previous stations from your mind and go into the next station with a positive and confident attitude.

EMT–BASIC SKILLS PERFORMANCE SHEETS

The Skills Sheets

TIP

Verbalize everything you do, even if it is obvious, during your examination.

The National Highway Traffic Safety Administration has provided the following skills performance sheets. These sheets adhere to the National Standard Curriculum and offer a comprehensive approach to practical skills. Each sheet contains a set of steps that you must complete to pass a specific station on the practical skills examination. The sheets also outline the critical failures for each station. If your course uses state-specific sheets for testing, do not memorize these sheets.

Institutions throughout the United States use the National Standard Curriculum templates as an evaluation tool for the EMT–Basic.

Station 1

Patient Assessment/Management–Trauma

Instructions to the Candidate

At this station, you will perform a patient assessment of a victim of multisystems trauma and "voice" treat all conditions and injuries discovered. You must conduct your assessment as you would in the field. This includes communicating with the patient. Verbalize everything you are assessing during this time. The examiner will provide you with clinical information not obtainable through visual or physical assessment after you demonstrate how you would obtain this information in the field. You may assume that you have two EMTs working with you who are carrying out the verbal treatments you indicate. You have 15 minutes to complete this skill station. Do you have any questions?

NOTE

You will receive your results at the end of the examination. Even if you fail a station or two, most examiners will allow you to retest the stations that you failed. Many institutions will even allow you to retest on the same day.

NOTES

PATIENT ASSESSMENT/MANAGEMENT
TRAUMA

		Points Possible	Points Awarded
Takes or verbalizes body substance isolation precautions		1	
SCENE SIZE-UP			
Determines the scene is safe		1	
Determines the mechanism of injury		1	
Determines the number of patients		1	
Requests additional help if necessary		1	
Considers stabilization of spine		1	
INITIAL ASSESSMENT			
Verbalizes general impression of patient		1	
Determines responsiveness		1	
Determines chief complaint/apparent life threats		1	
Assesses airway and breathing	Assessment	1	
	Initiates appropriate oxygen therapy	1	
	Assures adequate ventilation	1	
	Injury management	1	
Assesses Circulation	Assesses for and controls major bleeding	1	
	Assesses pulse	1	
	Assesses skin (color, temperature and condition)	1	
Identifies priority patients/makes transport decision		1	
FOCUSED HISTORY AND PHYSICAL EXAM/RAPID TRAUMA ASSESSMENT			
Selects appropriate assessment (focused or rapid assessment)		1	
Obtains or directs assistant to obtain baseline vital signs		1	
Obtains SAMPLE history		1	
DETAILED PHYSICAL EXAMINATION			
Assesses the head	Inspects and palpates the scalp and ears	1	
	Assesses the eyes	1	
	Assesses the facial area including oral and nasal area	1	
Assesses the neck	Inspects and palpates the neck	1	
	Assesses for JVD	1	
	Assesses for tracheal deviation	1	
Assesses the chest	Inspects	1	
	Palpates	1	
	Auscultates the chest	1	
Assesses the abdomen/pelvis	Assesses the abdomen	1	
	Assesses the pelvis	1	
	Verbalizes assessment of genitalia/perineum as needed	1	
Assesses the extremities	1 point for each extremity includes inspection, palpation, and assessment of pulses, sensory and motor activities	4	
Assesses the posterior	Assesses thorax	1	
	Assesses lumbar	1	
Manages secondary injuries and wounds appropriately **1 point for appropriate management of secondary injury/wound**		1	
Verbalizes reassessment of the vital signs		1	
	TOTAL:	40	

CRITICAL CRITERIA

___ Did not take or verbalize body substance isolation precautions
___ Did not assess for spinal protection
___ Did not provide for spinal protection when indicated
___ Did not provide high concentration of oxygen
___ Did not find or manage problems associated with airway, breathing, hemorrhage, or shock (hypoperfusion)
___ Did not differentiate patient's needing transportation versus continued on-scene assessment
___ Does other detailed physical examination before assessing airway, breathing, and circulation
___ Did not transport patient within ten (10) minute time limit

Station 2

Patient Assessment/Management–Medical

Instructions to the Candidate

At this station, you will perform a patient assessment of a patient with a chief complaint of a medical nature and "voice" treat all conditions discovered. You must conduct your assessment as you would in the field. This includes communicating with the patient. Verbalize everything you are assessing during this time. The examiner will provide you with clinical information not obtainable through visual or physical assessment after you demonstrate how you would obtain this information in the field. You may assume that you have two EMTs working with you who are carrying out the verbal treatments you indicate. You have 15 minutes to complete this skill station. Do you have any questions?

NOTES

PATIENT ASSESSMENT/MANAGEMENT
MEDICAL

		Points Possible	Points Awarded
Takes or verbalizes body substance isolation precautions		1	
SCENE SIZE-UP			
Determines the scene is safe		1	
Determines the mechanism of injury/nature of illness		1	
Determines the number of patients		1	
Requests additional help if necessary		1	
Considers stabilization of spine		1	
INITIAL ASSESSMENT			
Verbalizes general impression of patient		1	
Determines responsiveness/level of consciousness		1	
Determines chief complaint/apparent life threats		1	
Assesses airway and breathing	Assessment	1	
	Initiates appropriate oxygen therapy	1	
	Assures adequate ventilation	1	
Assesses Circulation	Assesses/controls major bleeding	1	
	Assesses pulse	1	
	Assesses skin (color, temperature and condition)	1	
Identifies priority patients/makes transport decision		1	
FOCUSED HISTORY AND PHYSICAL EXAM/RAPID ASSESSMENT			
Signs and Symptoms (Assess history of present illness)		4	

Respiratory	Cardiac	Altered Mental Status	Allergic Reaction	Poisoning/ Overdose	Environmental Emergency	Obstetrics	Behavioral
•Onset? •Provokes? •Quality? •Radiates? •Severity? •Time? •Interventions?	•Onset? •Provokes? •Quality? •Radiates? •Severity? •Time? •Interventions?	•Description of the episode •Onset? •Duration? •Associated symptoms? •Evidence of trauma? •Interventions? •Seizures? •Fever?	•History of allergies? •What were you exposed to? •How were you exposed? •Effects? •Progression? •Interventions?	•Substance? •When did you ingest/become exposed? •How much did you ingest? •Over what time period? •Interventions? •Estimated weight? •Effects?	•Source? •Environment? •Duration? •Loss of consciousness? •Effects - General or local?	•Are you pregnant? •How long have you been pregnant? •Pain or contractions? •Bleeding or discharge? •Do you feel the need to push? •Last menstrual period? •Crowning?	•How do you feel? •Determine suicidal tendencies •Is the patient a threat to self or others? •Is there a medical problem? •Interventions?

		Points Possible	Points Awarded
Allergies		1	
Medications		1	
Past medical history		1	
Last Meal		1	
Events leading to present illness (rule out trauma)		1	
Performs focused physical examination Assesses affected body part/system or, if indicated, completes rapid assessment		1	
VITALS (Obtains baseline vital signs)		1	
INTERVENTIONS Obtains medical direction or verbalizes standing order for medication interventions and verbalizes proper additional intervention/treatment		1	
TRANSPORT (Re-evaluates transport decision)		1	
Verbalizes the consideration for completing a detailed physical examination		1	
ONGOING ASSESSMENT (verbalized)			
Repeats initial assessment		1	
Repeats vital signs		1	
Repeats focused assessment regarding patient complaint or injuries		1	
Checks interventions		1	
CRITICAL CRITERIA	**TOTAL:**	34	

___ Did not take or verbalize body substance isolation precautions if necessary
___ Did not determine scene safety
___ Did not obtain medical direction or verbalize standing orders for medication interventions
___ Did not provide high concentration of oxygen
___ Did not evaluate and find conditions of airway, breathing, circulation
___ Did not find or manage problems associated with airway, breathing, hemorrhage, or shock (hypoperfusion)
___ Did not differentiate patient's needing transportation versus continued assessment at the scene
___ Does detailed or focused history/physical examination before assessing airway, breathing, and circulation
___ Did not ask questions about the present illness
___ Administered a dangerous or inappropriate intervention

Station 3

Cardiac Arrest Management/AED

Instructions to the Candidate

This station assesses your ability to manage a prehospital cardiac arrest by integrating CPR skills, defibrillation, airway adjuncts, and patient/scene management skills. There will be an assistant EMT at this station. The assistant EMT will only follow your instructions. When you arrive on the scene, you will encounter a patient in cardiac arrest. A first responder will be performing single rescue CPR on the patient. You must immediately establish control of the scene and begin resuscitation of the patient using an automated external defibrillator. At the appropriate time, you must ventilate the patient's airway or direct the ventilation using adjunctive equipment. You may use any equipment available in this room. You have 15 minutes to complete this skill station. Do you have any questions?

NOTES

CARDIAC ARREST MANAGEMENT/AED

	Points Possible	Points Awarded
ASSESSMENT		
Takes or verbalizes body substances isolation precautions	1	
Briefly questions rescuer about events	1	
Directs rescuer to stop CPR	1	
Verifies absence of spontaneous pulse *(skill station examiner states "no pulse")*	1	
Turns on defibrillator power	1	
Attaches automated defibrillator to patient	1	
Ensures all individuals are standing clear of the patient	1	
Initiates analysis of rhythm	1	
Delivers shock (up to three successive shocks)	1	
Verifies absence of spontaneous pulse *(skill station examiner states "no pulse")*	1	
TRANSITION		
Directs resumption of CPR	1	
Gathers additional information on arrest event	1	
Confirms effectiveness of CPR (ventilation and compressions)	1	
INTEGRATION		
Directs insertion of a simple airway adjunct (oropharyngeal/nasopharyngeal)	1	
Directs ventilation of patient	1	
Assures high concentration of oxygen connected to the ventilatory adjunct	1	
Assures CPR continues without unnecessary/prolonged interruption	1	
Re-evaluates patient/CPR in approximately one minute	1	
Repeats defibrillator sequence	1	
TRANSPORTATION		
Verbalizes transportation of patient	1	
TOTAL:	20	

CRITICAL CRITERIA

___ Did not take or verbalize body substance isolation precautions

___ Did not evaluate the need for immediate use of the AED

___ Did not direct initiation/resumption of ventilation/compressions at appropriate times

___ Did not assure all individuals were clear of patient before delivering each shock

___ Did not operate the AED properly (inability to deliver shock)

Station 4A

Spinal Immobilization–Seated Patient

Instructions to the Candidate

At this station, you will provide spinal immobilization on a patient using a short spine immobilization device. You and an assistant EMT arrive on the scene of an automobile accident. The scene is safe and there is only one patient. After completing the initial assessment, the assistant EMT reports that the patient does not have any critical conditions requiring intervention. For the purpose of this station, the patient's vital signs remain stable. You must treat the specific, isolated problem of an unstable spine using a short spine immobilization device. The assistant EMT will only follow your instructions. You should transfer and immobilize the patient to the long backboard verbally. You have 10 minutes to complete this skill station. Do you have any questions?

NOTES

SPINAL IMMOBILIZATION
SEATED PATIENT

	Points Possible	Points Awarded
Takes or verbalizes body substance isolation precautions	1	
Directs assistant to place/maintain head in neutral in-line position	1	
Directs assistant to maintain manual immobilization of the head	1	
Reassesses motor, sensory, and distal circulation in extremities	1	
Applies appropriate size extrication collar	1	
Positions the immobilization device behind the patient	1	
Secures the device to the patient's torso	1	
Evaluates torso fixation and adjusts as necessary	1	
Evaluates and pads behind the patient's head as necessary	1	
Secures the patient's head to the device	1	
Verbalizes moving the patient to a long board	1	
Reassesses motor, sensory, and distal circulation in extremities	1	
TOTAL:	12	

CRITICAL CRITERIA

____ Did not immediately direct or take manual immobilization of the head
____ Releases or orders release of manual immobilization before it was maintained mechanically
____ Patient manipulated or moved excessively, causing potential spinal compromise
____ Device moves excessively up, down, left, or right on patient's torso
____ Head immobilization allows for excessive movement
____ Torso fixation inhibits chest rise, resulting in respiratory compromise
____ Upon completion of immobilization, head is not in the neutral position
____ Did not reassess motor, sensory, and distal circulation after voicing immobilization
 to the long board
____ Immobilized head to the board before securing the torso

Station 4B

Spinal Immobilization–Supine Patient

Instructions to the Candidate

At this station, you will provide spinal immobilization on a patient using a long spine immobilization device. You arrive on the scene with an assistant EMT. The scene is safe and there is only one patient. After completing the initial assessment, the assistant EMT reports that the patient does not have any critical conditions requiring intervention. For the purpose of this station, the patient's vital signs remain stable. You must treat the specific, isolated problem of an unstable spine using a long spine immobilization device. Instruct the assistant EMT and the examiner to assist you when moving the patient to the device. The assistant EMT should control the patient's head and cervical spine as you and the examiner move the patient to the immobilization device. You are responsible for the direction and actions of the assistant EMT. You have 10 minutes to complete this skill station. Do you have any questions?

NOTES

SPINAL IMMOBILIZATION
SUPINE PATIENT

	Points Possible	Points Awarded
Takes or verbalizes body substance isolation precautions	1	
Directs assistant to place/maintain head in neutral in-line position	1	
Directs assistant to maintain manual immobilization of the head	1	
Assesses motor, sensory, and distal circulation in extremities	1	
Applies appropriate size extrication collar	1	
Positions the immobilization device appropriately	1	
Directs movement of the patient onto device without compromising the integrity of the spine	1	
Applies padding to voids between the torso and the boards as necessary	1	
Immobilizes the patient's torso to the device	1	
Evaluates the pads behind the patient's head as necessary	1	
Immobilizes the patient's head to the device	1	
Secures the patient's legs to the device	1	
Secures the patient's arms to the device	1	
Reassesses motor, sensory, and distal circulation in extremities	1	
TOTAL:	14	

CRITICAL CRITERIA

___ Did not immediately direct or take manual immobilization of the head

___ Releases or orders release of manual immobilization before it was maintained mechanically

___ Patient manipulated or moved excessively, causing potential spinal compromise

___ Patient moves excessively up, down, left, or right on the device

___ Head immobilization allows for excessive movement

___ Upon completion of immobilization, head is not in the neutral in-line position

___ Did not reassess motor, sensory, and distal circulation after immobilization to the device

___ Immobilized head to the board before securing torso

Station 5A

Immobilization Skills–Long-Bone Injury

Instructions to the Candidate

This station tests your ability to immobilize a closed, nonangulated long-bone injury. You must treat the specific, isolated injury to the extremity. The scene size-up and initial assessment are complete. During the focused assessment, you detected a closed, nonangulated injury of the _____ (radius, ulna, tibia, fibula). It is unnecessary to continue assessment of the patient's airway, breathing, and central circulation while completing this skill station. You may use any equipment available in this room. You have 10 minutes to complete this skill station. Do you have any questions?

NOTES

IMMOBILIZATION SKILLS
LONG-BONE INJURY

	Points Possible	Points Awarded
Takes or verbalizes body substance isolation precautions	1	
Directs application of manual stabilization	1	
Assesses motor, sensory, and distal circulation	1	
NOTE: The examiner acknowledges present and normal		
Measures splint	1	
Applies splint	1	
Immobilizes the joint above the injury site	1	
Immobilizes the joint below the injury site	1	
Secures the entire injured extremity	1	
Immobilizes hand/foot in the position of function	1	
Reassesses motor, sensory, and distal circulation	1	
NOTE: The examiner acknowledges present and normal		
TOTAL:	10	

CRITICAL CRITERIA

____ Grossly moves injured extremity

____ Did not immobilize adjacent joints

____ Did not assess motor, sensory, and distal circulation before and after splinting

Station 5B

Immobilization Skills–Joint Injury

Instructions to the Candidate

This station tests your ability to immobilize a noncomplicated shoulder injury. You must treat the specific, isolated injury to the shoulder. The scene size-up and initial assessment are complete. During the focused assessment, you detected the shoulder injury. It is unnecessary to continue assessment of the patient's airway, breathing, and central circulation while completing this skill station. You may use any equipment available in this room. You have 10 minutes to complete this skill station. Do you have any questions?

```
NOTES




















```

IMMOBILIZATION SKILLS
JOINT INJURY

	Points Possible	Points Awarded
Takes or verbalizes body substance isolation precautions	1	
Directs application of manual stabilization of the injury	1	
Assesses motor, sensory, and distal circulation	1	
NOTE: The examiner acknowledges present and normal		
Selects proper splinting material	1	
Immobilizes the site of the injury	1	
Immobilizes bone above injured joint	1	
Immobilizes bone below injured joint	1	
Reassesses motor, sensory, and distal circulation	1	
NOTE: The examiner acknowledges present and normal		
TOTAL:	8	

CRITICAL CRITERIA

____ Did not support the joint so that the joint did not bear distal weight

____ Did not immobilize bone above and below injured joint

____ Did not reassess motor, sensory, and distal circulation before and after splinting

Station 5C

Immobilization Skills–Traction Splinting

Instructions to the Candidate

This station tests your ability to immobilize a midshaft femur injury using a traction splint. An assistant EMT will help you with the application of the device by applying manual traction under your direction. You must treat the specific, isolated injury to the femur. The scene size-up and initial assessment are complete. During the focused assessment, you detected the femur injury. It is unnecessary to continue assessment of the patient's airway, breathing, and central circulation while completing this skill station. You may use any equipment available in this room. You have 10 minutes to complete this skill station. Do you have any questions?

NOTES

IMMOBILIZATION SKILLS
TRACTION SPLINTING

	Points Possible	Points Awarded
Takes or verbalizes body substance isolation precautions	1	
Directs application of manual stabilization of the injured leg	1	
Directs the application of manual traction	1	
Assesses motor, sensory, and distal circulation	1	
NOTE: The examiner acknowledges present and normal.		
Prepares/adjusts splint to the proper length	1	
Positions the splint at the injured leg	1	
Applies the proximal securing device (e.g., ischial strap)	1	
Applies the distal securing device (e.g., ankle hitch)	1	
Applies mechanical traction	1	
Positions/secures the support straps	1	
Re-evaluates the proximal/distal securing devices	1	
Reassesses motor, sensory, and distal circulation	1	
NOTE: The examiner acknowledges present and normal		
NOTE: The examiner must ask candidate how he/she would prepare the patient for transportation.		
Verbalizes securing the torso to the long board to immobilize the hip	1	
Verbalizes securing the splint to the long board to prevent movement of the splint	1	
TOTAL:	14	

CRITICAL CRITERIA:

___ Loss of traction at any point after it is assumed

___ Did not reassess motor, sensory, and distal circulation before and after splinting

___ The foot is excessively rotated or extended after splinting

___ Did not secure the ischial strap before taking traction

___ Final immobilization failed to support the femur or prevent rotation of the injured leg

___ Secures leg to splint before applying mechanical traction

NOTE: If the Sager splint or Kendrick Traction Device is used without elevating the patient's leg, application of manual traction is not necessary. The candidate should be awarded 1 point as if manual traction were applied.

NOTE: If the leg is elevated at all, manual traction must be applied before elevating the leg. The ankle hitch may be applied before elevating the leg and used to provide manual traction.

Station 5D

Bleeding Control/Shock Management

Instructions to the Candidate

This station tests your ability to control hemorrhage. This is a scenario-based testing station. As you progress through the scenario, the examiner will give you various signs and symptoms appropriate for the patient's condition. Base your management of the patient on these signs and symptoms. The examiner will read the scenario aloud to you. You will have the opportunity to ask questions about the scenario, but you will not receive answers to any questions about how to perform the procedure. You may use any equipment available in this room. You have 5 minutes to complete this skill station. Do you have any questions?

NOTES

BLEEDING CONTROL/SHOCK MANAGEMENT

	Points Possible	Points Awarded
Takes or verbalizes body substance isolation precautions	1	
Applies direct pressure to the wound	1	
Elevates the extremity	1	
NOTE: The examiner must now inform the candidate that the wound continues to bleed.		
Applies an additional dressing to the wound	1	
NOTE: The examiner must now inform the candidate that the wound still continues to bleed. The second dressing does not control the bleeding.		
Locates and applies pressure to appropriate arterial pressure point	1	
NOTE: The examiner must now inform the candidate that the bleeding is controlled.		
Bandages the wound	1	
NOTE: The examiner must now inform the candidate that the patient is showing signs and symptoms indicative of hypoperfusion.		
Properly positions the patient	1	
Applies high-concentration oxygen	1	
Initiates steps to prevent heat loss from the patient	1	
Indicates need for immediate transportation	1	
TOTAL:	10	

CRITICAL CRITERIA

___ Did not take or verbalize body substance isolation precautions
___ Did not apply high concentration of oxygen
___ Applies tourniquet before attempting other methods of bleeding control
___ Did not control hemorrhage in a timely manner
___ Did not indicate a need for immediate transportation

Station 5E

Airway, Oxygen, and Ventilation Skills–Upper Airway Adjuncts and Suction

Instructions to the Candidate

This isolated skills test comprises three separate skills. The station tests your ability to measure, insert, and remove an oropharyngeal airway and a nasopharyngeal airway. You must also suction the patient's upper airway. You may use any equipment available in this room. You have 5 minutes to complete this skill station. Do you have any questions?

NOTES

AIRWAY, OXYGEN, AND VENTILATION SKILLS
UPPER AIRWAY ADJUNCTS AND SUCTION

OROPHARYNGEAL AIRWAY

	Points Possible	Points Awarded
Takes or verbalizes body substance isolation precautions	1	
Selects appropriate size airway	1	
Measures airway	1	
Inserts airway without pushing the tongue posteriorly	1	
NOTE: The examiner must advise the candidate that the patient is gagging and becoming conscious.		
Removes oropharyngeal airway	1	

SUCTION

	Points Possible	Points Awarded
NOTE: The examiner must advise the candidate to suction the patient's oropharynx/nasopharynx.		
Turns on/prepares suction device	1	
Assures presence of mechanical suction	1	
Inserts suction tip without suction	1	
Applies suction to the oropharynx/nasopharynx	1	

NASOPHARYNGEAL AIRWAY

	Points Possible	Points Awarded
NOTE: The examiner must advise the candidate to insert a nasopharyngeal airway.		
Selects appropriate airway	1	
Measures airway	1	
Verbalizes lubrication of the nasal airway	1	
Fully inserts the airway with the bevel facing toward the septum	1	
TOTAL:	13	

CRITICAL CRITERIA

____ Did not take or verbalize body substance isolation precautions

____ Did not obtain a patent airway with the oropharyngeal airway

____ Did not obtain a patent airway with the nasopharyngeal airway

____ Did not demonstrate an acceptable suction technique

____ Inserts any adjunct in a manner dangerous to the patient

Station 5F

Mouth-to-Mask with Supplemental Oxygen

Instructions to the Candidate

This is an isolated skills test. This station tests your ability to ventilate a patient with supplemental oxygen using a mouth-to-mask technique. You may assume that mouth-to-barrier device ventilation is in progress and that the patient has a central pulse. The only patient management required is ventilator support using a mouth-to-mask technique with supplemental oxygen. You must ventilate the patient for at least 30 seconds. The examiner will evaluate you on the appropriateness of ventilatory volumes. You may use any equipment available in this room. You have 5 minutes to complete this skill station. Do you have any questions?

NOTES

MOUTH-TO-MASK WITH SUPPLEMENTAL OXYGEN

	Points Possible	Points Awarded
Takes or verbalizes body substance isolation precautions	1	
Connects one-way valve to mask	1	
Opens patient's airway or confirms patient's airway is open (manually or with adjunct)	1	
Establishes and maintains a proper mask to face seal	1	
Ventilates the patient at the proper volume and rate (800–1,200 ml per breath/10–20 breaths per minute)	1	
Connects mask to high concentration oxygen	1	
Adjusts flow rate to 15 liters/minute or greater	1	
Continues ventilation at proper volume and rate (800–1,200 ml per breath/10–20 breaths per minute)	1	
NOTE: The examiner must witness ventilations for at least 30 seconds.		
TOTAL:	8	

CRITICAL CRITERIA

___ Did not take or verbalize body substance isolation precautions

___ Did not adjust liter flow to 15 L/min. or greater

___ Did not provide proper volume per breath
   (more than 2 ventilations per minute are below 800 ml)

___ Did not ventilate the patient at 10–20 breaths per minute

___ Did not allow for complete exhalation

Station 5G

Oxygen Administration

Instructions to the Candidate

This is an isolated skills test. This station tests your ability to assemble the equipment needed to administer supplemental oxygen in the prehospital setting. The examiner will ask you to assemble an oxygen tank and a regulator. You will administer the oxygen to the patient using a nonrebreather mask. When the examiner informs you that the patient cannot tolerate the mask, you must switch to a nasal cannula. After you initiate oxygen administration using the nasal cannula, the examiner will instruct you to discontinue oxygen administration completely and shut off all equipment. You may only use the equipment available in this room. You have 5 minutes to complete this skill station. Do you have any questions?

NOTES

OXYGEN ADMINISTRATION

	Points Possible	Points Awarded
Takes or verbalizes body substance isolation precautions	1	
Assembles regulator to tank	1	
Opens tank	1	
Checks for leaks	1	
Checks tank pressure	1	
Attaches non-rebreather mask	1	
Prefills reservoir	1	
Adjusts liter flow to 12 liters/minute or greater	1	
Applies and adjusts mask to the patient's face	1	
NOTE: The examiner must advise the candidate that the patient is not tolerating the non-rebreather mask. Medical direction has ordered you to apply a nasal cannula to the patient.		
Attaches nasal cannula to oxygen	1	
Adjusts liter flow up to 6 liters/minute or less	1	
Applies nasal cannula to the patient	1	
NOTE: The examiner must advise the candidate to discontinue oxygen therapy.		
Removes the nasal cannula	1	
Shuts off the regulator	1	
Relieves the pressure within the regulator	1	
TOTAL:	15	

CRITICAL CRITERIA

____ Did not take or verbalize body substance isolation precautions
____ Did not assemble the tank and regulator without leaks
____ Did not prefill the reservoir bag
____ Did not adjust the device to the correct liter flow for the non-rebreather mask
     (12 L/min. or greater)
____ Did not adjust the device to the correct liter flow for the nasal cannula (up to 6 L/min.)

SUMMING IT UP

- You must successfully complete a practical skills examination to receive your EMT–Basic certification.

- Due to classroom time restraints, students should practice practical skills as much as possible outside the classroom.

- Skill performance sheets chart a student's proficiency in each skill area.

PART IV

PRACTICE TEST

Practice Test 2

ANSWER SHEET PRACTICE TEST 2

1. Ⓐ Ⓑ Ⓒ Ⓓ	21. Ⓐ Ⓑ Ⓒ Ⓓ	41. Ⓐ Ⓑ Ⓒ Ⓓ	61. Ⓐ Ⓑ Ⓒ Ⓓ	81. Ⓐ Ⓑ Ⓒ Ⓓ
2. Ⓐ Ⓑ Ⓒ Ⓓ	22. Ⓐ Ⓑ Ⓒ Ⓓ	42. Ⓐ Ⓑ Ⓒ Ⓓ	62. Ⓐ Ⓑ Ⓒ Ⓓ	82. Ⓐ Ⓑ Ⓒ Ⓓ
3. Ⓐ Ⓑ Ⓒ Ⓓ	23. Ⓐ Ⓑ Ⓒ Ⓓ	43. Ⓐ Ⓑ Ⓒ Ⓓ	63. Ⓐ Ⓑ Ⓒ Ⓓ	83. Ⓐ Ⓑ Ⓒ Ⓓ
4. Ⓐ Ⓑ Ⓒ Ⓓ	24. Ⓐ Ⓑ Ⓒ Ⓓ	44. Ⓐ Ⓑ Ⓒ Ⓓ	64. Ⓐ Ⓑ Ⓒ Ⓓ	84. Ⓐ Ⓑ Ⓒ Ⓓ
5. Ⓐ Ⓑ Ⓒ Ⓓ	25. Ⓐ Ⓑ Ⓒ Ⓓ	45. Ⓐ Ⓑ Ⓒ Ⓓ	65. Ⓐ Ⓑ Ⓒ Ⓓ	85. Ⓐ Ⓑ Ⓒ Ⓓ
6. Ⓐ Ⓑ Ⓒ Ⓓ	26. Ⓐ Ⓑ Ⓒ Ⓓ	46. Ⓐ Ⓑ Ⓒ Ⓓ	66. Ⓐ Ⓑ Ⓒ Ⓓ	86. Ⓐ Ⓑ Ⓒ Ⓓ
7. Ⓐ Ⓑ Ⓒ Ⓓ	27. Ⓐ Ⓑ Ⓒ Ⓓ	47. Ⓐ Ⓑ Ⓒ Ⓓ	67. Ⓐ Ⓑ Ⓒ Ⓓ	87. Ⓐ Ⓑ Ⓒ Ⓓ
8. Ⓐ Ⓑ Ⓒ Ⓓ	28. Ⓐ Ⓑ Ⓒ Ⓓ	48. Ⓐ Ⓑ Ⓒ Ⓓ	68. Ⓐ Ⓑ Ⓒ Ⓓ	88. Ⓐ Ⓑ Ⓒ Ⓓ
9. Ⓐ Ⓑ Ⓒ Ⓓ	29. Ⓐ Ⓑ Ⓒ Ⓓ	49. Ⓐ Ⓑ Ⓒ Ⓓ	69. Ⓐ Ⓑ Ⓒ Ⓓ	89. Ⓐ Ⓑ Ⓒ Ⓓ
10. Ⓐ Ⓑ Ⓒ Ⓓ	30. Ⓐ Ⓑ Ⓒ Ⓓ	50. Ⓐ Ⓑ Ⓒ Ⓓ	70. Ⓐ Ⓑ Ⓒ Ⓓ	90. Ⓐ Ⓑ Ⓒ Ⓓ
11. Ⓐ Ⓑ Ⓒ Ⓓ	31. Ⓐ Ⓑ Ⓒ Ⓓ	51. Ⓐ Ⓑ Ⓒ Ⓓ	71. Ⓐ Ⓑ Ⓒ Ⓓ	91. Ⓐ Ⓑ Ⓒ Ⓓ
12. Ⓐ Ⓑ Ⓒ Ⓓ	32. Ⓐ Ⓑ Ⓒ Ⓓ	52. Ⓐ Ⓑ Ⓒ Ⓓ	72. Ⓐ Ⓑ Ⓒ Ⓓ	92. Ⓐ Ⓑ Ⓒ Ⓓ
13. Ⓐ Ⓑ Ⓒ Ⓓ	33. Ⓐ Ⓑ Ⓒ Ⓓ	53. Ⓐ Ⓑ Ⓒ Ⓓ	73. Ⓐ Ⓑ Ⓒ Ⓓ	93. Ⓐ Ⓑ Ⓒ Ⓓ
14. Ⓐ Ⓑ Ⓒ Ⓓ	34. Ⓐ Ⓑ Ⓒ Ⓓ	54. Ⓐ Ⓑ Ⓒ Ⓓ	74. Ⓐ Ⓑ Ⓒ Ⓓ	94. Ⓐ Ⓑ Ⓒ Ⓓ
15. Ⓐ Ⓑ Ⓒ Ⓓ	35. Ⓐ Ⓑ Ⓒ Ⓓ	55. Ⓐ Ⓑ Ⓒ Ⓓ	75. Ⓐ Ⓑ Ⓒ Ⓓ	95. Ⓐ Ⓑ Ⓒ Ⓓ
16. Ⓐ Ⓑ Ⓒ Ⓓ	36. Ⓐ Ⓑ Ⓒ Ⓓ	56. Ⓐ Ⓑ Ⓒ Ⓓ	76. Ⓐ Ⓑ Ⓒ Ⓓ	96. Ⓐ Ⓑ Ⓒ Ⓓ
17. Ⓐ Ⓑ Ⓒ Ⓓ	37. Ⓐ Ⓑ Ⓒ Ⓓ	57. Ⓐ Ⓑ Ⓒ Ⓓ	77. Ⓐ Ⓑ Ⓒ Ⓓ	97. Ⓐ Ⓑ Ⓒ Ⓓ
18. Ⓐ Ⓑ Ⓒ Ⓓ	38. Ⓐ Ⓑ Ⓒ Ⓓ	58. Ⓐ Ⓑ Ⓒ Ⓓ	78. Ⓐ Ⓑ Ⓒ Ⓓ	98. Ⓐ Ⓑ Ⓒ Ⓓ
19. Ⓐ Ⓑ Ⓒ Ⓓ	39. Ⓐ Ⓑ Ⓒ Ⓓ	59. Ⓐ Ⓑ Ⓒ Ⓓ	79. Ⓐ Ⓑ Ⓒ Ⓓ	99. Ⓐ Ⓑ Ⓒ Ⓓ
20. Ⓐ Ⓑ Ⓒ Ⓓ	40. Ⓐ Ⓑ Ⓒ Ⓓ	60. Ⓐ Ⓑ Ⓒ Ⓓ	80. Ⓐ Ⓑ Ⓒ Ⓓ	100. Ⓐ Ⓑ Ⓒ Ⓓ

answer sheet

Practice Test 2

Directions: Each question has a maximum of four possible answers. Choose the letter that best answers the question and mark your choice on the answer sheet.

1. Cyanosis, blue-gray skin, is usually a sign of
   (A) carbon monoxide poisoning.
   (B) hyperthermia.
   (C) liver failure.
   (D) lack of oxygen in the blood.

2. When clamping a newborn's umbilical cord during delivery, place the first clamp six inches from the newborn's abdomen. Then place the second clamp _____ inches from the first clamp.
   (A) ten
   (B) six
   (C) three
   (D) one

3. All of the following are part of the lower-respiratory system EXCEPT the
   (A) alveoli.
   (B) lung.
   (C) bronchioles.
   (D) esophagus.

4. Which of the following is NOT a sign of an upper-airway obstruction?
   (A) Tightening of the chest
   (B) Gasping for air
   (C) Choking
   (D) Wheezing

5. The normal respiratory rate for a three-year-old child is about _____ breaths per minute.
   (A) twelve to twenty
   (B) fifteen to thirty
   (C) twenty-five to fifty
   (D) forty to sixty

6. Which of the following patients should be treated with activated charcoal?
   (A) A thirty-two-year-old who accidentally overdosed on blood pressure medication 3 hours ago
   (B) A three-year-old who had an allergic reaction to cold medication 2 hours ago
   (C) A fifty-six-year-old who ingested carbon monoxide 1 hour ago
   (D) A ten-year-old who accidentally drank antifreeze 5 hours ago

7. The carotid artery carries blood from the heart to the
   (A) legs.
   (B) lungs.
   (C) head.
   (D) arms.

8. A harsh, high-pitched sound heard when breathing usually indicates
   (A) fluid in the airways.
   (B) an upper-airway obstruction.
   (C) an inflammation of the pleura.
   (D) a narrowing of the lower airways.

9. You are called to the scene of a restaurant where a patient is choking from an apparent upper-airway obstruction. You use the Heimlich maneuver (subdiaphragmatic abdominal thrusts), but the patient loses consciousness. You should

(A) perform a jaw thrust.

(B) use a succession of blind finger sweeps.

(C) begin cardiopulmonary resuscitation.

(D) continue abdominal thrusts in rapid succession.

10. Patients take nitroglycerin during a heart attack to

(A) strengthen blood vessels.

(B) dilate blood vessels.

(C) increase heart rate.

(D) constrict blood vessels.

11. After auscultating a patient's lungs, you find that the patient has normal breath sounds. This means that the patient has normal bronchial and _____ sounds.

(A) strider

(B) tracheal

(C) vesicular

(D) pleural

12. To stop the tongue from obstructing an unconscious elderly patient's airways, you should use an oropharyngeal airway (OPA). Before you insert this adjunct, you should

(A) turn it upside down.

(B) lubricate the tip.

(C) use a tongue depressor.

(D) elicit the gag reflex.

13. When treating patients at a crime scene, you must take extra care to avoid

(A) upsetting law enforcement.

(B) destroying evidence.

(C) talking to the media.

(D) missing important details.

14. You are called to the scene of an automobile accident. On your arrival, you see that the police are not yet there, and a car has hit a tree. The driver of the car is outside of the vehicle. He is bleeding and appears to have a head injury. He is shouting and kicking the car. He appears to be intoxicated. At least one passenger in the car appears to be unconscious. The windshield is broken, and glass is scattered around the vehicle. What should you do?

(A) Try to get around the driver to help the passenger in the car

(B) Work with another responder to use force to subdue to driver

(C) Talk to the driver slowly and softly, and get him away from the car

(D) Stay by the ambulance, and wait for law enforcement to arrive

15. When you describe a patient's level of consciousness using the AVPU scale, the letter A represents whether the

(A) patient's eyes are open and whether the patient speaks.

(B) patient is unconscious to any stimulant.

(C) patient responds to your voice.

(D) patient opens eyes or moves to painful stimulation.

16. All of the following are signs of respiratory distress in an adult EXCEPT

(A) pulmonary edema.

(B) tachypnea.

(C) stiff lungs.

(D) seesaw breathing.

17. The diaphragm expands when the body senses a buildup of

(A) CO_2.

(B) O_2.

(C) N_2.

(D) H_2.

18. You would assess the mechanism of injury (MOI) for which of the following patients?

    (A) An elderly man having a heart attack

    (B) An elderly woman who has fallen

    (C) A family suffering from carbon monoxide poisoning

    (D) A young woman with a severe stomach flu

19. The detailed physical exam should include assessing the neck for

    (A) large distended veins.

    (B) firmness or softness.

    (C) paradoxical motion.

    (D) bony crepitus.

20. You respond to a fifty-six-year-old male who is not breathing and does not have a pulse. When you perform CPR, at what depth should your compressions be?

    (A) One-half to one inch

    (B) One to one-and-a-half inches

    (C) One-and-a-half to two inches

    (D) Two to three inches

21. When treating trauma patients with serious injuries, you will most likely discover the most life-threatening injuries during the

    (A) detailed physical exam.

    (B) focused history.

    (C) initial assessment.

    (D) ongoing assessment.

22. You are called to the scene of a crash on an interstate involving multiple vehicles. What is the first question you should ask yourself when you arrive at the scene?

    (A) How many patients are there?

    (B) Are there any witnesses?

    (C) How severe are patients' injuries?

    (D) What caused the crash?

23. When examining a patient who is in pain, which of the following questions should you ask the patient?

    (A) Does the pain radiate?

    (B) How severe is the pain?

    (C) Is the pain sharp, dull, crushing, or burning?

    (D) All of the above

24. An adult's heart beats about _____ beats per minute.

    (A) 40

    (B) 70

    (C) 120

    (D) 160

25. You respond to an eighteen-year-old boy who is in his backyard and has been bitten by a snake on his left leg. His mother's description of the snake matches that of a rattlesnake. You try to keep the boy calm, administer oxygen, and immobilize his injured leg. It is also important that you

    (A) apply ice to the wound.

    (B) keep the leg lower than the heart.

    (C) cut the wound and drain the poison.

    (D) stop the blood flow from the affected area.

26. Which part of the heart receives oxygenated blood from the lungs?

    (A) Left atrium

    (B) Right atrium

    (C) Left ventricle

    (D) Right ventricle

27. Which pulse should you assess first in a young woman who is alert and responsive?

    (A) Femoral

    (B) Brachial

    (C) Radial

    (D) Carotid

28. You are assisting a patient's ventilation with a bag-valve-mask. Which is a sign that the patient's breathing has improved?

(A) A reduced tidal volume

(B) Coughing up sputum

(C) Obvious chest rise and fall

(D) A drop in oxygenation

29. You are called to the scene of an apartment in a high-rise building. An infant is making a high-pitched crowing sound. An anxious young mother answers the door. You see several other young children inside. You should immediately suspect that the infant has

(A) suffered trauma to the head or neck.

(B) a severe ear infection.

(C) a partial-airway obstruction.

(D) been exposed to poisonous chemicals.

30. A patient whose ventricles are beating too fast to sufficiently pump blood is suffering from

(A) angina pectoris.

(B) ventricular fibrillation.

(C) asystole.

(D) ventricular tachycardia.

31. All of the following may indicate that a patient is suffering a heart attack EXCEPT

(A) radiating pain.

(B) pale skin.

(C) nausea or vomiting.

(D) vision problems.

32. In a _____ fracture, the bone is broken into two pieces that pierce the skin.

(A) complete

(B) simple

(C) compound

(D) comminuted

33. If you arrive at a scene and determine that a patient is not a priority patient, what should you do next?

(A) Perform a focused exam en route.

(B) Do a focused history and physical exam.

(C) Carefully assess the scene.

(D) Give the patient high-flow oxygen.

34. When taking a patient's SAMPLE history, what action should you take for the letter M?

(A) Determine the patient's medical history.

(B) Inquire as to what medications the patient takes.

(C) Determine if the patient can move his or her arms and legs.

(D) Give the patient relevant medical advice.

35. You are called to the scene of a forty-three-year-old woman. Her blood pressure is 125/70, her pulse is 75, and her respirations are 42. The woman's symptoms are referred to as

(A) bradypnea.

(B) tachypnea.

(C) dyspnea.

(D) tachycardia.

36. When placing automated external defibrillation (AED) pads on a patient's chest, one pad should be placed on the upper-right quadrant of the patient's chest. The other pad should be placed on the patient's chest in the _____ quadrant.

(A) upper-right

(B) upper-left

(C) lower-left

(D) lower-right

37. When you are splinting a fracture, you should do all of the following EXCEPT
    (A) cover wounds with dry, sterile dressing.
    (B) remove clothes around injury to inspect it.
    (C) move the patient before splinting the fracture.
    (D) record distal neurovascular function before and after splinting.

38. When a patient is dead on scene, you should do all of the following EXCEPT
    (A) document the absence of vital signs.
    (B) contact the coroner.
    (C) move the body near the ambulance.
    (D) contact law enforcement.

39. Bones are held together by tough fibers called
    (A) cartilage.
    (B) tissue.
    (C) nerves.
    (D) ligaments.

40. You are called to the scene of a sixty-two-year-old male who is suffering severe chest pain after shoveling snow. His wife explains that he has had a heart attack once before and hands you his nitroglycerin. The patient is alert but breathing heavily. He is sweating. He tells you the pain began 20 minutes ago and has not stopped. His blood pressure is 164/96, and his pulse is 104. What should you do before transporting him to the hospital?
    (A) Assist him with his nitroglycerin.
    (B) Perform CPR.
    (C) Deliver defibrillations.
    (D) Treat him for shock.

41. The bones in the cranium are held together by zigzagged joints called
    (A) sutures.
    (B) parietal bones.
    (C) fontanels.
    (D) zygomatic bones.

42. The _____ artery is in the thigh. You can palpate pulsations from this artery in the groin area.
    (A) carotid
    (B) radial
    (C) femoral
    (D) brachial

43. When a patient suffers cardiac arrest, an EMT should begin CPR as soon as possible to oxygenate the blood. CPR is a combination of chest compressions and artificial
    (A) oxidation.
    (B) ventilation.
    (C) diffusion.
    (D) circulation.

44. Which of the following is a physiological manifestation of stress?
    (A) A decrease in respiration and pulse
    (B) Constricted pupils
    (C) A decrease in blood pressure
    (D) Cool, clammy skin

45. If an EMT causes a patient to fear immediate bodily harm, the EMT is guilty of
    (A) negligence.
    (B) libel.
    (C) slander.
    (D) assault.

46. The center of the brain responsible for conscious perception and response is the
    (A) cerebrum.
    (B) cerebellum.
    (C) brain stem.
    (D) temporal lobe.

47. Which of the following is NOT a good way for an EMT–Basic to reduce stress?

(A) Get plenty of sleep.

(B) Drink coffee.

(C) Talk to friends.

(D) Go for a walk.

48. You are called to the scene of a house in a middle-class neighborhood. A fifty-two year-old is semiconscious. His wife says that he has been cutting grass in the sun. The temperature is more than 80 degrees. Upon assessment, you note that his skin is hot and dry. His skin is flushed but not sweaty. You suspect that he has suffered

(A) a stroke.

(B) heatstroke.

(C) cardiac arrest.

(D) dehydration.

49. All of the following are symptoms of a cerebral contusion EXCEPT

(A) tearing of the brain tissue.

(B) loss of consciousness.

(C) vomiting.

(D) unequal pupils.

50. In the AVPU system, the V stands for

(A) able to vocalize sounds.

(B) vertigo.

(C) responds to verbal stimulation.

(D) voice.

51. When splinting a fracture, you should splint the

(A) joint above and below the fracture.

(B) bone above and below the joint.

(C) joint above the fracture only.

(D) bone above the joint only.

52. Brain damage after cardiac arrest becomes irreversible in _____ minutes.

(A) 4 to 6

(B) 8 to 10

(C) 12 to 16

(D) 20

53. Patient information may be released to all of the following EXCEPT

(A) a patient's employer.

(B) a billing company.

(C) law enforcement officers.

(D) those ensuring continued care.

54. Express consent is NOT required if the patient is

(A) over eighteen.

(B) mentally competent.

(C) aware of the risks.

(D) unresponsive.

55. When assessing a patient's pupils using the PEARL acronym, E stands for

(A) even.

(B) enlarged.

(C) equal.

(D) elevated.

56. While assisting during childbirth, you see that the umbilical cord is wrapped around the newborn's neck. The first thing you should do is

(A) clamp and cut the cord.

(B) gently tug on the cord until you can move it.

(C) keep the cord moist.

(D) gently slide the cord from around the neck.

57. When treating a patient suffering a seizure, your primary concern is

(A) ensuring that the patient receives proper ventilation.

(B) suctioning secretions from the patient's mouth.

(C) restraining the patient.

(D) prying open the patient's mouth.

58. The part of the brain responsible for automatic functions below the level of consciousness, such as heart rate and blood pressure, is the

(A) brain stem.

(B) spinal cord.

(C) cerebrum.

(D) cerebellum.

59. When treating a patient with a sucking chest wound, called open pneumothorax, you should apply an occlusive dressing to the wound mainly to

(A) reduce tension.

(B) stop the bleeding.

(C) keep air out of the wound.

(D) apply pressure to the wound.

60. All of the following are bones in the lower extremity EXCEPT

(A) fibula.

(B) tarsals.

(C) tibia.

(D) ulna.

61. The amount of blood pumped by the heart in one beat is called

(A) stroke volume.

(B) cardiac output.

(C) blood pressure.

(D) diastolic pressure.

62. You are called to the scene of a nineteen-year-old girl who has overdosed on Vicodin, a narcotic. Until paramedics arrive, your main objective should be to keep the patient

(A) calm.

(B) breathing.

(C) awake.

(D) warm.

63. Which of the following is a sign of imminent delivery?

(A) Blood or mucous show

(B) Gush of amniotic fluid

(C) Dilation of the rectal sphincter

(D) Menstrual-like cramps

64. All of the following are signs of insulin shock EXCEPT

(A) loss of coordination.

(B) numbness in hands and feet.

(C) chest pain.

(D) very pale skin.

65. Which of the following will give a patient the greatest concentration of oxygen?

(A) Nonbreather facemask

(B) Resuscitation mask

(C) Rescue breathing

(D) Nasal cannula

66. A patient has an altered mental status, slow, shallow breathing, and constricted pupils. You suspect that the patient may have overdosed on

(A) narcotics.

(B) marijuana.

(C) barbiturates.

(D) amphetamines.

67. When treating a patient suffering from a migraine, you should do all of the following EXCEPT

(A) administer oxygen.

(B) monitor vital signs often.

(C) shine a light in the eyes.

(D) assist the patient in lying supine.

68. You are called to respond to a patient with shortness of breath. The patient displays symptoms of an airway obstruction but has suffered trauma to the head and neck. To open his airways, you should use
    (A) the jaw-pull maneuver.
    (B) the head-tilt chin-lift maneuver.
    (C) a soft-tip catheter.
    (D) the jaw-thrust maneuver.

69. When assisting with childbirth, what should you do as the head delivers?
    (A) Keep gentle pressure on the head
    (B) Suction the mouth and nose
    (C) Feel for the cord behind the top ear
    (D) Gently lift the head

70. According to the Glasgow Coma Scale, a patient who is confused receives a Verbal Response grade of
    (A) 5.
    (B) 4.
    (C) 3.
    (D) 1.

71. When managing a head injury in a responsive patient, you should do which of the following?
    (A) Control hyperventilation
    (B) Apply pressure to the fracture
    (C) Stop the flow of blood from the nose
    (D) Remove penetrating objects

72. The spinal column has _____ thoracic vertebrae.
    (A) twelve
    (B) seven
    (C) five
    (D) four

73. The part of the brain responsible for receiving sensations from the surface of the body is the _____ lobe.
    (A) frontal
    (B) occipital
    (C) temporal
    (D) parietal

74. How many breaths per minute should you administer when performing rescue breathing on a child?
    (A) Ten
    (B) Twenty
    (C) Thirty
    (D) Forty

75. Which of the following causes rhonchi, sounds in the chest that resemble snoring?
    (A) A popping open of small airways
    (B) A blockage of large airways
    (C) A blockage of airflow
    (D) A narrowing of airways

76. You are called to the scene of a thirty-five-year-old patient who is eight months pregnant. She has suddenly gained weight, and her hands and feet are swollen. She has a headache and says her vision has become blurry. She is most likely suffering from
    (A) supine hypotensive syndrome.
    (B) preeclampsia.
    (C) abruptio placenta.
    (D) miscarriage.

77. You need to lift a patient from a supine position onto a stretcher. What type of stretcher should you use?
    (A) Scoop
    (B) Flexible
    (C) Basket
    (D) Portable

78. All of the following are risk factors for suicide EXCEPT

(A) previous self-destructive behavior.

(B) the recent loss of a loved one.

(C) the recent start of new job.

(D) the recent diagnosis of a serious illness.

79. During pregnancy, the exchange of nutrients and wastes takes place in the

(A) cervix.

(B) placenta.

(C) amniotic sac.

(D) uterus.

80. If a patient is lying on his back with a 45-degree bend at the hips, he is in which of the following positions?

(A) Fowler's position

(B) Trendelenburg's position

(C) Supine position

(D) Shock position

81. All mental and physical activities are part of a patient's

(A) outlook.

(B) comprehension.

(C) behavior.

(D) perception.

82. All of the following are signs of potential patient violence EXCEPT

(A) anxiously sitting on the edge of a seat.

(B) threatening to take one's own life.

(C) clenching fists.

(D) shouting obscenities.

83. You are called to the scene of a teenage girl who is agitated and anxious. She is moving quickly and speaking so fast that you have trouble deciphering her words. You suspect that she may be

(A) manic.

(B) paranoid.

(C) psychotic.

(D) depressed.

84. Meconium is foul-smelling fecal matter excreted by an infant. If meconium is present during delivery, it is a sign of

(A) imminent labor.

(B) a breech birth.

(C) a precipitative delivery.

(D) severe fetal distress.

85. When using a suction device to clear foreign objects from a patient's airways, you should do all of the following EXCEPT

(A) suction farther than you can see.

(B) insert the catheter before suctioning.

(C) use the least possible pressure.

(D) suction only the mouth and oropharnyx.

86. You are called to the scene of a patient who says she has a knife inside her jacket. The patient tells you that she is thinking of stabbing herself with the knife. You should

(A) avoid treating her unless you know for sure she is unarmed.

(B) suspect that she is trying to get attention and proceed as usual.

(C) ask her to show you the knife to determine if she is serious.

(D) calmly ask her to explain why she wants to hurt herself.

87. A terminally ill patient is quiet and seems to have retreated into her own world. She does not want to get out of bed and does not seem to hear your questions. She is likely in which of the following emotional stages of death?

    (A) Bargaining

    (B) Acceptance

    (C) Depression

    (D) Denial

88. The responsibility of a safe rescue operation begins with

    (A) law enforcement.

    (B) your commander.

    (C) public participation.

    (D) you, the EMT.

89. When assisting in childbirth, you should take the following body substance isolation precautions:

    (A) a mask, a gown, gloves, and eye protection.

    (B) a mask, a gown, gloves, and footwear.

    (C) a mask and gloves only.

    (D) a mask and eye protection only.

90. You are called to a scene and discover a twenty-five-year-old male on the floor on his side with his knees drawn to his chest. From his positioning, you suspect that he is suffering from

    (A) respiratory distress.

    (B) cardiac arrest.

    (C) severe abdominal pain.

    (D) severe back pain.

91. An EMT ambulance may carry all of the following medications EXCEPT

    (A) oral glucose.

    (B) nitroglycerin.

    (C) oxygen.

    (D) activated charcoal.

92. If a patient is suffering respiratory distress, the EMT may assist the patient in taking which of the following medications?

    (A) Epinephrine

    (B) Decadron

    (C) Albuterol

    (D) Digoxin

93. When you receive an order from medical direction, you should

    (A) ask to hear the order again.

    (B) repeat the order.

    (C) write down the order.

    (D) tell your partner the order.

94. All of the following are signs of an ingested toxin overdose EXCEPT

    (A) abdominal pain.

    (B) unequal pupils.

    (C) vomiting.

    (D) altered mental status.

95. Which of the following is part of the upper-respiratory system?

    (A) Bronchioles

    (B) Trachea

    (C) Bronchi

    (D) Alveoli

96. Diastolic blood pressure measures the pressure in blood vessels when the heart

    (A) beats.

    (B) expands.

    (C) contracts.

    (D) rests.

97. You are called to the scene of a sixty-two-year-old woman who has been scalded. Upon assessment, you conclude that the epidermis and part of the dermis on both arms have been burned. This type of burn is a _____ burn.

    (A) first-degree
    (B) partial-thickness
    (C) fourth-degree
    (D) full-thickness

98. Most of the heat in the body is lost through

    (A) evaporation.
    (B) radiation.
    (C) condensation.
    (D) convection.

99. What is the best way to remove a bee stinger?

    (A) Scrape it with a credit card.
    (B) Make an incision and remove it.
    (C) Soak it in warm water.
    (D) Remove it with tweezers.

100. A patient with an Eye Opening grade of 3 on the Glasgow Coma Scale has

    (A) no eye opening.
    (B) eyes open to pain.
    (C) eyes open to speech.
    (D) spontaneous eye opening.

ANSWER KEY AND AND EXPLANATIONS

1. D	21. C	41. A	61. A	81. C
2. C	22. A	42. C	62. B	82. B
3. D	23. D	43. B	63. C	83. A
4. A	24. B	44. D	64. C	84. D
5. B	25. B	45. D	65. A	85. A
6. A	26. A	46. A	66. A	86. A
7. C	27. C	47. B	67. C	87. C
8. B	28. C	48. B	68. D	88. D
9. C	29. C	49. A	69. A	89. A
10. B	30. D	50. C	70. B	90. C
11. C	31. D	51. A	71. A	91. B
12. A	32. C	52. B	72. A	92. C
13. B	33. B	53. A	73. D	93. B
14. D	34. B	54. D	74. B	94. B
15. A	35. B	55. C	75. B	95. B
16. D	36. C	56. D	76. B	96. D
17. A	37. C	57. A	77. A	97. B
18. B	38. C	58. A	78. C	98. B
19. A	39. D	59. C	79. B	99. A
20. C	40. A	60. D	80. A	100. C

1. **The correct answer is (D).** Cyanosis indicates a lack of oxygen in the blood. Reddish skin is a sign of hyperthermia or a late stage of carbon monoxide poisoning. Yellow skin (jaundice) is a sign of liver failure.

2. **The correct answer is (C).** The second clamp should be three inches from the first clamp. You should then cut between the two clamps. Neither end of the umbilical cord should be bleeding.

3. **The correct answer is (D).** The alveoli, carina, bronchi, lung, and bronchioles make up the lower-respiratory system or the lower airway. The esophagus is part of the upper respiratory system.

4. **The correct answer is (A).** Signs of an upper-airway obstruction include agitation, cyanosis, changes in consciousness, choking, wheezing, difficulty breathing, and confusion. A tightening of the chest might be a sign of another illness, such as chronic obstructive pulmonary disease (COPD).

5. **The correct answer is (B).** The normal respiratory rate for a child is about fifteen to

thirty breaths per minute. Choice (A) gives the normal respiratory rate for an adult. Choice (C) is the normal respiratory rate for an infant, and choice (D) is the normal respiratory rate for a newborn.

6. **The correct answer is (A).** Activated charcoal is used to treat ingested poisonings. The drug may have been ingested up to 4 hours prior to the administration of activated charcoal.

7. **The correct answer is (C).** Two carotid arteries, one on each side of the neck, carry blood to the head and neck. A blockage in a carotid artery will cause a patient to suffer a serious stroke.

8. **The correct answer is (B).** A harsh high-pitched sound heard when breathing is called a stridor, and it usually indicates an upper-airway obstruction. Fluid in the airways might be indicated by cracking noises or a gurgling sound. A sound like dried pieces of leather rubbing together indicates an inflammation of the pleura, and wheezing indicates a narrowing of the lower airways.

9. **The correct answer is (C).** If a patient loses consciousness, he or she is more likely to benefit from CPR (cardiopulmonary resuscitation) than the Heimlich maneuver, which is referenced in choice (D). Blind finger sweeps are not recommended because they might harm the patient and/or the rescuer. A jaw thrust would not be the first line of therapy.

10. **The correct answer is (B).** Nitroglycerin dilates blood vessels, which release pressure on the heart by allowing it to receive more oxygen.

11. **The correct answer is (C).** The two normal breath sounds are bronchial and vesicular. Bronchial sounds are heard over the tracheo-bronchial tree. Vesicular sounds are heard over lung tissue.

12. **The correct answer is (A).** Before you insert the oropharyngeal airway, you should invert it so that the scoop is upward toward the nose. There is no need to lubricate it. You might use a tongue depressor instead of an oropharyngeal airway if you are treating an infant. An unconscious patient doesn't have a gag reflex. If the patient did have a gag reflex, you would not use an oropharyngeal airway but would instead use a nasopharyngeal airway (NPA).

13. **The correct answer is (B).** When treating patients at a crime scene, you should only move or touch objects when necessary for patient care. You should be careful where you step and inform law enforcement if you have accidentally moved something.

14. **The correct answer is (D).** When you assess the scene, you should conclude that it is not safe. The driver may be violent. The glass presents another danger. You should wait for law enforcement to arrive before approaching the vehicle and helping the driver and passenger or passengers.

15. **The correct answer is (A).** When you assess a patient's mental status using the AVPU scale, A stands for alert: whether the patient's eyes are open and whether the patient speaks to you. V stands for verbal: whether the patient opens eyes and responds to your voice and speaks. P stands for pain: whether the patient opens his or her eyes or moves to painful stimulation. U stands for unconscious to any stimulus.

16. **The correct answer is (D).** Seesaw breathing is a movement of the chest and stomach in opposite directions. It is a symptom of a respiratory problem suffered by infants. Other signs of respiratory distress in adults include wheezing, pale or gray skin with a bluish color around the mouth, increased breathing rate, and sweating.

answers practice test 2

17. **The correct answer is (A).** When the body senses a buildup of carbon dioxide (CO_2), the brain sends a message to the respiratory muscles and the diaphragm expands. Then air flows into the airways.

18. **The correct answer is (B).** You would assess the mechanism of injury (MOI) for patients who have suffered trauma. For the patients in the other answer choices, you would most likely assess the nature of illness (NOI).

19. **The correct answer is (A).** The jugular vein on either side of the neck should not be distended when the patient is supine. You would inspect the chest for paradoxical motion and bony crepitus.

20. **The correct answer is (C).** Your compressions should have a depth of one-and-a-half to two inches for an adult. If you were administering CPR compressions on a child, your compressions should be one-third to one-half the depth of the child's chest.

21. **The correct answer is (C).** You will usually discover serious injuries during the initial assessment. Injuries that are a threat to a patient's life should be treated as soon as they are discovered.

22. **The correct answer is (A).** Before you can begin to help patients, you need to know how many there are. If you don't, you run the risk of inadvertently avoiding a patient who may be seriously injured.

23. **The correct answer is (D).** You should ask a patient in pain all of these questions. You should also inquire when the pain began and what seems to make it worse.

24. **The correct answer is (B).** An adult's heart beats about 60 to 100 beats per minutes. A newborn's heart beats 100 to 160 beats per minute. The heart of a child under ten beats about 70 to 120 beats per minute.

25. **The correct answer is (B).** It is important to keep the leg lower than the heart. You should not apply ice to the wound. Doing so could cause blood vessels to constrict, which would cause the poison to go deeper into circulation. Cutting the wound could cause an infection, and you should never stop the blood flow from the affected area.

26. **The correct answer is (A).** The left atrium receives oxygenated blood from the lungs. The right atrium receives deoxygenated blood from the body. The right ventricle sends deoxygenated blood to the lungs, and the left ventricle sends oxygenated blood to the body.

27. **The correct answer is (C).** You would first assess the young woman's radial pulse at the groove in the wrist beneath the thumb. You would assess the brachial pulse in an infant and the carotid pulse in a patient who is unconscious.

28. **The correct answer is (C).** A patient who is breathing well will have an obvious chest rise and fall. Coughing up sputum and a reduced tidal volume do not indicate that a patient is breathing well. A drop in oxygenation is a sign that a patient is having difficulty breathing.

29. **The correct answer is (C).** Crowing is an upper-airway sound indicating a partial-airway obstruction. Treatment should include rapid transport, the administration of oxygen, and positioning if the patient is breathing adequately. If the patient stops breathing adequately or becomes unresponsive, the EMT should begin the airway obstruction/CPR algorithm.

30. **The correct answer is (D).** Angina pectoris is chest pain that subsides in less than 15 minutes. Ventricular fibrillation is a condition in which the ventricles are quivering. Patients suffering asystole have no electrical activity in their heart.

31. **The correct answer is (D).** A patient who suddenly has trouble seeing in one or both eyes may be suffering a stroke. Other signs of a heart attack include a feeling of heaviness in the chest, dyspnea, anxiety, an abnormal pulse or blood pressure reading, and stomach pain.

32. **The correct answer is (C).** In a complete fracture, the bone is broken into two pieces that move out of line, but don't pierce the skin. In a simple fracture, the bone is broken into two pieces that remain in line and don't pierce the skin. In a comminuted fracture, the bone is shattered into many small pieces.

33. **The correct answer is (B).** If you determine that a patient is not a priority patient, meaning you did not find a problem with the patient during your initial assessment, you should do a focused history and physical exam. If the patient is a priority patient, you would do this en route to the hospital. You should carefully assess the scene before you examine the patient, and you would give a patient high-flow oxygen after inserting an adjunct if he or she had a blocked airway.

34. **The correct answer is (B).** When taking a patient's SAMPLE history, S stands for signs and symptoms; A stands for allergies; M stands for medications; P represents past medical history; L is last oral intake; and E represents the events taking place when the patient's problem occurred.

35. **The correct answer is (B).** She is breathing abnormally fast, a condition called tachypnea. An adult usually takes about 12 to 24 breaths per minute. Bradypnea is slow breathing, dyspnea is a shortness of breath, and tachycardia is a fast heart rate.

36. **The correct answer is (C).** The second pad should be placed in the lower-left quadrant of the patient's chest.

37. **The correct answer is (C).** You should not move the patient before splinting unless the patient is in danger.

38. **The correct answer is (C).** If you discover a patient dead on scene, you should not disturb or move the body.

39. **The correct answer is (D).** Bones are held together by tough fibers called ligaments. Bones form from cartilage, a rubbery material. Bones are made from tissue. Nerves send information to the brain.

40. **The correct answer is (A).** You can assist the patient with his nitroglycerin by helping him place the tablet under his tongue. However, make sure you follow the "5 rights": right patient, right route, right medication, right dosage, and right time. You can also place the patient on oxygen.

41. **The correct answer is (A).** The bones in the cranium are held together by sutures. The parietal bone is one of the main bones in the cranium. Babies have soft spaces between the bones in their cranium. These spaces are called fontanels. The zygomatic bones shape the cheeks.

42. **The correct answer is (C).** The femoral artery is in the thigh. The carotid artery is in the neck. The radial artery is in the lower arm, and the brachial artery is in the upper arm.

43. **The correct answer is (B).** External chest compressions are used to circulate blood if the heart is not beating. These chest compressions are combined with artificial ventilation to oxygenate the blood.

44. **The correct answer is (D).** In addition to cool, clammy skin, signs of a physiological manifestation of stress include an increase in respiration and pulse, dilated pupils, an increase in blood pressure, tensed muscles, an increase in blood sugar levels, perspiration, and decreased circulation to GI tract.

45. The correct answer is (D). Assault is the fear of immediate bodily harm. Negligence is the failure to provide reasonable care. Libel and slander harm a person's reputation.

46. The correct answer is (A). Conscious perception and response takes place in the cerebrum. Motor control takes place in the cerebellum. Basic vital functions such as breathing take place in the brain stem. The temporal lobe is responsible for hearing and speech. It is one of four lobes in the cerebellum.

47. The correct answer is (B). Coffee contains caffeine, which is likely to make a person feel additional stress. EMTs may also reduce stress by eating a balanced diet, talking to a counselor, and reestablishing a normal schedule/routine.

48. The correct answer is (B). Symptoms of heatstroke include a change in consciousness and hot, dry skin. Symptoms of dehydration are somewhat different and include thirst, dry mouth, fatigue, vomiting, fever, and chills.

49. The correct answer is (A). A cerebral contusion is a traumatic brain injury in which the brain tissue is bruised. A tearing of the brain tissue is a symptom of a cerebral laceration. Another symptom of cerebral contusion is one-sided paralysis.

50. The correct answer is (C). AVPU stands for alert (A), responds to verbal stimulation (V), response to painful stimulus (P), and unresponsive (U).

51. The correct answer is (A). When you splint a fracture, you should splint the joint above and below the fracture. When you splint a dislocation, you should splint the bone above and below the joint.

52. The correct answer is (B). Brain damage begins occurring 4 to 6 minutes after cardiac arrest and becomes irreversible in 8 to 10 minutes.

53. The correct answer is (A). Patient information may not be released to a patient's employer. It may only be released if it is subpoenaed or if the patient signs an information release form.

54. The correct answer is (D). You do not need the patient's express consent if the patient is unresponsive and in need of medical care. Denying such care may be considered negligence.

55. The correct answer is (C). When assessing patient's pupils using the acronym PEARL, P standards for pupils; E stands for equal; A stands for and; R stands for reactive; and L stands for light.

56. The correct answer is (D). The first thing you should do is gently slide the cord from around the neck. If this doesn't work, clamp and cut the cord.

57. The correct answer is (A). Death from seizures is most commonly caused by hypoxia. Therefore, you need to ensure that the patient receives proper ventilation.

58. The correct answer is (A). The brain stem is responsible for automatic functions such as heart rate, respirations, blood pressure, and body temperature. The spinal cord serves as a center for reflex action. The cerebrum is the center for conscious perception and response. The cerebellum is responsible for posture, balance, equilibrium, and fine motor skills.

59. The correct answer is (C). A sucking chest wound is very serious; air in the wound will cause the patient to suffer respiratory distress. The occlusive dressing should be secured on three sides, so air can leave the wound through the fourth side. If an object is stuck in the chest, you should not remove it.

60. **The correct answer is (D).** The ulna is a bone in the forearm and is part of the upper extremity. Choices A, B, and C are bones in the lower extremity. The fibula is the calf bone, the tarsals are bones in the foot, and the tibia is the shinbone.

61. **The correct answer is (A).** Stroke volume is the amount of blood pumped by the heart in one beat. Cardiac output is the amount of blood pumped by the heart in one minute.

62. **The correct answer is (B).** Narcotics cause the heart rate and breathing to slow. The EMT–Basic should try to keep the patient breathing. Paramedics are allowed to administer a drug that can reverse the effects of narcotics.

63. **The correct answer is (C).** Dilation of the rectal sphincter is one sign of imminent delivery. Other signs include strong urge to bear down, move bowels, or push; increased bloody show; and bulging of the perineum. Choices (A), (B), and (D) are signs of early labor.

64. **The correct answer is (C).** Insulin shock does not usually cause chest pain. Other signs of insulin shock include irritability, a sudden onset of hunger, and shakiness.

65. **The correct answer is (A).** A nonbreather facemask system will give a patient an oxygen concentration of at least 90 percent. A resuscitation mask delivers a concentration of 35 to 55 percent, while a nasal cannula gives a concentration of 24 to 44 percent. Rescue breathing delivers the lowest concentration of oxygen, only about 16 percent.

66. **The correct answer is (A).** Narcotics will cause an altered mental status, slow, shallow breathing and constricted pupils. Marijuana is a hallucinogen and amphetamines are a stimulant; neither will produce these effects. Barbiturates will cause many of the same symptoms as narcotics except that the patient's pupils will dilate.

67. **The correct answer is (C).** Shining a light in the eyes of a patient with a headache will cause the headache to worsen and the patient to suffer additional pain.

68. **The correct answer is (D).** The correct maneuver for a patient with an airway obstruction who has suffered head and/or neck trauma is the jaw thrust maneuver. This maneuver is more difficult than the head-tilt chin-lift maneuver.

69. **The correct answer is (A).** You should keep gentle pressure on the head and perineum until the chin emerges.

70. **The correct answer is (B).** For Verbal Response on the Glasgow Coma Scale, a patient receiving a grade of 5 is oriented; a patient who is confused receives a grade of 4; a patient who uses inappropriate words receives a grade of 3; and a patient who makes only incomprehensible sounds receives a grade of 1.

71. **The correct answer is (A).** Controlling hyperventilation is very important when treating a head injury in a responsive patient. Patients should receive 100 percent oxygen. You should NOT apply pressure to the fracture, attempt to stop the flow of blood or CSF from the nose, or remove penetrating objects.

72. **The correct answer is (A).** The spinal column has twelve thoracic vertebrae, seven cervical vertebrae, five lumbar vertebrae, five sacrum vertebrae, and four coccyx vertebrae.

73. **The correct answer is (D).** Sensations from the body surface are received by the parietal lobe, one of the four lobes of the cerebrum. The frontal lobe is responsible for foresight, planning, and judgment along with movement. The occipital lobe is responsible for

hearing. The temporal lobe is responsible for hearing and speech.

74. **The correct answer is (B).** After you position the child and open the airway, check for breathing. If the child is not breathing, perform rescue breathing of twenty breaths per minute until you see signs of circulation and breathing.

75. **The correct answer is (B).** Rhonchi is caused by a blockage of large airways. Rales are caused by a popping open of small airways, and stridor is caused by a blockage of air flow or an upper-airway obstruction. Wheezes are caused by a narrowing of airways. Breathing sounds may indicate that the patient has chronic or acute bronchitis, asthma, emphysema, a foreign-body obstruction, or pneumonia.

76. **The correct answer is (B).** The woman's symptoms are consistent with those of pre-eclampsia. Supine hypotensive syndrome is a reduction in blood pressure that occurs when the woman lies on her back and the uterus compresses the vena cava. Abruptio placenta is the separation of the placenta from the place of implantation in the uterus before delivery. Symptoms include abdominal pain and vaginal bleeding. Symptoms of a miscarriage include severe menstrual cramping and vaginal bleeding.

77. **The correct answer is (A).** You should use a scoop stretcher to move a patient in a supine position onto a stretcher. This type of stretcher is hinged and opens at the head and feet, so you can use it to "scoop" the patient onto the stretcher by putting the stretcher under and around the patient. A flexible stretcher is often used to carry a patient from an upper floor to a ground floor, since it offers great flexibility. A basket stretcher is used in rescue situations, and a portable stretcher is used in areas where a

wheeled stretcher—the most common type of stretcher—won't fit.

78. **The correct answer is (C).** The recent loss of a job, not the start of one, is a risk factor in suicide. Other risk factors include age over forty, a divorce from or death of a spouse, alcoholism, depression, a recent arrest or an imprisonment, and living in a destructive environment.

79. **The correct answer is (B).** The exchange of nutrients and wastes takes place in the placenta. The cervix is the lower end of the uterus, which opens into the vagina. The amniotic sac is the sac in which the fetus develops, and the uterus is the organ in which the fetus grows.

80. **The correct answer is (A).** Most commonly used to reduce respiratory distress, Fowler's position requires that the patient lie on the back with a 45-degree bend at the hips. Patients in Trendelenburg's position, are lying on the back on an incline with the feet above the head. Supine simply means the patient is lying flat on the back. Patients in the shock position are lying on the back with the feet elevated about fifteen inches.

81. **The correct answer is (C).** The manner in which people act is behavior, which includes both physical and mental activities.

82. **The correct answer is (B).** Threatening to take one's own life is a sign of suicide, not potential patient violence. Other signs that a patient may become violent include moving quickly toward the EMT–Basic, throwing things, and holding a potentially dangerous object.

83. **The correct answer is (A).** The patient is displaying signs that she is manic. A paranoid patient may think that others are plotting against her. A psychotic patient may panic and be a danger to herself or others.

A depressed patient may be lethargic and refuse to answer questions.

84. **The correct answer is (D).** The presence of meconium means that the infant's life is in danger. You should suction the airway to remove all traces of meconium.

85. **The correct answer is (A).** You should only suction as far as you can see to avoid injuring the patient. Choices (B), (C), and (D) are true. In addition, you should use less pressure and extra care when suctioning children. For both children and adults, don't suction for more than 15 seconds.

86. **The correct answer is (A).** You should never treat a patient who is armed and may injure you or those around you. Report the situation to law enforcement or other emergency personnel.

87. **The correct answer is (C).** The patient is exhibiting signs of depression. The five stages of death include denial, anger, bargaining, depression, and acceptance.

88. **The correct answer is (D).** As an EMT, you have to assess whether an operation is safe and look out for your own safety as well as the safety of those around you.

89. **The correct answer is (A).** Remember that BSI precautions are meant to protect the EMT from coming into contact with body fluid. Since fluids may splash during childbirth, the EMT should wear a mask, a gown, gloves, and eye protection during delivery.

90. **The correct answer is (C).** The patient is in the fetal position. This position relieves some of the tension in the abdominal region.

91. **The correct answer is (B).** An EMT ambulance may carry oral glucose, oxygen, and activated charcoal. It may not carry nitroglycerin, but an EMT may help a patient administer his or her own nitroglycerin if needed.

92. **The correct answer is (C).** The EMT may assist patients in taking bronchodilators. Albuterol is one such drug. Epinephrine is used to treat patients in shock. Decadron is a chemotherapy drug. Digoxin is used to treat congestive heart failure.

93. **The correct answer is (B).** When you receive an order from medical direction, you should repeat the order word for word to ensure that you have heard it correctly.

94. **The correct answer is (B).** Pupils may be dilated, but they are not usually unequal in a patient who has suffered an overdose. Other signs of an ingested toxin overdose include nausea, diarrhea, chemical burns around the mouth, and bad breath.

95. **The correct answer is (B).** The trachea is part of the upper respiratory system or upper airway. The nasal air passages, nasopharynx, soft and hard palates, pharynx, mouth, tongue, epiglottis, oropharynx, vocal cords, and larynx are also part of the upper respiratory system. Choices (A), (C), and (D) list organs that are part of the lower airway.

96. **The correct answer is (D).** Diastolic blood pressure, the bottom number, measures the pressure in the blood vessels when the heart rests, and systolic pressure, the top number, measures the pressure in the blood vessels when the heart contracts.

97. **The correct answer is (B).** A burn that affects both the epidermis and dermis is a partial-thickness, or second-degree, burn. A first-degree burn affects only the epidermis. A third-degree burn is a full-thickness burn. With a fourth-degree burn, the epidermis and the dermis are destroyed and other organs are damaged as well.

98. **The correct answer is (B).** The majority of heat is lost through radiation. It is lost through the hands, feet, and head.

99. **The correct answer is (A).** The best way to remove a bee stinger is to scrape it with a credit card or a butter knife. There is no need to make an incision, and you should not soak it in warm water. Removing it with tweezers is likely to make the poison enter deeper into the body.

100. **The correct answer is (C).** According to the Eye Opening portion of the Glasgow Coma Scale, a score of 3 indicates eyes open to speech. A grade of 1 indicates no eye opening; a grade of 2 indicates eyes open to pain; a grade of 4 indicates spontaneous eye opening.

APPENDIXES

APPENDIX A   Availability of Training

APPENDIX B   Professional EMS Organizations
              and Journals

Availability of Training

AVAILABILITY OF TRAINING

EMS training is widely available in every state. Most states offer training that is easily accessible to interested parties. Fire and Rescue departments may offer EMS programs. In addition, some states may have dedicated EMS training facilities.

Some states also have a Regional Medical Advisory Committee (REMAC), which is a subset of the State Emergency Medical Advisory Committee (SEMAC). The Public Health Law states that REMAC "shall develop policies, procedures and triage, treatment and transportation protocols which are consistent with the standards of the State Emergency Medical Advisory Committee and which address specific local conditions." The statute goes on to detail other responsibilities of the REMAC, including approval of online medical control physicians and participation in Quality Improvement (QI) programs. Provision is made for physician membership on REMAC from each of the hospitals in the region, plus representative membership from the nursing and EMS communities.

Good QI programs and the assurance of appropriate physician oversight is a real need in every region. After all, prehospital Advanced Life-Support (ALS) care must be practiced under a physician's license, according to law.

Without the dedication and cooperation of agency medical directors and REMAC physician members, ALS as we know it could not take place. In so many ways, EMS remains a highly interdependent effort.

Each state has an EMS division within the state Department of Health, Department of Transportation, or other state organization. Providers who are interested in EMS training should contact the EMS organization in their home state for additional information. The following pages contain the addresses, phone numbers, and Web sites (if applicable) of EMS offices within the fifty states and Washington, D.C.

appendix a

ALABAMA

Alabama Department of Public Health
Emergency Medical Services Division
RSA Tower, Suite 750
201 Monroe Street
Montgomery, AL 36104
Phone: 334-206-5383
Fax: 334-516-5132
Web site: www.adph.org/ems

ALASKA

Community Health and Emergency Medical
    Services
410 Willoughby, Suite 109
P.O. Box 110616
Juneau, AK 99811-0616
Phone: 907-465-3141
Fax: 907-465-4101
Web site: www.chems.alaska.gov

ARIZONA

Arizona Department of Health Services
Bureau of Emergency Medical Services
150 N. 18th Avenue, Suite 540
Phoenix, AZ 85007
Phone: 602-364-3186
Fax: 602-364-3568
Web site: www.azdhs.gov/bems/index.htm

ARKANSAS

Arkansas Department of Health
Emergency Medical Services
4815 W. Markham
Little Rock, AR 72205
Phone: 501-661-2262
Fax: 501-280-4901
Web site: www.healthy.arkansas.gov/
    programsServices/hsLicensingRegulation/
    EmsandTraumaSystems/Pages/default.aspx

CALIFORNIA

California EMS Authority
1930 9th Street
Sacramento, CA 95811
Phone: 916-322-4336 (Main)
916-323-9875 (Paramedic Licensure)
Fax: 916-324-2875
Web site: www.emsa.ca.gov

COLORADO

Colorado Department of Public Health and
    Environment
Emergency Medical and Trauma Services
4300 Cherry Creek Drive South
Denver, CO 80246-1530
Phone: 303-692-2980
Fax: 303-691-7720
Web site: www.cdphe.state.co.us/em/index.
    html

CONNECTICUT

Connecticut Department of Public Health
Office of Emergency Medical Services
410 Capitol Avenue
MS #12 EMS
P.O. Box 340308
Hartford, CT 06134-0308
Phone: 860-509-7975
Fax: 860-509-7987
Web site: www.dph.state.ct.us/OHCPHHO/
    EMS_Office/welcome_to_oems.htm

DELAWARE

Delaware Health and Social Services
Division of Public Health
417 Federal Street
Dover, DE 19901
Phone: 302-744-5400
Fax: 302-744-5429
Web site: www.dhss.delaware.gov/dhss/dph/
    ems/ems.html

DISTRICT OF COLUMBIA

Department of Health
Fire and Emergency Medical Services
1923 Vermont Avenue, NW, Suite 102
Washington, DC 20001
Phone: 202-673-3331
Fax: 202-645-0526
Web site: http://fems.dc.gov/fems/site/default.
   asp

FLORIDA

Florida Department of Health
Division of Emergency Medical Operations
4025 Esplanade Way
Tallahassee, FL 32301
Phone: 850-245-4440
Fax: 850-921-8162
Web site: www.doh.state.fl.us/demo/EMS/
   index.html

GEORGIA

Georgia Division of Public Health
Emergency Medical Services and Trauma
Two Peachtree Street, NW
Atlanta, GA 30303-3186
Phone: 404-657-2700
Web site: http://ems.ga.gov/

HAWAII

State Department of Health
State Emergency Medical Services & Injury
   Prevention System
3675 Kilauea Avenue
Honolulu, HI 96816
Phone: 808-733-9210
Fax: 808-733-9216
Web site: www.hawaii.gov/health/family-
   child-health/ems/index.html

IDAHO

Department of Health & Welfare
Emergency Medical Services
450 West State Street
Boise, ID 83720
Phone: 208-334-5500
Web site: www.healthandwelfare.idaho.gov/
   site/3344/default.aspx

ILLINOIS

Illinois Department of Public Health
Division of EMS and Highway Safety
535 West Jefferson Street
Springfield, IL 62761-0001
Phone: 217-782-4977
Fax: 217-782-3987
Web site: www.idph.state.il.us/ems/index.htm

INDIANA

EMS Division
Indiana Department of Homeland Security
Indiana Government Center South
302 West Washington Street, Room E208
Indianapolis, IN 46204
Phone: 317-233-0208
Web site: www.in.gov/dhs/2341.htm

IOWA

Iowa Department of Public Health
Bureau of Emergency Medical Services
Lucas State Office Building
321 East 12th Street
Des Moines, IA 50319
Phone: 515-281-7689
Web site: www.idph.state.ia.us/ems/default.
   asp

KANSAS

Kansas Board of Emergency Medical Services
Landon State Office Building, Room 1031
900 SW Jackson Street
Topeka, KS 66612
Phone: 785-296-7296
Fax: 785-296-6212
Web site: www.ksbems.org

KENTUCKY

Emergency Medical Services Branch
Department for Health Services
275 E. Main Street
Frankfort, KY 40621
Phone: 502-564-8963
Fax: 502-564-6533
Web site: http://kbems.kctcs.edu/

LOUISIANA

Louisiana Department of Health and Hospitals
Bureau of Emergency Medical Services
8919 World Ministry Avenue, Suite A
Baton Rouge, LA 70821
Phone: 225-763-5700
Fax: 225-763-5702
Web site: www.dhh.louisiana.gov/
offices/?ID=220

MAINE

Maine Emergency Medical Services
Department of Public Safety
152 State House Station
Augusta, ME 04333-0152
Phone: 207-626-3860
Fax: 207-287-6251
Web site: www.state.me.us/dps/ems

MARYLAND

The Maryland Institute for Emergency
Medical Services Systems
653 W. Pratt Street, Room 105
Baltimore, MD 21201-1536
Phone: 410-706-3666
Fax: 410-706-2367
Web site: www.miemss.org

MASSACHUSETTS

Office of Emergency Medical Services
99 Chauncy Street, 11th Floor
Boston, MA 02111
Phone: 617-753-7300
Fax: 617-753-7320
Web site: www.mass.gov/dph/oems/oems

MICHIGAN

Michigan Department of Community Health
Lewis Cass Building
320 South Walnut Street, 6th Floor
Lansing, MI 48913
Phone: 517-373-3740
Web site: www.michigan.gov/mdch

MINNESOTA

Minnesota Emergency Medical Services
Regulatory Board
2829 University Avenue SE, Suite 310
Minneapolis, MN 55414
Phone: 612-627-6000
Fax: 612-627-5442
Web site: www.emsrb.state.mn.us

MISSISSIPPI

EMS/Trauma Care System
P.O. Box 1700
Jackson, MS 39215-1700
Phone: 601-576-7380
Fax: 601-576-7373
Web site: www.ems.doh.ms.gov/ems/index.
html

MISSOURI

State of Missouri Department of Health &
    Senior Services
Unit of Emergency Medical Services
P.O. Box 570
Jefferson City, MO 65102-0570
Phone: 573-751-6356
Fax: 573-751-6348
Web site: www.dhss.mo.gov/EMS

MONTANA

Montana Department of Public Health &
    Human Services
EMS & Trauma Systems
P.O. Box 202951
Helena, MT 59620
Phone: 406-444-3895
Fax: 406-444-1814
Web site: www.dphhs.mt.gov/ems

NEBRASKA

Nebraska Department of Health & Human
    Services
P.O. Box 95026
Lincoln, NE 68509-5007
Phone: 402-471-3578
Web site: www.hhs.state.ne.us/ems/emsindex.
    htm

NEVADA

Nevada State Health Commission
Emergency Medical Services
1550 E. College Parkway, Suite 158
Carson City, NV 89706
Phone: 775-687-3065
Fax: 775-684-5313
http://health.nv.gov/EMS_EmergencyMedical.
    htm

NEW HAMPSHIRE

Department of Safety
Bureau of Emergency Medical Services
33 Hazen Drive
Concord, NH 03305
Phone: 800-371-4503
Web site: http://webster.state.nh.us/safety/fst/
    index.html

NEW JERSEY

New Jersey Department of Health and Senior
    Services
Office of Emergency Medical Services
50 East State Street
P.O. Box 360
Trenton, NJ 08625-0360
Phone: 609-633-7777
Fax: 609-633-7954
Web site: www.state.nj.us/health/ems/index.
    shtml

NEW MEXICO

New Mexico Department of Health
EMS Bureau
1301 Siler Road, Building F
Santa Fe, NM 87507
Phone: 505-476-8200
Fax: 505-467-8201
Web site: http://nmems.org

NEW YORK

New York State Department of Health
Bureau of Emergency Medical Services
One Fulton Street
Troy, NY 12180-3298
Phone: 518-408-5318
Fax: 518-408-5392
Web site: www.health.state.ny.us/nysdoh/ems/
    main.htm

NORTH CAROLINA

The North Carolina Office of EMS
701 Barbour Drive
Raleigh, NC 27603
Phone: 919-855-3935
Fax: 919-733-7021
Web site: www.ncems.org

NORTH DAKOTA

North Dakota Department of Health
Division of Emergency Medical Services
600 East Boulevard Avenue, Department 301
Bismarck, ND 58505-0200
Phone: 701-328-2388
Fax: 701-328-1702
Web site: www.ndhealth.gov/ems

OHIO

Ohio Department of Public Safety
Emergency Medical Services Division
P.O. Box 182073
1970 West Broad Street
Columbus, OH 43218-2073
Phone: 800-233-0785
Fax: 614-466-9461
Web site: www.ems.ohio.gov

OKLAHOMA

Oklahoma State Department of Health
Emergency Medical Services Division
1000 NE 10th, Room 1104
Oklahoma City, OK 73117
Phone: 405-271-4027
Web site: www.ok.gov/
   health/Protective_Health/
   Emergency_Medical_Services

OREGON

DHS, EMS & Trauma Systems
800 NE Oregon Street, Suite 607
Portland, OR 97232
Phone: 971-673-0520
Fax: 971-673-0555
Web site: www.oregon.gov/DHS/ph/ems/
   index.shtml

PENNSYLVANIA

Pennsylvania Department of Health
Pennsylvania EMS Office
P.O. Box 90
Harrisburg, PA 17108
Phone: 717-787-8740
Web site: www.dsf.health.state.pa.us/health

RHODE ISLAND

Rhode Island Department of Health
Emergency Medical Services
3 Capitol Hill
Providence, RI 02908
Phone: 401-222-2231
Fax: 401-222-6548
Web site: www.health.ri.gov/hsr/professions/
   amb.php

SOUTH CAROLINA

Department of Health and Environmental
   Control
2600 Bull Street
Columbia, SC 29201
Phone: 803-545-4200
Web site: www.scdhec.gov/hr/ems

SOUTH DAKOTA

Emergency Medical Services
South Dakota Department of Health
118 W. Capitol
Pierre, SD 57501-5070
Phone: 605-773-4031
Web site: www.state.sd.us/dps/ems/index.htm

TENNESSEE

Tennessee Department of Health
Division of Emergency Medical Services
Heritage Place, Metro Center
227 French Landing, Suite 303
Nashville, TN 37243
Phone: 615-741-2584
Fax: 615-741-4217
Web site: http://health.state.tn.us/ems/index.
htm

TEXAS

Texas Department of Health
Bureau of Emergency Management
P.O. Box 149347
Austin, TX 78714-9347
Phone: 512-834-6700
Fax: 512-834-6736
Web site: www.dshs.state.tx.us/
emstraumasystems/default.shtm

UTAH

Utah Department of Health
Bureau of Emergency Medical Services
P.O. Box 142004
Salt Lake City, UT 84114-2004
Phone: 801-273-6666
Web site: http://health.utah.gov/ems

VERMONT

Vermont Department of Health
Division of Health Protection
EMS and Injury Prevention
108 Cherry Street
P.O. Box 70
Burlington, VT 05402
Phone: 802-863-7200
Fax: 802-865-7754
Web site: http://healthvermont.gov/hc/ems/
ems_index.aspx

VIRGINIA

Virginia Department of Health
Office of Emergency Medical Services
109 Governor Street, Suite UB-55
Richmond, VA 23219
Phone: 804-864-7600
Fax: 804-864-7580
Web site: www.vdh.virginia.gov/OEMS/
Contact_Us/index.htm

WEST VIRGINIA

West Virginia Department of Health & Human
Resources
Office of Emergency Management Services
350 Capitol Street
Charleston, WV 25301-3714
Phone: 304-558-3956
Fax: 304-558-3856
Web site: www.wvoems.org

WASHINGTON

Washington State Department of Health
Office of Emergency Medical Services and
Trauma System
P.O. Box 47853
Olympia, WA 98504-7853
Phone: 360-236-4700
Fax: 360-236-2829
Web site: www.doh.wa.gov/hsqa/emstrauma

WISCONSIN

EMS Systems Section
P.O. Box 2659
Madison, WI 53701-2659
Phone: 608-266-1568
Fax: 608-261-6392
Web site: http://dhs.wisconsin.gov/ems/

WYOMING

Wyoming Office of Emergency Medical
   Services and Injury Control
Hathaway Building, 4th Floor
2300 Capitol Avenue
Cheyenne, WY 82002
Phone: 307-777-7955
Fax: 307-777-5639
Web site: http://wdh.state.wy.us/sho/ems/
   trainingprograms.html

Professional EMS Organizations and Journals

Numerous professional organizations and journals are dedicated to serving and educating the people who work in the field of Emergency Medical Services. Review the objectives and mission statements for each of the following organizations and publications and become a member or subscriber of those that suit your needs for continued education.

National Association of Emergency Medical Technicians
P.O. Box 1400
Clinton, MS 39060-1400
Phone: 800-34-NAEMT (toll-free)
Web site: www.naemt.org

National Registry of Emergency Medical Technicians
Rocco V. Morando Building
6610 Busch Boulevard
P.O. Box 29233
Columbus, OH 43229
Phone: 614-888-4484
Web site: www.nremt.org

National Association of EMS Educators
Foster Plaza 6
681 Andersen Drive
Pittsburgh, PA 15220-2766
Phone: 412-920-4775
Web site: www.naemse.org

National Association of EMS Physicians
P.O. Box 15945-281
Lenexa, KS 66285-5945
Phone: 913-895-4611
        800-228-3677 (toll-free)
Fax: 913-895-4652
Web site: www.naemsp.org

Emergency Medical Services Magazine
1233 Janesville Ave.
Fort Atkinson, Wisconsin 53538
Phone: 920-563-6388
        800-547-7377 (toll-free)
Web site: www.emsresponder.com

Journal of Emergency Medical Services (JEMS)
JEMS Communications
525 B Street, Suite 1900
San Diego, CA 92101
Phone: 619-687-3272
Fax: 619-699-6396
Web site: www.jems.com

appendix b

WITHDRAWN